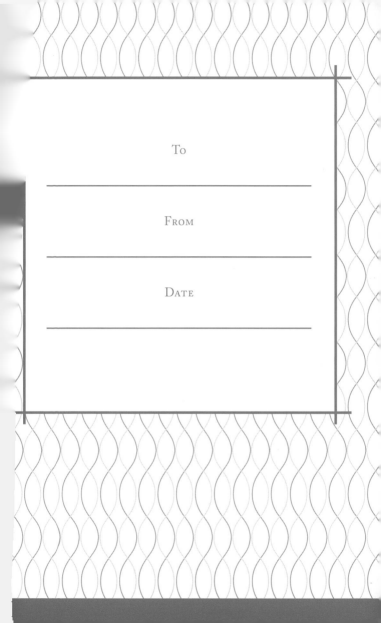

To

_____

From

_____

Date

_____

DEVOTIONS
FOR A
DEEPER LIFE

DEVOTIONS FOR A DEEPER LIFE

A DAILY DEVOTIONAL

OSWALD CHAMBERS

AUTHOR OF *MY UTMOST FOR HIS HIGHEST*
EDITED BY GLENN D. BLACK

 ZONDERVAN®

Devotions for a Deeper Life

Copyright © 1986 by Oswald Chambers

Requests for information should be addressed to:

Zondervan, 3900 Sparks Dr., SE, Grand Rapids, MI 49546

ISBN 978-0-310-08359-7

Library of Congress Cataloging-in-Publication Data

Chambers, Oswald., 1874–1917
Devotions for a deeper life
p. cm.
Excerpts from articles originally published in the periodical God's revivalist.
1907–1916
ISBN: 0-310-38710-8
1. Devotional calendars. I. Black, Glenn D. II. Title.
BV4811.C452 1986
242'.2 86–5537

Cover design: Faceout
Interior design: James Phinney

Printed in China

16 17 18 19 20 /DSC/ 22 21 20 19 18 17 16 15 14 13 12 11 10 9 8 7 6 5 4 3 2 1

FOREWORD

A s the editor of *God's Revivalist* from 1976 to 1985, I had the privilege of reviewing and researching past issues of that historic periodical, the official publication of God's Bible School and College in Cincinnati, Ohio. I became particularly interested in the writings of certain authors—among who was Oswald Chambers. From 1907 to 1916, 181 articles by Chambers appeared in *God's Revivalist*.

While en route from England to Japan in 1906, Chambers stopped in Cincinnati and visited the campus of God's Bible School. He was invited by the administration to remain on campus and teach some Bible courses. He did so for six months before he continued on his missionary journey to Japan. *God's Revivalist* published many of the notes from his classroom lectures and the Bible studies that he led at the Salvation Park Holiness Camp, sponsored by God's Bible School during the early years of its history. In subsequent years, Chambers contributed other articles to *God's Revivalist*.

The writings of Oswald Chambers contained in this volume were excerpted from these articles in *God's Revivalist*. Particular care was taken to use material heretofore unfamiliar to today's reader of Oswald Chambers. His writings in *God's Revivalist* have, for the most part, lay unresearched in the archives of the *Revivalist* office. Oswald Chambers is respected as an effective expositor of the Word of God, a prolific writer, and a practical Christian teacher whose disciplined mind explored the rich, redemptive truths of our Lord Jesus Christ. The writings of Oswald Chambers are cogent, challenging, and convincing. His pen etches the blessed truths of God, as revealed in the Holy Bible, with penetrating and passionate conviction. I commend this volume as a spiritual aid to all who seek to be more like Christ in Spirit-filled living for Him.

—GLENN D. BLACK, EDITOR

JANUARY

Peace I leave with you, my peace I give unto you; not as the world giveth, give I unto you. Let not your heart be troubled, neither let it be afraid.

—John 14:27

WHAT IS PEACE? YOU HAVE seen a water puddle in the road, I'm sure. It is peaceful. There is not the slightest stirring in it. The water is smooth and unruffled. The colors of nature are reflected in it. That is not peace, but stagnant death!

Have you ever seen a child spinning a top? When the top is going its fastest, it is at perfect rest. The peace of God is perfection of energy; it is a healthy vigor of the soul.

The peace of God is not the peace of stoicism or passivity. It is the most intense activity. Some people say that they are tired of life; they mean to say that they are tired of dying. They are tired of the spiritual death that stops activity. They are tired of life getting so sluggish.

What does Jesus say? "I am come that they might have life, and that they might have it more abundantly" (John 10:10). Everything in this natural world is pitted against you, and unless you have His life you will never have real peace.

May the Lord have a new year in you!

Prayer Thought: Lord, thank You for inner peace in the midst of a troubled world.

SUGGESTED READING: ISAIAH 26:3–4

But as many as received him, to them gave he power to become the sons of God, even to them that believe on his name.

—John 1:12

Our Lord Jesus Christ did not come into this world to do the work of a social reformer, a political administrator, a judge, or simply a ruler in the affairs of men and women.

Jesus came as the Light of the World, to perform a work of grace in the hearts of individuals that will impart a new disposition of righteousness. This heartfelt transformation will make God real in our lives.

Jesus Christ is a Savior who saves, not by the impressions we derive from a study of His character, but through the work He did by the shedding of His blood on the cross. Jesus Christ is a Sanctifier who sanctifies, not by our sympathetic imitation of Him, but by the fact of what He works in us.

Our Lord was not only without sin, but He also provides a work of grace whereby you and I might be without sin. Our Lord not only obeyed the good and perfect will of God perfectly, but He also makes it possible for us to fully obey God's perfect will. Our Lord Jesus Christ was our personal substitute on the cross, and our participation in His salvation depends on our acknowledgment of this glorious deed in our behalf.

Prayer Thought: Father, I acknowledge my salvation through the shed blood of Jesus on the cross.

SUGGESTED READING: JOHN 1:6–14

Surely he hath borne our griefs, and carried our sorrows.

—Isaiah 53:4

BEWARE OF ANY TEACHING THAT makes repentance the ransom that persuades God to forgive sin. Repentance is only the avenue whereby God enables us to see that our sinful condition is hopeless unless God does a remarkable work of grace and redemption in our lives.

Just as I am without one plea,
But that Thy blood was shed for me,
And that Thou bidst me come to Thee,
Oh, Lamb of God, I come, I come.

Isaiah reminds us that Jesus was "was wounded for our transgressions, he was bruised for our iniquities: the chastisement of our peace was upon him; and with his stripes we are healed" (53:5). This is the only scriptural understanding of how sin can be forgiven. It is the only way that God's character is clearly vindicated and His unutterable love exhibited: by making His only-begotten Son the scapegoat for every man, woman, and child.

Prayer Thought: Lord of mercy, I bow humbly, confessing my personal need of Your grace and redemption.

SUGGESTED READING: ISAIAH 53

I will arise and go to my father, and will say unto him, Father, I have sinned against heaven, and before thee.

—Luke 15:18

THE WORD *repentance* IS OFTEN misunderstood. This word, as we know it in the English language, does not fully convey the idea that God wants us to understand.

Repentance does not simply mean sorrow for sin. No! The prodigal son had remorse and sorrow while he fed pigs. In despair, he said, "How many hired servants of my father's have bread enough and to spare, and I perish with hunger!" (Luke 15:17).

But was that repentance? Obviously not. The prodigal left the pigs and husks, and went back to his father. He said, "[I] Father, I have sinned against heaven, and before thee, and am no more worthy to be called thy son: make me as one of thy hired servants" (Luke 15:18–19). Almost before he realized it, two strong arms of love embraced him, and the father clasped him to his bosom. That is repentance! The New Testament meaning of *repentance* is "going back."

Have you gone back? Have you returned to your heavenly Father? Remorse is not complete repentance. Returning to God is repentance!

Prayer Thought: Thank You, heavenly Father, for outstretched arms of mercy as You receive us in forgiveness.

SUGGESTED READING: LUKE 15:11–32

But God commendeth his love toward us, in that, while we were yet sinners, Christ died for us.

—Romans 5:8

WHEN A PERSON IS CONVICTED of sin, he cries out, "Against Thee, and Thee only, have I sinned!" From the biblical point of view, sin is ignoring God's claims and maintaining one's right to oneself. Sin is sometimes esteemed among human beings, but it is an abomination in the sight of God.

Sin is not an abstraction; it is a terrible and personal reality. Any person who has heard that Jesus Christ saves from sin, and continues in sin, is a damned soul already.

The wages of sin is death. But God postponed the penalty of death by allowing His only begotten Son to become the great Victim for the whole world. "For God so loved the world, that he gave his only begotten Son, that whosoever believeth in him should not perish, but have everlasting life" (John 3:16).

My sins, my sins, my Saviour,
Oh, sad on Thee they fall,
Seen through Thy tender patience,
I tenfold feel them all.
I know they are forgiven,
But, oh, their pain to me,
Is all the grief and anguish,
They laid, my Lord, on Thee.

Prayer Thought: I accept responsibility for my sins. O God, I need Your forgiveness.

SUGGESTED READING: ROMANS 5:6–21

Wherefore in all things it behoved him to be made like unto his brethren, that he might be a merciful and faithful high priest in things
pertaining to God, to make reconciliation for the sins of the people.

—Hebrews 2:17

THE GREATEST WORK IN THE world is the work of Christ's
reconciliation of mankind with God. Sin put each one of
us at enmity with God and God at enmity with us.

We have too often forgotten God's hatred of sin. The
consequence is that our sense of salvation becomes merely a sentiment; we presume that God, being love, will forgive any sinner
at any time. But if we teach that people are saved by "simply
looking to Jesus," we are quite mistaken—unless we understand
what the Bible means by looking to Jesus. If we declare that
there is no other name given among men whereby we must be
saved, all well and good; but if by that we mean looking to Jesus
as a representation of God, if we are "lost in wonder, love, and
praise" as we meditate upon that fact, and if we accept that sense
of wonder as a sign of our salvation—then we are deceived.

Beware of any teaching that says "loving Jesus" means that
your soul is saved. This simply is not true, either in Scripture or
in the common experience of life. There are scores of men and
women who love Jesus, but who loathe the doctrine of forgiveness of sins by the shed blood of Jesus.

Prayer Thought: Gracious Lord, the love You
expressed toward us through Your death and
resurrection gives me hope. I praise You for it.

SUGGESTED READING: HEBREWS 2

God . . . commandeth all men every where to repent.

—Acts 17:30

TRUE REPENTANCE IS KEENLY PAINFUL, but very beneficial in its results. Some people easily forget their period of repentance; others never do. I am referring to the period when a person fully feels what one has been. I do not believe the Spirit of God allows Christians to lose all memory of the horrible pit and miry clay of sins out of which God has delivered them. The apostle Paul never forgot what he was; and that memory reminded him that he became what he "now is" by the marvelous grace of God.

Repentance does not mean that you will never commit those sins again.

It means that you have, by God's grace, reached a place where you do positively the other things. The only truly repentant person, in the fullest analysis, is the person who allows God to deal with what was wrong—sin.

Set your heart and mind toward God and let the holy light of Jesus Christ search through every nook and cranny. The result will be a marvelous readjustment of your whole life.

Prayer Thought: Search me, Lord. Enable
me to forsake all sin and live for You.

SUGGESTED READING: ACTS 17:22–31

To the end he may stablish your hearts unblameable in holiness before God, even our Father, at the coming of our Lord Jesus Christ with all his saints.

—1 Thessalonians 3:13

A TRUE SAINT HAS RECEIVED CHRIST Jesus our Lord. A saint's conduct does not spring from adherence to external rules, but is the spontaneous outcome of an inward life of holiness and love. A true saint is free from condemnation (Romans 8:1), fully forgiven of sins (1 Corinthians 6:11; Ephesians 1:7), justified by God (Romans 3:24), sanctified wholly (Hebrews 13:12; 1 Thessalonians 5:23; 1 Corinthians 1:30), a child of God (John 1:12; 1 John 4:1–3), and the possessor of all things (1 Corinthians 3:21–23).

Saintliness is not a divine anticipation; it can be a fact now! Oh, for more holy boldness to claim what is ours through the atonement of Jesus Christ our Lord!

> *Thou know'st He died not for Himself, nor for Himself arose;*
> *Millions of souls were in His heart, and thee for one He chose.*
> *Upon the palms of His pierced hands engraven was thy name,*
> *He for thy cleansing had prepared,*
> *His water and His flame.*
> *Make sure thou with Him art risen: and now with Him thou*
> *   must go forth.*
> *And He will lend thy sick soul health, thy*
> *   strivings might and worth.*

Prayer Thought: I am not worthy to be called a saint, Lord; but help me to be one in all my attitudes and actions.

SUGGESTED READING: I THESSALONIANS 3:7–13

For our light affliction, which is but for a moment, worketh for us a
far more exceeding and eternal weight of glory.

—2 Corinthians 4:17

THE DOMINANT TRAIT OF A true saint is a personal, passionate, and overwhelming devotion to the Lord Jesus Christ. Experiences of inward ecstasy are secondary. A saint wants to know Him.

In spite of disastrous circumstances, a saint yearns to know more of the providence of God. The apostle Paul was imprisoned, shipwrecked, starved, and stoned, yet we hear him speaking about "our light affliction, which is but for a moment . . ." (2 Corinthians 4:17). He unhesitantly says, "Who shall separate us from the love of Christ? shall tribulation, or distress, or persecution, or famine, or nakedness, or peril, or sword? . . . For I am persuaded, that neither death, nor life, nor angels, nor principalities, nor powers, nor things present, nor things to come, nor height, nor depth, nor any other creature, shall be able to separate us from the love of God, which is in Christ Jesus our Lord" (Romans 8:35, 38–39).

It is not reward that a saint looks for; it is to hear our Lord say, "Well done, good and faithful servant."

Prayer Thought: Father, with Your help, I will be faithful to You.

SUGGESTED READING: 2 CORINTHIANS 4:14–18

The eyes of your understanding being enlightened; that ye may know what is the hope of his calling, and what the riches of the glory of his inheritance in the saints.

—Ephesians 1:18

SAINTLINESS IS NOT BUILT ON admiration for Jesus Christ. It is not simply a reflected glory due to one's nearness to our blessed Lord. It is not refined sensitivity or a subtle religious genius. The stately beauty of a saint is not a reformed edition of carnality.

A saint is the work of our Master Workman, the Lord Jesus Christ. The saint is one who—on this good old mother earth, amid the sordid and sacred days of time—has the glory of the Lord.

Saintliness is the product of Calvary and Pentecost where our Lord

> *Jesus Christ dug our souls,*
> *From central gloom,*
> *And heated hot with burning fears,*
> *And dipped in baths of hissing tears,*
> *And battered by the shocks of doom,*
> *To shape and use.*

The saint is one who loves the Lord with all his heart, soul, mind, and strength and loves his neighbor as himself (Mark 12:30–31). Saints tread this earth with human feet while creation "groaneth and travaileth in pain," waiting for full redemption (Romans 8:22).

If this life is so glorious now, what will it be when our Lord returns?

Prayer Thought: Many times, Lord, I sense my need of more of You, so that I may better understand how to be a true saint of God.

SUGGESTED READING: [15]Wherefore I also, after I heard of your faith in the Lord Jesus, and love unto all the saints, [16]Cease not to give thanks for you, making mention of you in my prayers; [17]That the God of our Lord Jesus Christ, the Father of glory, may give unto you the spirit of wisdom and revelation in the knowledge of him: [18]The eyes of your understanding being enlightened; that ye may know what is the hope of his calling, and what the riches of the glory of his inheritance in the saints, [19]And what is the exceeding greatness of his power to us-ward who believe, according to the working of his mighty power, [20]Which he wrought in Christ, when he raised him from the dead, and set him at his own right hand in the heavenly places, [21]Far above all principality, and power, and might, and dominion, and every name that is named, not only in this world, but also in that which is to come: [22]And hath put all things under his feet, and gave him to be the head over all things to the church, [23]Which is his body, the fulness of him that filleth all in all.

—EPHESIANS 1:15–23

With the mind I myself serve the law of God; but with the flesh the law of sin.

—Romans 7:25

L UNACY, IN THE NATURAL WORLD, means that a person has alternating personalities. The most popular literary presentation of this type of behavior is Robert Louis Stevenson's study *Strange Case of Dr. Jekyll and Mr. Hyde.*

One of the greatest tragedies with regard to spiritual matters is this very thing. When the Holy Spirit first convicts a person's conscience, and uncovers a personality that fights against the light of God, the consequence is spiritual conflict. It is this tragedy of tragedies to which Paul is alluding in Romans 7.

The ultimate outcome of this spiritual tragedy is either our sinking back into the old unity of the personality of sin, or being lifted up to a new unity of the personality of holiness. Man is what his "will" makes him, and sin's seat of operation is in the human will. A person's attitude toward God depends on the simplicity of a personal choice.

Prayer Thought: Father, unless You empower me to live victoriously, I will miserably fail You.

SUGGESTED READING: ROMANS 7:14–17

O wretched man that I am! who shall deliver me from the body of this death?

—Romans 7:24

ROMANS 7 IS UNIQUE. THE very best things said or written about it still leave this chapter unique.

Verse 24 of the seventh chapter of Romans is a heart-rending cry from the depths of despair. It is difficult to think of this as exactly St. Paul's own experience. As a Christian, he seems above it, as a Pharisee, below it. Self-satisfaction was too engraved on his Pharisaic temper.

The performance of the Pharisaic righteousness was too well within the compass of the average will, but St. Paul was not an ordinary Pharisee. He dealt too honestly with himself so that sooner or later the self-satisfaction, natural to the Pharisee, must give way, and his experience as a Christian would throw back a lurid light on those old days of which he was now ashamed. The whole description is so vivid and so sincere, so evidently rung from the anguish of direct personal experience, that it is difficult to think of it as largely imagination. It is really not so much imaginary as imaginative. It is not a literal engraving of any one stage of the apostle's career, but a constructive picture drawn by him in bold lines from elements supplied to him by introspection. . . . The process described comes to different men in different times and in different degrees; to one early, to another later. In one man it would lead up quickly and suddenly; in another, the slow growth of years. We can lay down no rule. *Sanday and Headlam's Commentary on Romans*, pp. 183, 186.

Prayer Thought: Lord, create within me a new heart, fully in unity with You and Your purposes.

SUGGESTED READING: [18] For I know that in me (that is, in my flesh,) dwelleth no good thing: for to will is present with me; but how to perform that which is good I find not. [19] For the good that I would I do not: but the evil which I would not, that I do. [20] Now if I do that I would not, it is no more I that do it, but sin that dwelleth in me. [21] I find then a law, that, when I would do good, evil is present with me. [22] For I delight in the law of God after the inward man: [23] But I see another law in my members, warring against the law of my mind, and bringing me into captivity to the law of sin which is in my members. [24] O wretched man that I am! who shall deliver me from the body of this death? [25] I thank God through Jesus Christ our Lord. So then with the mind I myself serve the law of God; but with the flesh the law of sin.

—ROMANS 7:18–25

To reveal his Son in me, that I might preach him among the heathen; immediately I conferred not with flesh and blood.

—Galatians 1:16

WHEN GOD TOLD PAUL TO do something for Him, the apostle did not consult with "flesh and blood." In other words, he did not ask for a human opinion about God's will for him. Do you?

Some people have told us, "Well, I was ready to receive the baptism of the Holy Spirit; but not now." Why? Because they went to their minister and asked his opinion, even though he is not filled with the Spirit. There is no way he can give guidance in an area he doesn't know anything about. Speak with God. Wait for Him. Take His way. Confer not with "flesh and blood."

There are some dear people on a foreign field who have no business being there. They should be at home. The reason they went to the mission field is because they listened to the passionate appeal of human pleas. God did not send them. They consulted with "flesh and blood."

Listen to God, not to the selfish voice of "flesh and blood."

Prayer Thought: Forgive me, Lord, for my tendency to let human voices crowd out the still, small voice of the Spirit of God.

SUGGESTED READING: GALATIANS 1:15–24

And now abideth faith, hope, charity, these three; but the greatest of these is charity.

—1 Corinthians 13:13

LOVE IS THE BEGINNING AND the middle and the end—the first sign, stamp, and seal—of the saint. Stronger than death, deeper than hell, higher than heaven, is this mighty, personal devotion to the Lord Jesus Christ. No one can ever destroy the individual whose heart is in personal, passionate devotion to Jesus.

Who that one moment has the least descried Him,
Dimly and faintly, hidden and afar,
Doth not despise all excellence beside Him,
Pleasures and powers that are not and that are.
Aye amid all men bear himself thereafter,
Smit with a solemn and a sweet surprise,
Dumb to their scorn and turning on their laughter,
Only the dominance of earnest eyes?
    (Frederic William Henry Myers)

Since my eyes were fixed on Jesus, I've lost sight of all besides. This is not sentiment; this is fact. When will this knowledge of Him be full? Never! Eternal life is to know Christ eternally; not eternal existence, but eternal knowledge of God; deeper depths and grander heights forever! Beware of your own inward experiences unless they have this dominant note of fervent love for God.

Prayer Thought: I love You, Lord, and I want to show the fruit of this passionate devotion toward others.

SUGGESTED READING: 1 CORINTHIANS 13:8–13

And Ananias went his way, and entered into the house; and putting his hands on him said, Brother Saul, the Lord, even Jesus, that appeared unto thee in the way as thou camest, hath sent me, that thou mightest receive thy sight, and be filled with the Holy Ghost.

—Acts 9:17

The Holy Spirit's work of grace is not finished in one's soul until that soul has had a personal Pentecost.

Have you had your Pentecost yet? Christ's work is not done, as He came to do it, until you are filled by God's Spirit. When a Christian is filled with the Spirit, the Spirit comes to dwell within, and the indwelling Holy Spirit will make him incandescent for the glory of God.

The gospel is not that God loves us with unmerited mercy and blots out our sins. The miraculous work that Jesus Christ came to do is the making of saints—stamped and sealed by Golgotha and Pentecost.

You cannot do God's work unless the Holy Spirit infills you completely. Allow God to complete His work in you.

Prayer Thought: Fill me, Spirit of God, with Your powerful presence as I labor for You.

SUGGESTED READING: ACTS 9:10–22

And put no difference between us and them, purifying their hearts by faith.

—Acts 15:9

Do you realize that you can be one with Jesus, as He is one with God? Christ's patience, holiness, purity, gentleness, prayerfulness, and faith can be so personally yours that you can say with the apostle Paul, "I live, yet not I, but Christ liveth in me" (Galatians 2:20).

God works this unspeakable mystery of entire sanctification in your life and mine. People try to seek the experience of entire sanctification in ways other than God's way; but the wonderful Spirit of God will remove confusion and enable us to see that the only means to obtain the experience of entire sanctification by faith is the grace of God.

Launch out in simple faith and ask God to make the sanctification of the New Testament yours. The unsearchable riches of Jesus Christ can be yours.

Prayer Thought: I praise You, dear Lord, for the truth of sanctification in Your Word.

SUGGESTED READING: ACTS 15:6–11

I am crucified with Christ: nevertheless I live; yet not I, but Christ liveth in me: and the life which I now live in the flesh I live by the faith of the Son of God, who loved me, and gave himself for me.

—Galatians 2:20

Entire sanctification means that the perfections of Jesus Christ have been imparted to me—not gradually, but instantly, in a crisis moment. This moment occurs when I enter into the full realization, by faith, of Christ's being made sanctification to me. Faith is the divine instrument given to us to make this wonderful spiritual blessing ours personally.

If you have been born again of the Spirit of God, the deep craving of your heart is to be holy. Just as you enter into regeneration by faith, so you enter into entire sanctification by faith.

The union of my soul with Christ in entire sanctification means that the unsearchable riches of our Lord Jesus Christ are made mine. We are invited to believe until the whole gospel of Christ is fully formed in us. The secret of a holy life is not in imitating Jesus, but in letting the perfections of Jesus be manifested in our mortal flesh.

Prayer Thought: Manifest Your holy beauty,
Lord Jesus, in and through me.

SUGGESTED READING: GALATIANS 2:16–21

But of him are ye in Christ Jesus, who of God is made unto us wisdom, and righteousness, and sanctification, and redemption.

—1 Corinthians 1:30

Jesus Christ did a twofold work for us and in us, technically called justification and sanctification. God justifies us as Christ was crucified and risen outside us; God sanctifies as Christ is crucified and risen within us. God glorifies in virtue of both, as Christ is enthroned in the fullness of power.

We have justification as we are seen in Him. We have sanctification as He is seen in us. We have increasing glory and ultimate redemption as both of these divine works of grace combine in the sovereign purpose of God.

The forgiveness of sins is not the sole purpose of the atonement; it is but the means to a redemptive purpose—namely, holiness. Justification is the road to holiness, and to stop spiritual progress at one without the other is to annul both. Our Lord's work of grace produces the greatest fact on earth, a saint—i.e., a holy man or woman.

Holiness, not love, is the greatest thing in the world; for holiness is the basis of love.

Prayer Thought: May my life always reflect the beauty of holiness as I grow in grace.

SUGGESTED READING: 1 CORINTHIANS 1:23–31

Likewise reckon ye also yourselves to be dead indeed unto sin, but alive unto God through Jesus Christ our Lord.

—Romans 6:11

ENTIRE SANCTIFICATION DEPENDS ENTIRELY ON my willing, conscious, definite break with sin at the cross, and by an act of faith, appropriating Christ on the throne. The world, the flesh, and the Devil are conquered.

The term *sanctification* is used by many religions. But any sanctification other than Christian sanctification leads to self-righteousness under the misleading guise of self-denial, self-sacrifice, self-inflicted seasons of prayer, self-appointed fasts, and self-torment.

Christian sanctification is the indwelling holiness that guides our lives as spontaneously as its breathing. It depends not on my longings, yearning, praying, fasting, weeping, or howling, but entirely on my will.

A word of caution is perhaps needed: It is dangerous to draw peace from the realization that we have turned from a wrong way of living to a right way. This is the very essence of pharisaic fanaticism. Holiness is the remaking of our inward and hidden desires and affections, when the Holy Spirit of God dwells in our mortal bodies.

Prayer Thought: Through Your mercy and grace,
Lord, I truly and completely yield myself to You.

SUGGESTED READING: JOHN 6:50–56

O God the Lord, the strength of my salvation, thou hast covered my head in the day of battle.

—Psalm 140:7

SPIRITUAL STRENGTH BELONGS TO THE entirely sanctified. That strength is the strength of the Lord God omnipotent. Nothing can destroy the person whom God backs.

People are always talking about "power" or "lack of power." Have you ever understood the magnitude of His power that is toward us who have believed? For what purpose is the call of God's hope in you? For what did He save you? To shout "Hallelujah"? To say you are "saved and sanctified"? No. But that He might be made manifest in your mortal flesh.

Prayer Thought: I am weak in my own strength.
Manifest Your power and strength in me!

SUGGESTED READING: PSALM 140

And the Lord said unto him, Now do ye Pharisees make clean the outside of the cup and the platter; but your inward part is full of ravening and wickedness.

—Luke 11:39

WHY PEOPLE WHO CLAIM TO be Christians must be told to refrain from such habits as smoking and chewing tobacco is to me an amazement. There is a big mistake somewhere, and it is either in them or God. (I rather think that man is a liar and God is true, because I know what He has done for me.)

Of course, if you refrain from all sorts of bad things that is no sign that you are regenerated, much less sanctified! Not one bit of it. Scores of people who have not a spark of salvation live a cleaner life than some folks who say they are Christians.

Entire sanctification is not mere outward cleanliness or moral living. That is your definition, not God's. But spirituality is based on the most intense morality.

Christianity is not the annulling of the Ten Commandments; to the contrary, it is a transfiguration of the will, which allows Jesus Christ to be manifested in every fiber of your being.

Prayer Thought: Heavenly Father, I give You all that I am and all I have. I am completely Yours.

SUGGESTED READING: LUKE 11:37–44

Wherefore Jesus also, that he might sanctify the people with his own blood, suffered without the gate.

—Hebrews 13:12

THERE IS NO USE LOOKING and longing for sanctification as a direct result of "our praying" or "our obedience." Sanctification is the direct gift of God, which comes by faith in Him and His Word.

Entire sanctification is "Christ in you." Some testimonies to sanctification seem to put the standard too high for any of us to attain in this life. But sanctification is the wonderful life of His imparted to me. I cannot merit it. I cannot earn it. I cannot pray it down. But, thanks be unto God, I can take it by faith in His blood.

If you have the slightest feeling that you can earn the blessing of sanctification, you will never receive it. But if you seek entire sanctification in a spirit of unworthiness, it will be given through God's sovereign grace. God will purify your heart and entirely sanctify you.

Prayer Thought: More of You, Christ
Jesus, I need and want in my life.

SUGGESTED READING: HEBREWS 13:8–13

And be not drunk with wine, wherein is excess; but be filled with the
Spirit.

—Ephesians 5:18

IF YOU SAY YOU ARE entirely sanctified and have never been
baptized in the Holy Spirit, you have deluded yourself. The
baptism in the Holy Spirit is Jesus Christ's seal on your regenerated and sanctified soul and is your inauguration in service
for your Master. A man and woman, when married, know it;
and they can tell you the day when they were. A person who is
baptized with the Holy Spirit knows the very moment, the very
place, the very spot the transaction was done, and will never
forget it.

I remember the place. I recall the old wooden pew in a
Baptist Church in the west of Scotland. It is so photographed
in my mind that I will never forget it through time and eternity.
Oh, bless God!

Unless you have had a definite, personal Pentecost, you are
suffering spiritually. Go down before God, and let Him do a
definite work of grace in your heart and life. Let Him fill you
with His Spirit.

Prayer Thought: Fill me, Holy Spirit, with
Your purity, power, and presence.

SUGGESTED READING: ACTS 2:1–4

Through sanctification of the Spirit, unto obedience and sprinkling of the blood of Jesus Christ: Grace unto you, and peace, be multiplied.

—1 Peter 1:2

SATAN TRIES RELENTLESSLY TO GET a saint to disbelieve that he maintains his Christian experience by faith. Satan attempts to convince us that we "must do this or that." But the Spirit of God will steadily remind us that only faith will keep us.

The best illustration of appropriating faith is the act of eating and drinking. Our Lord uses this illustration in John 6. Just as you take food into your body, you take Christ into your soul. Jesus did not say, "It is enough to see the bread and drink on the table." That's not faith. Only as you reach out and take the bread and drink are you showing faith.

If you had faith for the Lord Jesus Christ to save you, have faith exactly the same way for entire sanctification. His presence is the reality; the experience is the gift. And how much do you pay to earn a gift? Nothing. You simply accept it.

Obedience is the means whereby you show the earnestness of your desire to do God's will. Through obedience you will receive, as a gift of God, this perfect adjustment of the personality of holiness—the life of Jesus Christ manifested in your mortal flesh.

Prayer Thought: Yes, Lord, I will fully obey
and will heed Your call to holiness.

SUGGESTED READING: JOHN 6:5–14

For this is the will of God, even your sanctification.

—1 Thessalonians 4:3

WHEN A SOUL IS ENTIRELY sanctified, the chances are ten to one that the saint will stay there. The experience of sanctification is as stable as God's throne. The soul that slips out of it does not slip unconsciously, but deliberately withdraws from God. Do not take my word for it. Take the Bible and search, and you will learn what real backsliding is. It is "forgetting the first love" and going back (Revelation 2:4).

I do not believe that I have met many real backsliders, but I have met many people (and so have you) who never "slid forward," as someone has said. These souls come moping and mourning about, and are generally accepted as having backslidden, when they have never really gotten near God. But just let Jesus Christ get those souls into entire sanctification, and the chances are that they will go right on in the divine life. Do you know when I feel the most inclined to shout? It is when a believer says, "I thought I was sanctified, but I am not." Then I know that person will get to the place where God wants him.

Prayer Thought: Let me know the certainty
of being completely Yours, Lord.

SUGGESTED READING: I THESSALONIANS 4:3–8

Now we exhort you, brethren, warn them that are unruly, comfort the feebleminded, support the weak, be patient toward all men.

—1 Thessalonians 5:14

IF THERE IS ONE THING that God has taught me in the past six years, it is that He can minister to a mind diseased. He can breathe into that mind His cleanness, His balm, His restoration. And in this Scripture verse, by the inspiration of the Holy Spirit, Paul admonishes us to "comfort the feebleminded, support the weak, be patient toward all men."

Some servants of God find it very easy to obey the first command in that verse, but they forget the other two. It is far easier to warn the "unruly" than it is to comfort "the feebleminded."

I am apt to forget the long way it took God to bring me to this point in the divine life, and I lose patience with other folks if they do not see at once what I now see. But God's Word exhorts me to be patient with all people. It brings to mind the question, How long did it take God to put you where you are now?

Prayer Thought: O Lord, make me mindful of my own weakness when I am prone to lose patience with the weakness of another.

SUGGESTED READING: 1 THESSALONIANS 5:12–15

In every thing give thanks: for this is the will of God in Christ Jesus concerning you.

—1 Thessalonians 5:18

You do not grieve the Holy Spirit by taking a look over your past life. In fact, the Holy Spirit may take you back through your unregenerated days so that you may remember from where He took you, remember what you are, and remember He did it all. When the Holy Spirit begins to take you for a walk back, do not start to say it is a temptation of the Devil. It is a grand thing when the Holy Spirit takes a person for a walk down his unregenerated days. It will make the believer rejoice and understand that Jesus not only did it all, but is all.

Rejoice in everything if you are His child—no matter where you find yourself, no matter what your circumstances are, no matter what tribulations come. You can give thanks in all things because He remains the same. Nothing alters Him.

Prayer Thought: Knowing that You change not, Lord, I rejoice in everything You permit me to experience today.

SUGGESTED READING: 1 THESSALONIANS 5:16–22

And the very God of peace sanctify you wholly; and I pray God your whole spirit and soul and body be preserved blameless unto the coming of our Lord Jesus Christ.

—1 Thessalonians 5:23

Your entire spirit, entire soul, and entire body are to be preserved blameless. Until when? "Unto the coming of our Lord Jesus Christ."

Listen! "Faithful is he that calleth you, who also will do it" (v. 24). Do what? "Sanctify you wholly." And if He has not done it already, you are casting aside the completed work of Jesus Christ.

The gospel of Jesus Christ does not consist only in the forgiveness of sins, not by any means. The gospel does not end with the fact that God loved you with unmerited mercy and forgives you of your sins. That is only the beginning of it. But the full gospel of God is that He enables you to love others as He does. He permits you to live and walk and breathe and move in this natural body with the likeness of Jesus Christ. Oh, blessed be God!

If even a few people would enter into entire sanctification, who could measure the possibilities for the human race?

Prayer Thought: Holy Spirit of Christ, cleanse me completely and equip me to live in the likeness of my Lord, beginning today.

SUGGESTED READING: 1 THESSALONIANS 5:23–24

Sanctify them through thy truth: thy word is truth.

—John 17:17

FAITH IS TOO OFTEN VIEWED as a habit of the mind whereby we assent to a testimony, upon the authority of the one who testifies. But New Testament faith is infinitely more than this. When Jesus Christ testified of Himself, religious people of His day did not believe Him. He had to awaken their faith. Faith in the gospel became the very means of producing the wonderful life of God in them.

When Christ creates His marvelous sanctification in you, you will live this holy life moment by moment through faith in the Son of God. Entire sanctification is not receiving from our Lord power to live like Jesus; it is Christ in you, living out His life. This Christlike life of holiness will be seen in you and through you as you walk by faith.

By simple faith look up into God's face, trust entirely in His grace, and say, "Lord, make Thy sanctification in me as real as the sanctification that is stated in Thy Word."

Prayer Thought: Let my every thought and deed be filled with the holiness and beauty of Jesus.

SUGGESTED READING: HEBREWS 11:1–3

So likewise shall my heavenly Father do also unto you, if ye from your hearts forgive not every one his brother their trespasses.

—Matthew 18:35

THE FULL FRUIT OF SANCTIFICATION is biblically demanded of the one who has received the grace of sins forgiven. If the unmerited mercy of God shown to me is not reshown to others, my justification is annulled. If the unmerited forgiveness of God awarded to me is not exercised toward others, my justification is annulled.

Forgetting is the essence of divine forgiveness. Unless my forgiveness of other people "forgets" their trespasses against me, the grace of God in me is a mere painted flower, and I am a play actor.

Listen to this warning: "Be not deceived; God is not mocked: for whatsoever a man soweth, that shall he also reap" (Galatians 6:7).

Prayer Thought: Help me, O Lord, to forgive the trespasses of others.

SUGGESTED READING: MATTHEW 18:21–35

Now he that planteth and he that watereth are one: and every man shall receive his own reward according to his own labour.

—1 Corinthians 3:8

THE APOSTLE PAUL CAUTIONS US about a dangerous snare when he tells us not to "glory in men" (1 Corinthians 3:21). That is exactly where the Corinthian church was trapped. They gloried in their leaders' abilities, and this brought divisions. When will we learn that the best of men are but the best of men, and that the best of women are but the best of women?

These Corinthian Christians were dividing themselves by saying, "I believe Paul" or "I believe Apollos." Paul said, "Who then is Paul, and who is Apollos, but ministers by whom ye believed, even as the Lord gave to every man?" (v. 5).

Paul warned the Corinthians, and he warns us in our own day, against aligning ourselves with certain personalities within Christ's church, pitting ourselves against each other. We will always have leaders to instruct us in spiritual matters. But let us remember that we are Christ's and Christ is God's.

Prayer Thought: Let me learn that making other people my idols, even in church work, is an abomination to You, Lord.

SUGGESTED READING: 1 CORINTHIANS 3:1–8

FEBRUARY

If any man's work abide which he hath built thereupon, he shall receive a reward.

—1 Corinthians 3:14

Probably the most severe disillusionment we encounter in our walk with God is when He removes a teacher or leader because that person is worshiped.

Have you seen the picture of medieval saints with a circular halo on their heads? The saints of God are apt to install a halo on certain teachers, preachers, or leaders and put them up where God does not want them. God will remove the halo. And if you have been following these "haloed Christians" instead of God, you will go down in humiliation. God will break the props from underneath them—and us—and let us fall until we learn that it is "Jesus ever, Jesus only, Jesus all in all."

God is wonderful! He brings the friends we need just at the right time, and He removes them just at the right time. It is their removal that is the hardest lesson for us to accept.

Prayer Thought: On You, Lord, will I set my affections.

SUGGESTED READING: 1 CORINTHIANS 3:9–15

Stand fast therefore in the liberty wherewith Christ hath made us free, and be not entangled again with the yoke of bondage.

—Galatians 5:1

THE LORD JESUS CHRIST IS our Judge. Any standard of spiritual measurement and examination must be based on Him. This fundamental consideration is many times ignored.

Too often we find saints in bondage to one another's personal convictions. They suppose freedom will be theirs only if they live according to these human convictions. A false spirituality has increased this bondage among so many of us. This false spirituality is overly concerned lest it offends anyone's scruples.

Did our Lord hesitate to offend the scruples of the religious Jews when He strolled through the cornfields on the Sabbath and allowed His disciples to pluck the ripe ears and eat them? Did our Lord hesitate to heal the afflicted on the Sabbath, for fear of offending the Pharisees?

There is a major difference between "offending" other people and "causing them to stumble." Our Lord offended many, but He never caused one to stumble. His disciples must know the difference also!

Prayer Thought: Deliver me from bondage to other Christians. May I truly enjoy freedom in Christ.

SUGGESTED READING: GALATIANS 5:1–16

Jesus saith unto him, I am the way, the truth, and the life: no man cometh unto the Father, but by me.

—John 14:6

THERE IS A PERILOUS DANGER in having no standard of spirituality except our own inward impressions. If we allowed everybody the same liberty, this would end in religious anarchy. The New Testament utterly opposes such a practice among the saints of God.

The Lord Himself is the one standard of conduct and character in the New Testament. People do not object to a man or a woman becoming outwardly holy, but they do object to his or her becoming a personal devotee of Jesus Christ.

The standard for creed, conduct, and character is Jesus Christ only. The standard of my life must be the same as the Lord's—holiness of walk and character. My limitations and liberties must spring from my personal devotion to Jesus Christ and to nothing else. All who observe me should perceive that I have been with Jesus, not that I have formed some personal convictions about conduct and character, whereby I measure the Almighty and everybody else with whom I come into contact.

Prayer Thought: Lord Jesus, thank You for Your holy example.

SUGGESTED READING: JOHN 14:1–15

He that judgeth me is the Lord.

—1 Corinthians 4:4

WE DARE NOT JUDGE ONE another, and certainly not ourselves. When the Bible exhorts us to walk in the light, it does not mean the light of our own convictions, but the light of the Lord. The Light of the world is Jesus, and one's own point of view is darkness.

It is not obedience to a standard that matters to God, but the fulfillment of the highest standard by the Spirit that is within. Holiness and purity are not obedience to an actual law, but the unconscious natural characteristics of the indwelling Holy Spirit. No one can imitate either. This is why so many who have never experienced the baptism in the Holy Spirit are so stern and unChristlike, and such sticklers for obeying the letter of the truth. These carnal Christians are not spiritual in God's sight.

What a man is—not what he does or has done or hopes to do—will be the standard of judgment on the Judgment Day. There will be no acquittal or appeal.

Prayer Thought: Heavenly Father, cleanse me of self-righteousness. I want to obey You.

SUGGESTED READING: MATTHEW 7:1–5

Yea, I judge not mine own self.

—1 Corinthians 4:3

WHO HAS NOT MET SENSITIVE Christians who are so hyper-conscientious that they are almost afraid to breathe, lest they err? Such bondage is obviously not in accordance with the New Testament. There is no element of freedom about such a tyrannizing standard of introspective self-judgment, for perfect love casteth out fear. Such conscientiousness is selfishness, inverted from glowing pride into a creeping fear.

Paul was not bound or limited by his own introspection or by any subjective standard of judgment whatsoever. He did not live in the light of his own convictions. He walked in the light that produces convictions of the most definite order.

Prayer Thought: Not my will but Thine be done, Lord Jesus.

SUGGESTED READING: PSALM 139:23–24

Whether therefore ye eat, or drink, or whatsoever ye do, do all to the glory of God.

—1 Corinthians 10:31

I F AN INDIVIDUAL SAYS HE will be offended because I wear a necktie, or drink tea, or eat meat, then let him be offended. It is moral courage to ignore such bondage. But if I find that my wearing a necktie, or drinking tea, or eating meat makes any brother or sister to stumble, then I will never do those things again.

Offense arises from wounded personal opinion. Stumbling arises from following another person you love, rather than following Christ.

Most of our "isms" have arisen from following the prescribed limitations of someone's personal convictions, instead of the Lord. Most of these "isms" have a logical and sensible basis. Take "vegetarianism" for an example. A lot can be said in favor of it; but it becomes a law to me if I make it a standard for judgment of others.

Consequently, I put myself in a place where I cannot fulfill the rules of spiritual convictions as cited by the apostle Paul in 1 Corinthians 10.

Prayer Thought: May I not cause another to stumble, Lord.

SUGGESTED READING: 1 CORINTHIANS 10:23–33

If I must needs glory, I will glory of the things which concern mine infirmities.

—2 Corinthians 11:30

WHEN THE LETTER OF GOD'S LAW is enforced contrary to its spirit, or some unjust edict is passed, or some self-effacing step has to be taken by the Christian community, then the atmosphere grows ominous, hot, and sultry. Just at the moment when it seems most logical to compromise, when it seems so easy to compromise, when legitimate compromise seems the sanest and safest thing—to stand up calmly and say with Paul, "It is a very small thing that I should be judged of you," is beyond human language to describe.

This attitude of Paul was neither boyish exuberance nor a defiant shout. No! This was the profound statement of a cultured, somewhat delicate Jew who was passionately in love with the Lord Jesus Christ.

You can also humbly feel and express a holy love toward others and the Lord Jesus Christ.

Prayer Thought: Like You, Lord, help me to love others in spite of their conduct and circumstances.

SUGGESTED READING: 2 CORINTHIANS 11:23–33

But with me it is a very small thing that I should be judged of you, or of man's judgment.

—1 Corinthians 4:3

THIS SCRIPTURE VERSE IS NOT written in an irritated mood or a defiant spirit, but under the direct inspiration of the Holy Spirit, for the purpose of pointing to the one fundamental source of all Christian freedom. Paul regards it lightly that he was judged or scrutinized by his friends. He knew that his Lord was his Judge.

To be misjudged by those who are not one's friends is unimportant to a person who has real friends. But when the examination by one's own friends produces harsh and cruel judgment, it is hard to bear. None can endure this but the man or woman baptized in the Holy Spirit and fire.

The spiritual autobiographies of many lives are full of the pain suffered from the harsh condemnation of friends, until those sufferers took the attitude of Paul—not callously indifferent, but patient, with the large-hearted graciousness of one who endures "as seeing him who is invisible" (Hebrews 11:27).

Prayer Thought: O God, it hurts when friends falsely accuse me. But forgive me if I complain.

SUGGESTED READING: 1 CORINTHIANS 4:1–5

Neither murmur ye.

—1 Corinthians 10:10

PERHAPS THE MOST SUBTLE FALSE standard of spirituality arises from a selfish adherence to one's own convictions. A sad history of severities, stunted lives, broken hearts, and distorted visions of God has arisen from not understanding this wrong and warped method of Christian living.

There is a spiritual sensitiveness which makes one's own personal convictions the standard of spirituality, and which is more concerned about adherence to these convictions than obedience to the Lord. It is a moment of eternal value when we discover that God does not guide us by abstract principles, but by Jesus Christ our Lord.

When we worship the holiness of our own convictions instead of our holy Lord, there is an element in human nature that makes us all possible popes and intolerant upholders of our personal views.

Prayer Thought: From my heart I cry "Holy, holy, holy" is the Lord God omnipotent.

SUGGESTED READING: 1 CORINTHIANS 10:1–14

Who gave himself for our sins, that he might deliver us from this present evil world, according to the will of God and our Father.

—Galatians 1:4

THE NEAREST AND CHOICEST FRIENDS will at times misunderstand God's way with you and may even become very demons in advice, even as Peter was to Jesus.

At the very outset of the sanctified life, cruel judgments and condemnations by our friends will be encountered. In such moments as these, to stand with the silence of God in the heart and the clear understanding of the misjudgment of the dearest and innermost circle of friends is to know with Paul (and our Lord) the introduction to a larger and more useful life, through the hurt of a broken circle of friends.

It is perilously easy for us to react to the critical comments of our friends and to feel that, after all, "I may be wrong, for those I love and who love me see spiritual things so differently." Yet the inward heart knows, when alone with God, whether His way points differently.

Prayer Thought: Dear Lord, help me to remain steady and sure in the security of Your Word and its guidance.

SUGGESTED READING: GALATIANS 1:1–16

But we have this treasure in earthen vessels, that the excellency of
the power may be of God, and not of us.

—2 Corinthians 4:7

"THE UTMOST FOR THE HIGHEST" was the motto of that
great artist G. F. Watts. My utmost for His highest in
actual life, as depicted by Paul, involves loving attitudes and
holy actions on our part when there are not ideal conditions in
our lives. Through these attitudes and actions, we seek to carry
out the ideals of our heavenly Father.

The highest Christian love is not devotion to a certain
work or cause of God, but to Him. Causes and works are good,
but love for them will fail us. Our Lord was viewed as erratic
because He did not identify Himself with the cause of the
Pharisees or with the Zealots. Instead He laid down His life as
the servant of His Father.

Thank God, we have opportunities of identifying ourselves with our Lord's interests in other people, by manifesting
the love that never fails. That love "suffereth long, and is kind;
[love] envieth not; [love] vaunteth not itself, is not puffed up,
doth not behave itself unseemly, seeketh not her own, is not
easily provoked, thinketh no evil; rejoiceth not in iniquity, but
rejoiceth in the truth; beareth all things, believeth all things,
hopeth all things, endureth all things" (1 Corinthians 13:4–7).
Love never fails.

Prayer Thought: God of love, help me to
exhibit love in all I say and do.

SUGGESTED READING: 2 CORINTHIANS 4:7–11

It is better to trust in the LORD than to put confidence in man.

—Psalm 118:8

WITH OUR MINDS, WE NEVER receive a complete knowledge through mere research. Knowledge of God comes through our hearts—the windows of our souls.

During the Boxer uprising in China, a lady I knew learned of the murder of her husband and two of her children. Their bodies were found beheaded and mutilated. After this astounding catastrophe she testified: "I could not pray, have faith, or lay hold of God. But my heart knew Him and no matter how this tragedy seemed to contradict so many things, I rejoiced in Him." So many people believe in their beliefs, have faith in their faith, and are confident in their confidence. All of this is of no avail. It is our confidence in God that abides, faith in God that remains, and belief in God that lasts.

Hallelujah! Not joy or peace, but God is our God.

Prayer Thought: I worship You, heavenly Father, for You are full of grace and goodness, love and longsuffering.

SUGGESTED READING: PSALM 118:1–8

And whatsoever ye shall ask in my name, that will I do, that the Father may be glorified in the Son.

—John 14:13

THE ROYAL WAY IN WHICH we partake in Christ's sufferings is in intercession for others.

Do you know what God will do when you begin to take a soul before Him? He will put the condition of that soul on you until you go through all that person experiences, so to speak. And new converts will abide if you will present them steadfastly day and night, in the blood of your soul and the passion of your prayer, straight before God.

> *Though the Garden be before me,*
> *And the scornful Judgment Hall,*
> *Though the gloom of deepest midnight,*
> *Settle round me like a pall;*
> *Though the cross my path o'ershadows,*
> *Thou didst bear it once for me,*
> *And whate'er the pain or peril,*
> *"Jesus, I'll go through with Thee."*
> *Jesus Christ interceded for us. To be like*
> *Him, we must be intercessors.*

Prayer Thought: Give me a burden for the souls of mankind.

SUGGESTED READING: JOHN 14:12–14

He that believeth on me, as the scripture hath said, out of his belly shall flow rivers of living water.

—John 7:38

A LADY SAID TO ME THE other day, "Well, Brother Chambers, I am sure that I once was more visibly used of God than I am now; and yet I know God better now than I ever did. I do not know where the trouble is."

Jesus said, "Drink of me and out of you shall flow rivers of living water." Am I to watch the flow? Never. I am to pay attention to the source. He will then look after the flow.

Almost invariably, a preacher will tell you that at the beginning of his ministry God seemed to use him more mightily than at the present. Now he knows God tenfold better, and yet is not being used in the same way by God. What is the implication? God is making character.

I think that, at the beginning of our Christian experience, God encourages us by letting us see His wonderful doings and marvel at them. Then He quietly begins to be manifested through our mortal being in new ways. Allow Him to do so in your life. Do not complain.

Prayer Thought: God, use me for Your glory.
Help me not to question Your ways.

SUGGESTED READING: JOHN 7:32–39

Be merciful unto me, O Lord: for I cry unto thee daily.

—Psalm 86:3

WHEN THE HOLY SPIRIT REALLY grips someone in conviction of sin, there is only one of two places for that person—namely, an insane asylum or the cross of Jesus. Conviction can be the origin of saving faith. Justification is given to a sinful person who willingly, as a pauper, accepts the forgiveness of God on the basis of what Jesus did for him through His death on the cross and His resurrection from the grave.

Holiness is likewise a gift of grace, given to a surrendered soul by God. It comes whenever a justified person willingly gives up the right to oneself and presents one's body "a living sacrifice . . . acceptable unto God." (Romans 12:1).

A life of faith, after a supreme act of faith for salvation, is as natural and subconscious as breathing.

Not by wrestling, but by clinging,
Shall we be most blessed.
Wrestling only brings us sorrow;
Clinging brings us rest.
When we stay our feeble efforts,
And from struggling cease,
Unconditional surrender,
Brings us God's own peace.

Prayer Thought: I need You every hour, Lord Jesus. Thank You for Your promised presence.

SUGGESTED READING: PSALM 86:1–7

From that time many of his disciples went back, and walked no more with him.

—John 6:66

*F*aith, IN THE NEW TESTAMENT sense of the word, is the act of changing one's will and staking it determinedly on Jesus, the living Word of God.

Let me illustrate what I mean. A boy comes in for dinner and knows that the food on the table will satisfy him. He does not doubt it. He sees the food on the table and knows that it will satisfy. But when will he be satisfied? When he sees the meal? No, only when he eats the food. Not before.

This is what offended the disciples of Jesus. He told them, "Except ye eat the flesh of the Son of man, and drink his blood, ye have no life in you." The Word says, "From that time many of his disciples went back, and walked no more with him" (John 6:53, 66). They became deserters. You will be a deserter too, if you do not accept what God has given you in the Lord Jesus.

Prayer Thought: Consciously and willingly
I accept the truth of Your Word.

SUGGESTED READING: JOHN 6:51–66

For ye are all the children of God by faith in Christ Jesus.

—Galatians 3:26

WHO ARE THE CHILDREN OF Abraham—the Jews? Yes, but there are more. All who believe in Jesus Christ are the children of Abraham. All the promises of God are for every man and woman who believes.

What do I mean by believing? Believing is when people make a willful commitment of their all to God, and stake their all on Him.

For twenty centuries, God has not said another word. The Cross was His last word and Pentecost was the explanation of the Cross. Now God is waiting. When the next word is spoken, what do you think He will say to the hosts of people who have been playing loosely with the promises of God, as if they were nothing at all? When the wrath of the Lamb of God bursts forth, and the judgment of our God begins, it will be unspeakably terrible.

Take heed: "Neither is there salvation in any other: for there is none other name under heaven given among men, whereby we must be saved" (Acts 4:12). When we willfully yield to God, He will witness by the Holy Spirit to this act of faith on our part in response to His promises.

Prayer Thought: I love being a member of the family of God.

SUGGESTED READING: GALATIANS 3:17–29

That if thou shalt confess with thy mouth the Lord Jesus, and shalt believe in thine heart that God hath raised him from the dead, thou shalt be saved.

—Romans 10:9

SENTIMENTAL THEOLOGY SAYS THAT WE are saved by admiring Jesus. This makes about as much sense as saying that when the whitewashed gable of a house reflects the glory of sunlight, the sun is shining inside the house.

By voluntary sacrifice of Himself, Jesus became sin for us; He repaired the evil that Adam brought on the whole human race. Jesus became the recipient of the punishment that you and I should have received. God is satisfied with Jesus; and when we unite ourselves by faith to Jesus Christ, we find that God imputes to us His righteousness.

When Jesus saves us, He destroys the personality of sin and gives us a personality of holiness.

Prayer Thought: Lord, I am not worthy of salvation. With gratitude I will live for You.

SUGGESTED READING: ROMANS 10:1–10

Brethren, if a man be overtaken in a fault, ye which are spiritual, restore such an one in the spirit of meekness; considering thyself, lest thou also be tempted.

—Galatians 6:1

THE PROBABLE REASON THAT SOME Christians condemn other servants of God who have fallen and been reclaimed is that they have never encountered the same trials and testings. They have been shielded.

God have mercy on us when we forget the horrible pit and miry clay out of which the sovereign grace of God dug us! When we do forget, we are apt to allow spiritual pride to put a barrier between us and others.

Certain forms of sin shock us unspeakably. But the sin that shocks God and broke the heart of our Lord on Calvary is the sin of "my right to myself"—pride. God hates pride and will not tolerate this evil in sinners or saints.

We have no right to have a "holier-than-thou" attitude toward fallen men or women. A holy man does not keep his eyes on his own spiritual cleanness.

Prayer Thought: Forgive me if I tend to belittle and degrade others.

SUGGESTED READING: GALATIANS 6:1–5

I beseech you therefore, brethren, by the mercies of God, that ye present your bodies a living sacrifice, holy, acceptable unto God, which is your reasonable service.

—Romans 12:1

EVERY TIME GOD GAVE ABRAHAM the promise of a blessing, he erected an altar and gave it back to God. Paul says this should be true even in our lives. God gave us our bodies; we are to give them back to Him as living sacrifices. This is something that God cannot do for us. It is something we have to do. We have to give Him a definite gift of ourselves.

God grant that you will come to this point of giving! God grant that this passionate entreaty of Paul be mightily fulfilled in your life today, for the glory of the Lord!

The Lord will spoil you for this age. Your passionate love for God will refashion you from a love of this world.

Prayer Thought: Possess me fully, Lord, and fashion me according to Your will.

SUGGESTED READING: ROMANS 12:1–9

Thanks be to God, which giveth us the victory through our Lord Jesus Christ.

—1 Corinthians 15:57

THE FUNDAMENTAL CHARACTERISTIC OF A life of faith is a definite breaking away of everything that ruled our sinful past, and a determined and disciplined claiming of God's Word. The spiritual life of faith operates as unconsciously and naturally as our physical bodies, bringing us victory as a matter of course.

Sin rules our conscious lives apart from God. Entire sanctification removes this "personality of sin," upsetting the conscious life and all its human reasoning, and puts a new "saintly personality" in its place. So to speak, the power of God begins the construction of a new consciousness.

Jesus Christ finished on the cross the greatest work in the world. He overcame Satan, death, and sin, so that "whosoever will" may become in Him a victor over Satan, death, and sin.

Prayer Thought: Father, I claim victory by virtue of what Jesus Christ did on the cross for me.

SUGGESTED READING: 1 CORINTHIANS 15:55–58

Ye adulterers and adulteresses, know ye not that the friendship of the world is enmity with God? whosoever therefore will be a friend of the world is the enemy of God.

—James 4:4

THE PITY OF THIS MODERN age goes out to Judas, not to Christ. Pity does not overflow for that lonely Nazarene who came and died to save and sanctify us, but for the one who hated and betrayed Jesus. In the same line of thought, some modern Christians, if they had lived at the time of the Good Samaritan, would have pitied the thieves and left the poor victim still lying on the roadside.

Our sympathies have gone rotten! Anyone who is a friend of this age is the enemy of God; and anyone who befriends the enemy of God hates Jesus Christ.

If you are called of Christ and acquainted with His Cross—if you are not wedded to the present age—then share the message of the Cross and see if you will not be despised. Jesus said, "For whosoever shall do the will of my Father which is in heaven, the same is my brother, and sister, and mother" (Matthew 12:50).

Prayer Thought: Lord, help me to be Your true friend.

SUGGESTED READING: LUKE 10:30–37

Howbeit when he, the Spirit of truth, is come, he will guide you into all truth: for he shall not speak of himself; but whatsoever he shall hear, that shall he speak: and he will shew you things to come.

—John 16:13

GOD DOES NOT ALWAYS CONVICT people when I think they ought to be convicted. Do I think that people can be convicted just when I like? Never! My praying cannot make someone listen to God.

But if you are professing to be saved and sanctified, and God knows you are not, He will begin to convict you. To the soul who will listen, God will—with unerring finger—point to the one hindering thing.

Do not tell me, when you have not gotten through to God, that you do not know why it is. You do! If there is one faithful power on this earth, it is the power of the Holy Spirit. He will reveal to you the hindering thing. After you obey Him, then— and only then—will God give you faith.

Prayer Thought: Break my stubborn will, blessed Holy Spirit, and have Your complete way and will in my life.

SUGGESTED READING: JOHN 16:1–14

God that made the world and all things therein, seeing that he is Lord of heaven and earth, dwelleth not in temples made with hands.

—Acts 17:24

WHERE IN THE BIBLE DO you read that you must have a long, peaceful life? Paul held to this world very lightly. With magnificent meaning, he said to the Romans,

Who shall separate us from the love of Christ? shall tribulation, or distress, or persecution, or famine, or nakedness, or peril, or sword? . . . For I am persuaded, that neither death, nor life, nor angels, nor principalities, nor powers, nor things present, nor things to come, Nor height, nor depth, nor any other creature, shall be able to separate us from the love of God, which is in Christ Jesus our Lord (Romans 8:35, 38–39).

The soul that Jesus has saved and sanctified goes with a calm and unwavering tread through earth's heartbreaks, sorrows, and joys—through death itself—with the whisperings of Christ, "Let not your heart be troubled, for I have gone before you." Glory be to God!

Prayer Thought: Lord of life, I commit
my earthly days into Your hands.

SUGGESTED READING: ACTS 17:17–27

For we are the circumcision, which worship God in the spirit, and rejoice in Christ Jesus, and have no confidence in the flesh.

—Philippians 3:3

THE APOSTLE PAUL WAS OF a noble line of birth, had noble blood in his veins, and was a genius of heart and mind. And yet, this great man said, "[I] have no confidence in the flesh."

When you are having difficulty spiritually, physically, or financially, where do you go for help? If you are a child of God and your work for Him is experiencing serious problems, what are you doing about it? Do you put your trust in some preacher who has mighty gifts? That is to have confidence in the flesh!

We are to have no confidence in human wisdom. This was the very problem with the children of Israel; God told them to go over Jordan and possess the land, but they said no. They thought they could follow their human wisdom and do something better. But God banished and blighted them.

God will do the same thing to you if you insist upon having confidence in the flesh instead of faith in Him.

Prayer Thought: Your wisdom, dear Father in heaven, is my need this very hour.

SUGGESTED READING: PHILIPPIANS 3:1–7

And whosoever doth not bear his cross, and come after me, cannot be my disciple.

—Luke 14:27

W**HAT IS THE** C**HRISTIAN'S CROSS**? It is not the cross Christ carried. We cannot carry that; on that cross God took away the sin of the world. Nor does the Christian's cross consist of the trials one has to bear if one is a Christian. It is distinctly and emphatically the result of being one of the Lord's disciples.

The cross is my sign that I am crucified with Christ, dead to the world. If I am dead, how then can I live as before?

How much provision does one make for a corpse in the house? None. One must bury it. When Christ delivers you from sin, you are able to reckon the death of the "man of sin"; you make no provision for him.

Have you your cross, my friend? The cross is marked from the place of death, not to it. Conviction for sin is not the cross by which Jesus marks His disciples. The sign of the cross is that you are crucified with Christ; you are not your own. Jesus is first!

Do you desire this life in Christ?

Prayer Thought: Help me, God, to bear acceptably my cross for You in the days and months before me this year.

SUGGESTED READING: LUKE 14:25–33

Therefore thou art inexcusable, O man, whosoever thou art that judgest: for wherein thou judgest another, thou condemnest thyself; for thou that judgest doest the same things.

—Romans 2:1

To accuse "the brethren" is devilish in nature and practice. Yet many professing Christians do this. They are carnal! Carnality, in blunt American talk, is bossism. When self-appointed know-it-alls speak of things pertaining to holiness, they manifest carnal behavior.

Carnal behavior will not suffer long with others, is not kind to people, envies, always is rash in judgment and attitudes, seeks its own selfish ways, rejoices in iniquity when it is discovered, and will not rejoice in the truth.

Moral lepers are the first to detect moral leprosy in others; so carnal people see in others what is often within themselves. Carnality is the genius of discovering defects and sins in others, so that one can excuse sins and defects in oneself.

Carnality always ignores God's claim to us as creatures of His. It emphasizes the idea that "I have the truth of God and whoever does not agree with me shall be damned." But our Lord said to the carnal Pharisees in His day that they would not escape the damnation of hell (see Matthew 23:13–23).

Prayer Thought: Father, help me to be peaceable and not a source of trouble in the family of God.

SUGGESTED READING: MATTHEW 23:1–12

Finally, brethren, whatsoever things are true, whatsoever things are honest, whatsoever things are just, whatsoever things are pure, whatsoever things are lovely, whatsoever things are of good report; if there be any virtue, and if there be any praise, think on these things.

—Philippians 4:8

GENUINE SAINTS WILL DISCERN WHATSOEVER things are true, just, pure, lovely, and of good report. True holiness discerns virtuous and praiseworthy people and deeds, and delights in these.

The discerning of spirits is one of the gifts of the Spirit (see 1 Corinthians 12:10). Real discernment does not consist of the vague impressions of a lively imagination. Discernment works by the Word of God. The Holy Spirit glorified Jesus; and the Spirit-filled, sanctified saint intuitively discerns any person, teaching, or doctrine that does not glorify Him as Lord.

A sanctified person immediately recognizes spiritual error because the Holy Spirit will bring to remembrance all that Jesus taught. The Holy Spirit will lead one into all truth and will help every "sheep of the Lord" to detect a stranger's voice.

Spiritual discernment is keenly sensitive to the glory of God. A spiritually discerning saint walks in the light and with the Light who is Jesus Christ.

Prayer Thought: I desire to know truth. Grant to me, Lord, wisdom to discern the truth.

SUGGESTED READING: PHILIPPIANS 4:1–9

And ye shall be hated of all men for my name's sake: but he that endureth to the end shall be saved.

—Matthew 10:22

THERE ARE TIMES IN THE life of every Christian where one does not know what to do or say. Things look unclear and very difficult. Friend, such times of darkness come to discipline your character; they will increase your knowledge of the Lord. These seasons of darkness are for listening, not for speaking.

In times of darkness, our Lord shares the darkness with His disciple. He is there. He knows all about it. There must be a sense of mystery, for mystery requires you to be guided by someone who knows more than you do. This is true, both physically and spiritually speaking. Never forget this fact.

Let me mention a very important point in this matter of fellowshipping with God when darkness prevails all around us. You and I should not say in our hearts, "I must have a breakthrough; God must reveal Himself." God wants us to listen, not fuss with Him. Only "in quietness and confidence shall be your strength" (Isaiah 30:15).

The listening ear is characteristic of a Christian in darkness. We should not listen to the voices of sympathizing fellow Christians, nor to voices of self-pity. We should listen only to the voice of the Lord.

Prayer Thought: Speak to me, Lord, even throughout the dark circumstances of life.

SUGGESTED READING: MATTHEW 10:16–28

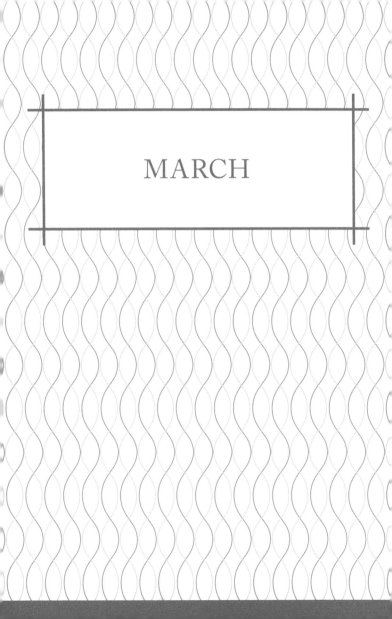

MARCH

My sheep hear my voice, and I know them, and they follow me.

—John 10:27

IT IS NOT WHAT A Christian utters in public prayer, preaches from the pulpit, or writes on paper that determines God's attitude and relation to him; it is what he says in his heart, which God alone can hear. This determines the believer's relationship with God.

Many people talk glibly about stupendous truths that they believe. But the Lord has never talked to them in the stillness of the dark and lonely moments of solitude, when only His voice gives light to see and understand.

Remember this: The Lord never gives private illumination to favored Christians. God's way of communication descends from divine illumination through His Word, for the development of spiritual character in His saints. Yet the Lord speaks, definitely and persuasively, to those who care to listen.

At first we may not hear the Lord's voice because our spiritual ears are untrained to detect it above the tumult and noise of the dark circumstances of our lives. But once we learn His voice, the finest of earth's voices are never again mistaken for the voice of the Lord.

Prayer Thought: Lord God, I have heard Your voice many times. It is always a source of strength to me.

SUGGESTED READING: PSALM 18:24–28

Ye are my friends, if ye do whatsoever I command you.

—John 15:14

WE LONG FOR PERENNIAL FRESHNESS in our Christian lives. It is indeed a blessing to enjoy spiritual freshness at camp meeting, during a revival meeting, and in our prayer meetings; but what we yearn to know is the secret source of abiding freshness.

Friendship with Jesus is the first source of abiding freshness in our Christian lives. What is a friend? A "friend" is one in agreement and attachment to the deepest and most fundamental things of a person's life. In order to be a friend of Jesus, I must be born again of the Spirit of God. Only then will I have a disposition like His.

It is an experience of perennial delight to any man or woman to know that he or she has a friend "that sticketh closer than a brother"! Jesus is this kind of friend. He understands the heart so thoroughly that He satisfies the last aching abyss of the heart. Jesus is ready to be your friend, if you will but come to Him. This attachment in holy friendship will bring freshness to your heart and life.

Prayer Thought: Thank You, Jesus, for being my personal friend.

SUGGESTED READING: MATTHEW 11:28–30

Labour not for the meat which perisheth, but for that meat which endureth unto everlasting life, which the Son of man shall give unto you: for him hath God the Father sealed.

—John 6:27

FRIENDSHIP WITH CHRIST IS ONLY one part of the sources of abiding spiritual freshness. Work is the other. Our Lord labored, and did so easily.

Much of the work done for God and the church today shatters the nervous system and strains the body. This must not continue if we are to have abiding freshness. It is not the work we do for God that keeps us fresh; it is the work we allow God to do through us. With a heart at leisure from itself, through abiding friendship with Jesus, we can have an indefatigable fund of energy for beneficial work.

In spite of all the opposition of the world, the flesh, and the Devil, we can know that God is doing His work through us. His fountain of living water can well up within us to eternal life, so that the thirsty and parched throughout the world may rejoice and be refreshed and uplifted, wherever we go!

Prayer Thought: O God, forgive me for being self-righteously busy for You. Give me a fresh touch of spiritual blessing and anointing, I pray.

SUGGESTED READING: JOHN 6:22–29

All things were made by him; and without him was not any thing made that was made. In him was life; and the life was the light of men.

—John 1:3–4

W E ARE CREATED THE CHILDREN of God, not the sons and daughters of God; Jesus Christ, through regeneration, makes us sons and daughters of God. The idea of the fatherhood of Jesus is revealed in Isaiah 9:6, where He is called the "everlasting Father."

Creative power is vested in Jesus Christ in a far more marvelous way than He manifested when He created the world. Jesus is the Being by whom you and I can be re-created into His own image.

In Jesus Christ, we are made new creatures—not merely given a new start. Jesus creates in us the image of God as it is in Himself. What Jesus Christ creates in us, He was and is. He becomes our sanctification. That is what the grand old hymn means,

My hope is built on nothing less,

Than Jesus' blood and righteousness.

We are sons and daughters of God by God's claim in creation; but we become sons and daughters of God in reality only by our choice and our will. Do you willingly choose to hand yourself over to God? Let Jesus Christ make His creation good in you.

Prayer Thought: O God, may I always reflect
Your image as a new creation in Christ.

SUGGESTED READING: COLOSSIANS 1:16–29

Because as he is, so are we in this world.

—1 John 4:17

THOSE OF US WHO ARE God's children stand in holy reverence when we read the above verse of Scripture. It can only mean one thing: The image, character, and holiness of Jesus Christ are in His sanctified ones. They are consequences of His sovereign right of creation.

Sanctification means that I am taken into that mystical union which no language can define. " Beloved, now are we the sons of God, and it doth not yet appear what we shall be: but we know that, when he shall appear, we shall be like him; for we shall see him as he is" (1 John 3:2).

It is one thing for God to claim me, quite another thing for me to allow Him to make that claim real. It is one thing to realize in speechless wonder that I can be sanctified, that my heart can be turned to worship; but it is another thing to tell God that I want Him to realize His claim in me.

I can hear someone say, "Do you mean to tell me, Brother Chambers, that I—an ordinary human being with ordinary, commonplace work, surrounded by ordinary, commonplace people with no particular education—that I can be a new creation in Christ Jesus?"

Yes, I am saying all of this. Let God realize His claim in you. Let Jesus Christ make His creation good in you.

Prayer Thought: Create in me the attributes of righteousness, Lord, which will identify me as Your child.

SUGGESTED READING: 1 JOHN 4:1–17

Verily thou art a God that hidest thyself, O God of Israel, the Saviour.

—Isaiah 45:15

THERE IS AN ASPECT OF God's nature that can be expounded in no other term than *astonishing*. It is probably best explained by saying that the sovereign will of God is really His free will; yet this presents a mystery so deep to His children that the Bible must say that we serve "a God that hideth Himself."

This hiding of God's face toward us is not on account of our sin or backsliding. God is simply working His sovereign will, trusting that His children will love Him, even when they do not understand His ways—as in the case of Job.

In this respect, one application of the Beatitudes is rarely explained by preachers. In Matthew 5:7, we read, "Blessed are the merciful: for they shall obtain mercy." As children of God we should, when God is putting us through strange and mysterious circumstances, convey a merciful impression to the minds of others regarding their attitude toward God! It is a real danger, and perilous to their souls, to allow people to sympathize so much with us in our suffering that they have resentful thoughts of God.

Prayer Thought: I accept what You permit to come into my life, heavenly Father, as Your will for me.

SUGGESTED READING: ISAIAH 45:1–15

And I will give thee the treasures of darkness, and hidden riches of secret places, that thou mayest know that I, the LORD, which call thee by thy name, am the God of Israel!

—Isaiah 45:3

"THE TREASURES OF DARKNESS" is a remarkable phrase. We can see the stars in our natural world because of the surrounding darkness. And it is because of the mysterious darkness of God's providences that the deep secrets of God are ever known to us.

The prophet Isaiah greeted God's message with the question, "Who is this?" (Isaiah 63:1). He was plainly astonished and almost staggered with the unfamiliarity of the revelation coming to him from God. Have you ever faced a similar situation? It is good for us to recall the "horror of the great darkness" that befell Abram, or the statement made by Moses that God "met him in an inn to put him to death." Or remember David, in the case where Uzzah put forth his hand and steadied the ark, and God smote him to death. We read that David was so astonished that he was "displeased" with God.

When the sovereign God brings us an astonishing revelation, we are to be a mouthpiece of God Almighty, not a systematic expounder of our own private convictions. The tendency to be true to our own convictions, not to the Lord, is apt to produce a troublesome attitude toward divine revelation.

Prayer Thought: Lord, I accept Your Word and the circumstances resulting from Your intentions in my life.

SUGGESTED READING: ISAIAH 63:1–6

Be of good cheer: it is I; be not afraid.

—Mark 6:50

A SUDDEN STORM AROSE ON THE Sea of Galilee. Apparently, Jesus Christ permitted this crisis to enter the lives of His disciples. The uproar of nature threatened to overthrow their boat. They were isolated in the terror of a storm. Why would the Lord God permit such an astonishing set of circumstances?

Whatever the reasons for our trouble, we must not allow our souls to become so overwhelmed that we think we have committed some "unpardonable sin." For out of all the terror comes the soothing voice of our Lord Himself, "Be of good cheer: it is I; be not afraid."

Too many disciples have faith in their faith, or in their joy in the Lord; and when a spiritual storm comes, they have neither faith nor joy. Only one thing can endure, and that is love for God. If such love is not there, we will not recognize the loving voice of God when He cries out to us that He is "our refuge and strength, a very present help in trouble. . . . Be still, and know that I am God" (Psalm 46:1, 10).

Prayer Thought: You are my God, and I seek strength and shelter in Your love and goodness.

SUGGESTED READING: MARK 6:45–50

But the Comforter, which is the Holy Ghost, whom the Father will send in my name, he shall teach you all things, and bring all things to your remembrance, whatsoever I have said unto you.

—John 14:26

THERE IS A CRAZE THESE days to hear something new from the Lord; but what we need to hear are those things we have heard all along, but have not listened to. The reason many people do not understand the leadings of God is their ignorance of His revealed Word.

We can be led through the guidance of the Bible. This is why we must preach and teach the Word by the passion of the indwelling Holy Spirit.

Your success consists in being completely loyal to God. If you are loyal, then God is responsible for the fruitage. Whether the results be gladness (as with the 3,000 converts when Peter preached on the Day of Pentecost) or madness (such as Stephen faced when he was stoned and martyred), one is equally as successful in God's sight as the other.

God have mercy on the soul who dares to stand for Jesus Christ and teach any other gospel, any other obedience, than the way of the cross of Jesus Christ.

Prayer Thought: Lord, I am completely open to Your marvelous way and will.

SUGGESTED READING: MATTHEW 7:24–29

This is the way, walk ye in it.

—Isaiah 30:21

WE CANNOT GROW INTO ENTIRE sanctification; but after we attain this experience, we must grow into all the fullness of Christ. We are not saved and filled with the Holy Spirit to do any special work, but simply to let God work through us.

Oh, we are so desperately concerned about erecting the scaffolding in our lives to build a great work! When God begins to remove it—the scaffolding of our works, etc.—we begin to totter. And when our scaffolding falls, and we are sitting among the ruins, the Holy Spirit whispers, "That was not my staff, upon which you should rest. So I am removing it. You are the work I am after, not your little works. I want you where I can work through you."

For God's sake, let Him do what He likes with you.

Prayer Thought: Help me, God, never to hesitate to embark on the path of duty You set before me.

SUGGESTED READING: ISAIAH 30:18–21

If ye abide in me, and my words abide in you, ye shall ask what ye will,
and it shall be done unto you.

—John 15:7

THE ONLY RELIABLE WAY TO be truly guided by God is
to assimilate the Word of God to your character. Yet even
that spiritual truth will damage instead of help you if the Holy
Spirit is not present.

Have you ever noticed that the most hardened people are
not the backsliders, but preachers or teachers who thunder out
the truth of Scripture, yet make no application of it to themselves? Scripture reveals God's will only if we allow His Holy
Spirit to apply it to our circumstances.

The Bible is not a book that you can open and say, "Now,
Lord, put some magic into my soul that will open up the meaning of this book." There is only one way really to understand
the Word, and that is through wrestling with the circumstances
and happenings of life. God will take His servants through
things no one else seems to endure, because He wants them to
understand the deep secrets of His Word.

Prayer Thought: When I complain, Lord Jesus,
about the circumstances of life, allow me to realize
that You are sharing the truth with me.

SUGGESTED READING: JOHN 15:1–8

But that no man is justified by the law in the sight of God, it is evident: for, The just shall live by faith.

—Galatians 3:11

G OD USES SYMBOLS IN His dealings with us human beings in order to get our attention. For example, He used a "pillar of cloud" to lead the children of Israel; study the Book of Exodus to learn more about this.

Yet God will sometimes remove symbols of guidance in our lives. Over and over again, God has removed the symbols whereby He has guided His people. And whenever He has done it, some of His followers proved to be wedded to the symbol instead of to God. As a result, the loss of God's symbol wrecked their lives.

When Jesus reinterpreted the Law, what did the Pharisees say? They called Jesus "an impostor" and thought He should be "put to death." They were wedded to their symbols, and not to the Lord.

When you begin to walk with God, He may permit you to walk by sight more than by faith. But after a while, He will begin removing the visible symbols and let you tremble. When that happens, you can be sure that He is about to teach you how to walk by faith.

Prayer Thought: O Lord, it is easier to walk by sight, but teach me how to walk with You by faith.

SUGGESTED READING: GALATIANS 3:1–12

He made known his ways unto Moses, his acts unto the children of Israel.

—Psalm 103:7

A SERVANT OF GOD IS TAKEN into God's counsels. A servant of God is one with whom God counsels, not one who counsels God.

Have you found that God is destroying your little human wisdom and knowledge? The Lord be praised! God wants to wound the pride of your intellect. God does not use the wisdom of this world to express His thoughts; nor should we think our own thoughts and then ask God to bless them. God wants to think His thoughts through us, and then make us a blessing to others.

I was but a hell-bound carnal vagabond; now I am saved and entirely sanctified by the sheer might and mercy of God. Who am I that I can bring you face to face with God?

Yet the servant of God should bring people to meet God. Then the servant should sink out of sight and let God "bind up the broken-hearted," "set at liberty the captive," and help men and women to make straight paths for their feet. This is the plan of divine guidance.

Prayer Thought: Lord, You must increase and I decrease in the hearts and minds of those around me.

SUGGESTED READING: PROVERBS 3:5–6

For thou art my rock and my fortress; therefore for thy name's sake lead me, and guide me.

—Psalm 31:3

WHEN YOU ARE WOUNDED AND stricken, seek refuge in God's abiding presence. Carry your burdens to Him. Pour your heaped-up troubles on Him. He understands, my precious friend, when the heart is apparently gone out of you. God pities you, as a father does his little child. The gentleness of a mother is harsh compared with the gentleness of God.

When perplexities and troubles come, go to Jesus. Listen as He says, "Let not your heart be troubled" (John 14:1). He will guide you by His sympathy. He will guide!

The prophet Isaiah shared with us a spiritual secret with these comforting words, "Thou wilt keep him in perfect peace, whose mind is stayed on thee: because he trusteth in thee" (Isaiah 26:3).

Prayer Thought: For Your glory and my good,
guide me onward, O King Eternal.

SUGGESTED READING: PSALM 31:1–3

Who are kept by the power of God through faith unto salvation ready to be revealed in the last time.

—1 Peter 1:5

CRISES REVEAL CHARACTER! THIS IS true in the natural and the spiritual worlds. When Jesus Christ was in the wilderness, being tempted of the Devil for forty days and nights with nothing to eat, what do you think kept Him? Divine character, secured by the indwelling presence of the Holy Spirit.

What about your home life in recent weeks and months? How did you behave when things went wrong? Did you have to suppress your real feelings? Be honest.

Unless you meet God at the altar, He will never alter you. The Devil will try to pawn all kinds of emotional defeats on you. After you are sanctified wholly, he will try to convince you that you are not sanctified. Then is the time for you to get out your handcuffs for the Devil and say, "I am crucified with Christ."

Character, not emotions, will keep and hold you by the power of God when the onslaughts of the Devil are leveled at you.

Prayer Thought: Lord Jesus, Your security, in the midst of my swirling emotions, is the rock on which I stand.

SUGGESTED READING: 1 PETER 1:3–9

And thou shalt love the Lord thy God with all thy heart, and with all thy soul, and with all thy mind, and with all thy strength: this is the first commandment. And the second is like, namely this, Thou shalt love thy neighbour as thyself. There is none other commandment greater than these.

—Mark 12:30–31

AFTER YOU START TO LIVE a holy life, I defy you to tell me how God is going to lead you. I defy you to tell me how God will lead anybody. We fall into great error when we get censorious and vindictive about other people's Christian experience. By meddling in their matters, we displease God.

Let me raise a hypothetical situation: Suppose that you are entirely sanctified and so am I. God brings us into a crisis. You have a solution, but I have my own idea. I decide that unless you see it my way, as far as I am concerned, you are wrong and not as spiritual as I. This unnecessary encounter is impudence and God will punish me for it.

The standard of holiness is that I love my neighbor as myself. But I am not loving you as myself when I presume to tell you what God wants you to do.

Prayer Thought: As You have loved me,
Lord, help me to love others.

SUGGESTED READING: MARK 12:28–34

But Peter said unto him, Although all shall be offended, yet . . . I will not deny thee in any wise.

—Mark 14:29, 31

WAS PETER BEING HONEST? I think he was. Then why did Jesus Christ discourage the very essence of his profession?

Are we called to profess our loyalty to Christ? Never!—no, ten thousand times never—are we to profess our loyalty. We are called to profess whose we are and what God has done. Realizing and acknowledging this, we are to stand upright in the hand of God. If we try to stand on our profession, we will fall as Peter did.

God wants to separate us from our profession. "Away with professions!" is God's attitude. He wants to possess us. He wants us to be His.

Prayer Thought: Jesus, strip all self-righteousness from my witness for You.

SUGGESTED READING: MARK 14:22–31

Keep thy heart with all diligence; for out of it are the issues of life.

—Proverbs 4:23

EVERY LIFE CARRIES AN ATMOSPHERE, and this atmosphere blesses or blights.

Have we not met people who enlarge our horizons and loosen the limitations about our hearts? This happens because of the very atmosphere they produce. We seem to grow nobler and purer for having met them and being with them.

On the other hand, have we not met people who make it "winter for our souls"? They create a cold atmosphere in which we shrivel and grow small. Generous thoughts about others do not survive in their presence.

Our personal atmosphere arises from the condition of our hearts, not from our surroundings. Watch the attitudes of your heart, "for out of it are the issues of life."

Prayer Thought: Heavenly Father, allow my life to have a positive, holy influence on others.

SUGGESTED READING: PROVERBS 4:23–27

And he went out, not knowing whither he went. . . . He sojourned in the land of promise.

—Hebrews 11:8–9

GOD DEMANDS SEPARATION. SOMETIMES HE wants us to separate ourselves from what we consider a good set of circumstances. That is exactly what He did with Abraham.

Jesus demands that we have freedom in Him by becoming detached from a particular set of opinions, from the way we look at things on the basis of our upbringing, and from our ideals and ambitions. Jesus requires separation from the most sacred of relationships. The most loving eyes that look on you will never understand. The tenderest hand that ever caressed you will not understand. Yet consecration to Christ entails this kind of separation.

Does this mean, then, that I must leave my country, my home, everything, to prove my love to Jesus? No, that is not Christianity. It may mean staying at home in your own country. This may require more sacrifice than leaving.

Prayer Thought: I am ready to go or ready to stay—ready to do Your will, heavenly Father.

SUGGESTED READING: HEBREWS 11:8–10

Wherefore let him that thinketh he standeth take heed lest he fall.

—1 Corinthians 10:12

THERE IS A TENDENCY TO take ourselves too seriously, until we really begin to wonder if God can do anything before we get up in the morning. We act as though He cannot do anything without our help. May God have mercy!

God shows us that a servant of His is not a necessary instrument. Remember how God visibly blessed and led in a certain happening in your past? But after a while, a spell of tribulation came. God laid you aside. Slowly you begin to see that an "instrument" is something that God takes up at His sovereign pleasure and puts down at His will. A "servant" is one who voluntarily chooses what God chooses. The servant chooses to do according to God's sovereign will.

God does the shaking of His servants, not the Devil. Why does He shake them? Because they are backslidden? Dear me, no. He shakes them partly to remove the parasites.

Has God shaken you lately? If so, fear not. He does so because He loves you.

Prayer Thought: Only You are truly great.
Forgive me when I think I am.

SUGGESTED READING: PSALM 100

Who, when he was reviled, reviled not again; when he suffered, he threatened not; but committed himself to him that judgeth righteously.

—1 Peter 2:23

EVERY PERSON WHO SUFFERS CAN measure, according to the depths of his own suffering, the sublimity and divinity of our Lord—who, when He suffered, "threatened not." Jesus did not retaliate or make threats toward the person or group who caused Him to suffer.

Jesus did not suffer because He was a wrongdoer. Oftentimes you and I have. One who suffers as a wrongdoer often responds in rancorous spite and with threats. Suffering, when the heart knows nothing of trust in God nor love for Him, is damning, not saving; it will respond in venomous threats and evil deeds.

Sarcasm, cynicism, slander, murder, war, and lawsuits spring from suffering—which springs from wrongdoing and a wrong temper.

Suffering is the heritage of the bad, the penitent, and the sons of God. All end at the Cross. The bad thief was crucified, the penitent thief was crucified, and the Son of God was crucified. All three represent the widespread history of suffering in our world.

In the cruel fire of sorrow,
Cast thy heart, do not faint or wail!
Let thy hand be firm and steady,
Do not let thy spirit quail!
But wait till the trial is over,
And take thy heart again;
For as gold is tried in fire,
So a heart must be tried by pain.

Prayer Thought: When I suffer, Lord,
I want to suffer like You—without
retaliation or a rancorous spirit.

SUGGESTED READING: [18]Servants, be subject to your masters with all fear; not only to the good and gentle, but also to the forward. [19]For this is thankworthy, if a man for conscience toward God endure grief, suffering wrongfully. [20]For what glory is it, if, when ye be buffeted for your faults, ye shall take it patiently? but if, when ye do well, and suffer for it, ye take it patiently, this is acceptable with God. [21]For even hereunto were ye called: because Christ also suffered for us, leaving us an example, that ye should follow his steps: [22]Who did no sin, neither was guile found in his mouth: [23]Who, when he was reviled, reviled not again; when he suffered, he threatened not; but committed himself to him that judgeth righteously: [24]Who his own self bare our sins in his own body on the tree, that we, being dead to sins, should live unto righteousness: by whose stripes ye were healed. [25]For ye were as sheep going astray; but are now returned unto the Shepherd and Bishop of your souls.

—1 PETER 2:18–25

Yea, they despised the pleasant land, they believed not his word: but murmured in their tents, and hearkened not unto the voice of the Lord.

—Psalm 106:24–25

ONE FORM OF SUFFERING FOSTERS the most dangerous isolation of pride, which produces a kind of human sphinx. Shrouded in mystery, the sufferer feels that his suffering is "profound" in nature. This type of suffering is preeminently cowardly as well as proud.

According to the personality make-up of the individual, this form of suffering may express itself through sullenness or quietism. It may be sullen and gloomy in expression, or mystic and remote in its quietism.

The ultimate result of sullen suffering is hatred toward the saints of God, envy and murmuring toward the messengers of God, and a sullen contempt toward God's Word. Suffering in the form of quietism produces a quietness that spends one's life in contemplation and reverie. It was a very common practice in medieval Christianity; but I believe it contradicts the very spirit of Christianity. Quietism is highly esteemed in nearly every religion, but it engenders a pseudo-mysticism that inevitably ends in private illuminations apart from the written Word. It leads to prayers that are actually "strong delusions," or false beliefs, resulting from a misleading of the mind.

Beware, my friend!

Prayer Thought: Help me to know the difference, Father, between suffering and sullenness, between praying and pouting.

SUGGESTED READING: PSALM 106

Wherefore let them that suffer according to the will of God commit the keeping of their souls to him in well doing, as unto a faithful Creator.

—1 Peter 4:19

HAVE YOU EVER HEARD OF what might be called active, well-doing suffering? It is commended to us by the apostle Peter (1 Peter 4:19).

The idea of a saint in the New Testament does not suggest a cloistered sentiment, or an emotion which encircles an individual like a halo of glory. A real saint is a holy person engaged in life with deeds of holiness. Saints live in the world, suffering "according to the will of God" and committing "the keeping of their souls to him in well doing."

The saint's life is not to be reduced to zero through renunciation, but raised to infinity through satisfaction. The essential difference between the stoic and the saint is just the point where they seem most alike. For instance, in overcoming the world and the ills of this life, both seem indifferent. The stoic's overcoming, however, is through a lack of passion. The saint's overcoming is by passion for Christ. This is godly suffering.

Prayer Thought: It is easier, Lord Jesus, simply to avoid those who inflict suffering on me; instead of behaving like this, though, I want to "suffer in well-doing."

SUGGESTED READING: 1 PETER 4:12–19

Casting all your care upon him; for he careth for you.

—1 Peter 5:7.

S UFFERING ACCORDING TO THE WILL of God is Christlike. To "be in the will of God" is a state of heart, not an intellectual discernment. The will of God in a sanctified heart is its implicit life, as natural as breath. As a sick person knows what health is intellectually, a sinful person knows what the will of God is intellectually. But only the sanctified heart expresses the will of God.

The motto of the holy heart is: My Father can do what He likes with me; He may bless me to death, or He may give me a bitter cup, or a cup of blessing. I delight to do His will.

Is this your motto? When you suffer according to the will of God, remember you do so under the watchful eye of a sovereign and faithful Creator. The sovereignty of God is of the greatest comfort to the saint. The saint is not responsible for suffering allowed by God and can relax in His care. The sanctified soul of the saint is in rapport with God.

God's predestinations are the voluntary choosings of the saint who is in the will of God. The eminent mystery in this statement is no more or less than the mysterious nature of love. This truth is discerned by the pure in heart, not by the powerful intellect.

Prayer Thought: Father, into Your loving care I commit my well-being as Your child in this world.

SUGGESTED READING: 1 PETER 5:6–10

Ye are my friends, if ye do whatsoever I command you.

—John 15:14

A DEFINITION OF *life*, *love*, OR *suffering* is not possible, for these words refer to the incalculable elements in human experience. Their very essence is implicit, not explicit.

Suffering is grand when the heart is right with God. Through suffering we gain a friendship with God. Oh, unspeakably blessed is the suffering of the sanctified! Lest you should faint or wail, hear our God reassure us, "Fear not . . . I am thy shield, and thy exceeding great reward" (Genesis 15:1). Catch the majesty, the might, the awe, the unspeakable satisfaction of that statement!

> *My goal is God Himself, not joy, nor peace,*
> *Nor even blessing, but Himself, my God;*
> *'Tis His to lead me there, not mine, but His—*
> *"At any cost, dear Lord, by any road."*

"In thy presence is fulness of joy; at thy right hand there are pleasures for evermore" (Psalm 16:11). This is ours by the sheer might of the Lord Jesus Christ, who gave Himself for us to cleanse us and reorient us, to baptize us in the Holy Spirit. That soul, incandescent with the Holy Spirit, then walks and talks with God as friend with friend, and lets God do as He wills with him.

Suffering according to the will of God—not so much for personal perfecting, but for enabling God to express His intentions for our lives—is the sublimity of the suffering of the sanctified!

Prayer Thought: Thank You, Lord, for expressing Your will through the suffering You permit in my life.

SUGGESTED READING: JOHN 15:10–17

For even hereunto were ye called: because Christ also suffered for us, leaving us an example, that ye should follow his steps.

—1 Peter 2:21

D O YOU SUFFER ON ACCOUNT of somebody else or for somebody else? In your agonizing prayers before the Lord on behalf of what you consider a "distressing situation," are you longing for release because the "distressing situation" hurts and discomforts you? If so, you are not having fellowship with His suffering. But if your soul, out of love, longs and bears in a voluntary and vicarious way for others, then you are having fellowship with Jesus in His sufferings.

When your Christian work seemingly is in ruins and you wail before God, is it because the work of your hands is in ruins? Are you tempted to say, "I thought this was to be my life work; now it is broken and blighted and shattered"? If so, you do not know what fellowship with His sufferings means. But when you see people defiling the work of God, making His house of worship a place for worldly business for the engendering of false affections and pursuits, and you agonize before the Lord with tears, then you are learning to have fellowship with our Lord in His sufferings.

Prayer Thought: Oh, to be like You—in suffering!

SUGGESTED READING: JUDE 21–25

Giving thanks unto the Father, which hath made us meet to be partakers of the inheritance of the saints in light. . . . In whom we have redemption through his blood, even the forgiveness of sins.

—Colossians 1:12, 14

A SAINT IS ONE, WHO, DISCOVERING himself at Calvary, lies in despair with the nature of sin uncloaked to him. Then, rising in the glamour of amazement and discerning Jesus Christ as a substitute for sin, calls out, "Jesus, I should be there." To his astonished spirit, he receives justification from all his sinfulness through the atonement at Calvary. Standing in the light of the atonement and placing, as it were, his hands over his Savior's crucified hands and his feet over His crucified feet, the saint has crucified forever his right to himself. The Lord Himself baptizes him in the Holy Spirit, giving him a new principle of life in which a new personality of holiness reflects an unmistakable likeness to Jesus Christ.

To be a friend of God, walking in communion with the Lord in suffering, and abiding with the Father, Son, and Holy Spirit as daily and hourly companions—this truly enables the human soul to look into the depths of pain that our Savior and Sanctifier endured. This gives us a key to understanding the shame, the agony, the mock trial, the Crucifixion, the Resurrection, and Pentecost.

Prayer Thought: Master, I know I can trust in Your shed blood for full salvation.

SUGGESTED READING: COLOSSIANS 1:1–18

For the Son of man is come to save that which was lost.

—Matthew 18:11

HAVE PEOPLE SCATHED AND SHAMED you because of your passionate devotion to the Lord of all suffering? If so, has your love of Jesus Christ prevailed? Have your own self-culture and education impeded your walk with the Lord, or has your love for Him been so passionate that you "love not your own life"?

John Wesley said, "To abandon all, to strip one's self of all, in order to seek and follow Jesus Christ to Bethlehem where He was born, to the hall where He was scourged, to Calvary where He died on the cross, is so great a mercy toward us, that the blessing of salvation and redemption is given but through faith in the Son of God."

The Cross of Jesus stands unique and alone. It is not our cross. Our cross is what is manifested before the world—the fact that we are sanctified to do nothing but the will of God. Our cross becomes our divinely appointed privilege by means of His Cross.

Prayer Thought: To bear my cross for You, Jesus,
is my desire in every circumstance of life.

SUGGESTED READING: MATTHEW 18:7–14

And if children, then heirs; heirs of God, and joint-heirs with Christ; if so be that we suffer with him, that we may be also glorified together.

—Romans 8:17

SPIRITUAL FREEDOM FULFILLS ALL THE law of God and transfigures that fulfillment into loving devotion. Oh, the sublimity of that freedom where, "sharing in the suffering of our Savior," we are released from being dupes of ourselves, our convictions, our temperaments, and we realize with John that "our fellowship is with the Father, and with his Son Jesus Christ" (1 John 1:3).

Let it be said with all reverence and in the deepest humility that suffering according to the will of God raises us to a freedom in God that baffles all language to express it to others. Do you know the unspeakable bliss of God abiding with you, making you one with Him? This is the sublime height of suffering according to the will of God.

When we are filled by the Spirit of the living God, we can be one in holiness, one in love, and one forever with God the Father, God the Son, and God the Holy Spirit.

Prayer Thought: Lord of all holiness, I seek to think, act, and respond in the beauty of holiness in every happening of life.

SUGGESTED READING: ROMANS 8:9–18

For the preaching of the cross is to them that perish foolishness; but unto us which are saved it is the power of God.

—1 Corinthians 1:18

THE HOLY SPIRIT WILL NOT allow us to forget the significance of the Cross of Christ. The burden of the apostle Paul was always the Cross of Jesus Christ. Whenever he spoke or wrote about the resurrection or the majesty of entire sanctification, he went back to the Cross.

The message of the Cross is not only that the vilest man or woman may be saved, or the foulest wretch on this earth be presented before the Throne of God whiter than snow; but it is that God may have His way through every one who will let Him.

Jesus Christ encountered self-seeking scholars who never understood what He meant by His Cross. You will find even today some souls who do not understand the Cross of Christ.

Do you? If you are ignorant about God's intentions through the Cross concerning you, you are to blame. It is not a question of intelligence or education, but a question of knowing the Bible; and the only interpreter of the Word of God is the Holy Spirit.

Prayer Thought: Father, teach me the true significance and message of the Cross of Christ.

SUGGESTED READING: 1 CORINTHIANS 1:17–22

And they understood none of these things: and this saying was hid from them, neither knew they the things which were spoken.

—Luke 18:34

As you enter the marvelous experience of entire sanctification, God will lead you directly to do His will. At this crisis point in your walk of faith, you will be face to face with God. Many people are so overwhelmed at this rushing out of God's power that they stagger.

The only persons who can bear the truth of the Cross are the ones who are sanctified. Nothing needs to defeat the sanctified because their whole heart, soul, and spirit are devoted to the Lord Jesus Christ. God grant that we will leave our ignorance behind us! We have no right to be ignorant concerning the things of God.

Prayer Thought: Yes, dear Lord Jesus, I want to be a true servant and saint of God. Lead me on, O King Eternal!

SUGGESTED READING: LUKE 18:31–34

APRIL

Set your affection on things above, not on things on the earth. For ye are dead, and your life is hid with Christ in God.

—Colossians 3:2–3

J ESUS CHRIST SAID, "AND BECAUSE iniquity shall abound, the love of many shall wax cold" (Matthew 24:12). Has yours?

The Cross of Jesus Christ calls us to pattern our lives after the example of Jesus. There is no sanctified life that is not crucified, or dead, to the lure of this present age. We are not saved and sanctified to see our Lord glorified in our way of thinking, but for God to take us victoriously along the pathway of obedience with Him. The characteristic of the sanctified life is obedience.

If you want to be spiritually weak and submissive to the spirit of this age, you will be popular. Carnal men and women would rather magnify the idea of the Cross than submit to the humiliation of the Cross. May God get us to the point of submission!

Prayer Thought: Forgive me, Lord, when I trust too much in material things and displease You.

SUGGESTED READING: COLOSSIANS 3:1–13

And he is before all things, and by him all things consist.

—Colossians 1:17

WHAT KIND OF ZEAL HAVE you? If it is only "moral zeal," then beware! But if your zeal, passion, and determination—yea, every fiber of your body—are motivated by a personal and passionate devotion to Jesus Christ, you are a humble worker of God.

Our Lord wants us to see this important distinction. Everything done from any motive other than a passionate devotion to the Lord, who died that He might save us by washing us from our sins through the shedding of His own blood, is unacceptable to Him. Hatred of sin is not enough. Even love for our fellow man falls short.

Jesus does not call us to be moral reformers. We are to concentrate our efforts on one thing, and the apostle Paul echoes it for us: " For I determined not to know any thing among you, save Jesus Christ, and him crucified" (1 Corinthians 2:2).

My right to myself must cease. My zeal in doing God's work my way must cease. My desire to take God's truth my way must cease. And my practice of preaching Jesus Christ my way must cease. I must magnify the Cross of Christ. My zeal and fervor must be lost in devotion to our Lord and Savior Jesus Christ.

Prayer Thought: Jesus, be the Lord of my
life and the Master of my mind.

SUGGESTED READING: COLOSSIANS 1:14–17

But Jesus answered and said, Ye know not what ye ask. Are ye able to drink of the cup that I shall drink of, and to be baptized with the baptism that I am baptized with? They say unto him, We are able. And he saith unto them, Ye shall drink indeed of my cup, and be baptized with the baptism that I am baptized with: but to sit on my right hand, and on my left, is not mine to give, but it shall be given to them for whom it is prepared of my Father.

—Matthew 20:22–23

How often has the Lord come with the cup He drank and offered it to you, and you told Him, "Now, Lord, I have far too much to do. I cannot drink the cup. I cannot go through the baptism of your sufferings just now. People are dying and I must go out and save them my way. I am consumed with a desire and love for the lost."

"Are you able to drink of My cup?" again Jesus asks.

What did Jesus do for the first thirty years of His life to save the lost? Absolutely nothing! He remained closeted up in silence. No one ever heard of Him, except the few at His birth and those who were confounded by His brilliance as the lad in the Temple. Then for three blazing years that have staggered time and eternity, He lived and died so that the gospel might be preached.

The world was not lost while the disciples waited in the Upper Room for Pentecost. God grant that we will drink the cup He wants us to drink—the cup of humble submission to Him.

Prayer Thought: Despite my eagerness to win the lost, Father, guide me in holy and humble submission to the will of the Savior.

SUGGESTED READING: MATTHEW 20:20–29

We ought to obey God rather than men.

—Acts 5:29

YOU KNOW EXACTLY IN WHAT respects you have refused to obey the Lord and persisted in having your own way. When He said, "Drink with Me," you responded, "No, Lord, I want to have the pattern and imprint of my church. I want to go their way. I want to live as they live and adhere to their decisions in my life." Instead of having fellowship with Him, you have preferred the fellowship of other Christians.

The Lord stands beside you very patiently, but in judgment as you refuse Him and obey others.

Do you want to know Paul's attitude about what other Christians thought of him? He said, "with me it is a very small thing that I should be judged of you, or of man's judgment (1 Corinthians 4:3).

Is this true with you, brother and sister? If the Christian crowd you mingle with judge you, so what? Are they your god, or is the crucified Lord and Savior, Jesus Christ? We are called to faithfulness to the Lord Jesus Christ. Any movement or person that contradicts Jesus, God will blast to pieces.

Prayer Thought: Deliver me from obeying
other people instead of You.

SUGGESTED READING: ACTS 5:17–32

But every man is tempted, when he is drawn away of his own lust, and enticed.

—James 1:14

TEMPTATION MAY BEST BE CALLED "that wild reach of possibility" which stretches one to fame or infamy; and the higher we walk, the more severe the temptation. Temptation simply indicates the sublime nobility of the character God is building within us.

It is impossible to be free from temptation; but temptation is not sin. If temptation were sin, then the Lord Jesus Christ was a sinner.

Two kinds of temptation are mentioned in the New Testament. First, we read of the temptation by Satan, such as that experienced by our Lord Jesus Christ. Secondly, we notice the temptation arising from the old disposition of sin within us (see James 1:14). We would avoid a lot of confusion if we clearly distinguished between these two types of temptation.

We are always responsible for temptation from our old disposition, because the atonement of the Lord Jesus Christ could radically alter that disposition if we would let Him. But we are not responsible for the temptation from Satan. That sort comes by the express permission of God, who at times seems to say to the Devil, "Do your worst. He that is in them is greater than you!"

Prayer Thought: Father, help me to resist Satan,
knowing that he will flee from me.

SUGGESTED READING: HEBREWS 2:6–18

And when the tempter came to him, he said, If thou be the Son of God, command that these stones be made bread.

—Matthew 4:3

THIS PASSAGE OF SCRIPTURE DESCRIBES a kind of socialistic temptation. Basically, Satan was saying: "Put man's needs first. Abolish hunger! Make Your appeal to their bodies, make Your appeal to their desire for fellowship, and the world will crown You king."

No one understood better the poignant needs of poverty and human suffering than our Lord. Remember that Jesus had come to be a Savior and King, and you will see at once the subtle appeal in this temptation of Satan.

The temptation to provide bread and abolish hunger occurred more than once in our Lord's life (see John 6:13–15). People instantly wanted to enthrone Jesus because of His ability to feed thousands. Jesus resisted. His goal was not to be a popular social leader, merely providing for physical needs.

World brotherhood was not His mission on earth, either (see Matthew 12:46–50). All men are not His brothers; only those who do His will and His Father's will are Christ's brothers. Jesus has deep compassion for all of humanity, and He has promised the communion of saints. But we cannot assume that He will gather all people into His fellowship.

The temptation to cater merely to the social needs of mankind was subtly alluring to Jesus Christ. It continues to allure modern Christians and the church.

Prayer Thought: With Christ, I cry, "Get thee behind me, Satan," for I am committed to doing God's will.

SUGGESTED READING: MATTHEW 4:1–4

Seeing then that we have a great high priest, that is passed into the heavens, Jesus the Son of God, let us hold fast our profession. For we have not an high priest which cannot be touched with the feeling of our infirmities; but was in all points tempted like as we are, yet without sin.

—Hebrews 4:14–15

JESUS WAS TEMPTED TO AMAZE humanity, daze people's senses, and overrule the natural laws of earth. Satan knew the power of the miraculous to gain the attention of human beings. Anything supernatural instantly sways us. But our Lord did not need to prove that He was the Son of God. He vehemently opposed giving "signs" to convince His critics of His mission on earth (see Matthew 12:38–39).

Jesus Christ could command forces that other men knew nothing about. To dazzle humanity by miracles would have been as easy for Him as breathing; but He restrained His miracle-working power.

Many modern Christians say, "If God would only perform signs and wonders, we would have a sweeping awakening." There are actually people who promote this concept. They seek supernatural gifts, with a desire to do "signs and wonders" among us; they seek to "amaze humanity" with their power.

In spite of all the warnings of Scripture, God's people are so easily led astray by signs and supernatural wonders. We must beware!

Prayer Thought: Spare me, Lord, from the onslaughts of Satan and of all earthly cults deceived by him.

SUGGESTED READING: MATTHEW 4:5–7

Then saith Jesus unto him, Get thee hence, Satan: for it is written, Thou shalt worship the Lord thy God, and him only shalt thou serve.

—Matthew 4:10

SATAN TEMPTED JESUS TO COMPROMISE with the evil that is in our world—with Satan himself. The Devil sought from the King of kings and Lord of lords a supremacy and sovereignty in this world.

Satan said that he could give the kingdoms of this world and the glory of them to Jesus if He would worship him. What was Satan's goal as he tempted our Master on this occasion? I believe he wanted to abolish hell. If he could convince the Son of God to worship him, Satan thought, he might spare himself from everlasting doom.

Satan is still trying to abolish hell. He wants all of us to banish hell from our beliefs and teachings. But Jesus would not, and we must not also.

Our Lord is opposed to all compromise with evil (Luke 14:28–33). We compromise with evil whenever we try to satisfy our desires at the expense of doing the will of God. The only people who do not see the enormous danger of compromising with evil are those who are ignorant of the snares of Satan.

Prayer Thought: Oh, I shun compromise with evil. I want the Holy Spirit to empower me to overcome evil with good.

SUGGESTED READING: MATTHEW 4:8–11

He that committeth sin is of the devil; for the devil sinneth from the beginning. For this purpose the Son of God was manifested, that he might destroy the works of the devil.

—1 John 3:8

OUR LORD'S LIFE CHALLENGES US to maintain an intense narrowness in our spiritual lives. I agree that walking arm in arm with the world is highly beneficial for the civilizing of a community. But I believe that civilization is not Christianity.

Modern Christians' craze for social refinement is effacing the rugged, sterling truth of the gospel of Jesus Christ. The fear of poverty makes many a Christian live in harmony with the world. The church that allows this worldly practice will, of course, gain the respect of this world; but if repentance does not come soon, that church will hear those words of Jesus, "I never knew you: depart from me, ye that work iniquity" (Matthew 7:23).

First John 3:8 clearly shows us that Jesus came to our world of sin to destroy the works of the Devil, not to renovate them. The Christian who yields to this temptation to gain supremacy in this world will be found ultimately to bear the scent of a spiritual corpse, with a horrible stench of evil corruption.

Prayer Thought: Strengthen me that I may not be defeated by the cares of this life and the deceitfulness of riches.

SUGGESTED READING: 1 JOHN 3:1–11

And in the morning, rising up a great while before day, he went out, and departed into a solitary place, and there prayed.

—Mark 1:35

THIS INCIDENT OCCURRED AFTER OUR Lord experienced a tremendous spiritual victory over Satan. He had endured the fierce onslaught of Satan in the wilderness. But after this ordeal "the angels ministered unto him" (Mark 1:13). There is a peril in assuming that we are strong after a victory, and Jesus realized this fact.

I wonder what was the subject of the Lord's early dawn experience in prayer? Jesus went with such easy power through life; what did He do in those solitary moments with God? The fame of the Lord Jesus Christ grew steadily; people brought all the diseased and the demon-possessed to Him, and He delivered them. Yet, in the midst of such a marvelous career of relieving and blessing people in need, He spent practically the whole night in prayer.

Do you realize that after eminent success in God's work, there is more need for prayer than when we are at the foothills of a struggle for survival? The moments of victory and success are more dangerous than moments of darkness and depression.

Prayer Thought: Dear Father, may the spiritual success I experience be fortified with seasons of earnest prayer.

SUGGESTED READING: MARK 1:28–39

We give thanks to God always for you all, making mention of you in our prayers.

—1 Thessalonians 1:2

WE DO NOT NEED TO be told that it is necessary to pray for our needy friends. It is obvious that the unsaved and those in difficult circumstances need our prayers.

But what about those who are full of sunshine, whose dispositions seem sweet with heavenly blessing? Do we pray for them as we should, or do we simply stand in awe of their joy and victory? Do we neglect to agonize in prayer for them? When our souls have been lifted into the presence of God and when the Spirit of God has stirred our aspirations at a camp meeting or convention, how much time do we spend in prayer for those who ministered to us?

When the ultimate truth is told, we may find to our horror that, though we have enjoyed and listened to men and women of God as they blessed our spiritual lives, we have been spiritually selfish. We have allowed ourselves to think that, because we have been blessed by their ministry, we would be presumptuous to pray for them. This is a snare of Satan.

Have we spent so much time in the exuberance of shouting, thanksgiving, and joy that we have forgotten that the safest place for us is on our knees?

Prayer Thought: Bless Your servants today, Lord.

SUGGESTED READING: 1 THESSALONIANS 1

Have not I commanded thee? Be strong and of a good courage; be not afraid, neither be thou dismayed: for the Lord thy God is with thee whithersoever thou goest.

—Joshua 1:9

EVERY RELIGION, EXCEPT CHRISTIANITY, REVERES the past. Christianity alone makes the best in the past seem poor, compared to the present—and the present seem poor, compared with what is yet to be.

When God announced to Joshua the death of His great servant Moses, did He announce plans for a memorial? Did He instruct Joshua to write a book of remembrance of Moses? No! God told Joshua, "Now therefore arise, go!" (Joshua 1:2). Moses was a mighty man of God; but a living babe is of more use in God's plans than a dead Moses.

For the saint of God there is no time as good as the present, unless it be the future. Even the splendid cry, "Back to the Bible," is not a call to return to the past; it springs from our need to return to the source of the mighty ocean of God's grand ideas for you and me.

Beware of people who worship reminiscences of the "good old times." Those who indulge in sentimentality do not savor the things of God. Every period of time in the Bible was better than the preceding age; and Christians know that the best is yet to be.

Prayer Thought: O God, lead and guide as You did Your servants Moses and Joshua.

SUGGESTED READING: JOSHUA 1:1–9

For we are saved by hope: but hope that is seen is not hope: for what a man seeth, why doth he yet hope for?

—Romans 8:24

WHEN I TELL YOU THAT the best is yet to be, I mean this in its profoundest sense, not in its obvious sense. God is not outdone, defeated, and beaten within the confines of human history. Only because I am confident that He is bringing His own purposes to pass, in His own way, can I say that every age of time is better than the last. But this reality is discernible only to the Spirit of God within me, not to the spirit of man within me.

The Bible stirs up an intense and unquenchable hope that an age of time is coming on this earth, inconceivably wonderful, when all that we have ever dreamed will fade into silly fancies beside the reality.

This will be when Christ reigns among us. Satan, the antagonist of God and the accuser of the saints, will be imprisoned by God and will be unable to harm or disturb the saints of God. The colossal pretensions of the Antichrist will be a thing of the past as the resurrected saints take active share in the manifestation of the kingdom of God on earth.

Prayer Thought: Father, my hope for
the future is completely in You.

SUGGESTED READING: ROMANS 8:22–25

Thou shalt hide them in the secret of thy presence from the pride of man: thou shalt keep them secretly in a pavilion from the strife of tongues.

—Psalm 31:20

WHEN HUMAN THOUGHT IS NAIVE, life looks simple, and history may be explained in ways that are simple and glib. For instance, some so-called scholars talk about "evolution." This system of thought is a simple and obvious development of modern reasoning. But when you and I talk about the Fall of man, the evolutionists think we are absurd.

However, when we are made to face life as it is, and history as it is recorded in Genesis, and the human soul in all its tragic features and triumphs, our minds are staggered. Our thinking then becomes subdued, and the human spirit is forced to cry out, "Oh, that I knew where I might find Him that I might even come before His presence!"

Prayer Thought: O Lord, keep me in the security of Your presence and the shelter of Your love.

SUGGESTED READING: PSALM 31:1–20

And it shall come to pass in that day, that the Lord shall punish the host of the high ones that are on high, and the kings of the earth upon the earth.

—Isaiah 24:21

ACCORDING TO THE HOLY BIBLE, there is a coming day of judgment. God reveals in the Scriptures that He has brought about many doomsdays but the final Doomsday has not yet come.

Because God has had several doomsdays in the history of the world, and things have gone afterwards as they went before, men and women have slipped into the notion that the final Doomsday will be simply like all the others. They seem to forget that the Bible states that the final Doomsday fixes the character of each individual forever, either in heaven or hell.

Destiny! Every person makes his own destiny. God's merciful judgment days warn us of the way our eternal character is developing and of the destiny that faces us.

The voice of Scripture earnestly warns us to heed the voice of God in these intermediate judgment days, lest, when the final Judgment Day comes, we will have no deliverance.

Prayer Thought: Prepare me, O Lord, for Judgment Day.

SUGGESTED READING: ISAIAH 24:13–23

For I say unto you, Among those that are born of women there is not a greater prophet than John the Baptist: but he that is least in the kingdom of God is greater than he.

—Luke 7:28

WHAT IS PROPHECY? THE PREVALENT popular notion is that a prophet is one who predicts things; and consequently, he is thought to be a kind of sanctified gypsy. As a result, delusions have played havoc within Christian communities.

From the Bible's point of view, a prophet is one who teaches under the direct influence of God, with a predictive ability to aid in proclaiming the moral purposes of God. No prophet of God, from the beginning of time until now, ever fully understood all he has said.

A prophet of God is a flesh-and-blood mortal whom God uses. Some glibly say that a prophet is "inspired of God." But this can be very misleading, because the word *inspiration* is made to mean just about anything—from a rise of high emotional feeling to the sublime beauty of the baptism in the Holy Spirit. The prophets of the Bible were not people who spoke and wrote merely from pious reflection. This is a popular idea today. Prophets of God were—and are—men and women moved by the Holy Spirit!

Prayer Thought: Move upon Your servants, God, so that they deliver to us the Word of God without fear or favor.

SUGGESTED READING: LUKE 7:24–30

I tell you that he will avenge them speedily. Nevertheless when the Son of man cometh, shall he find faith on the earth?

—Luke 18:8

F ROM GENESIS TO THE BOOK of Revelation, the Bible has spoken of a coming One—not a prophet, but One of whom all the prophets spoke.

Prophecies concerning Jesus were clear and obscure before He came to earth. Likewise, after He came the first time, prophecies concerning His coming again in the skies have been clear and obscure. Clearness and obscurity are the very characteristics of divine prophecy. To the pure in heart, the prophecies are clear, because the pure in heart know the way that passes knowledge. But to the lost, the prophecies are obscure.

Obscurity is common to human intelligence, because human intelligence can only perceive what has taken place in its own experience, not that which makes it what it is.

Those with a pure heart know that Jesus Christ is coming again in rapturous glory. They are looking for His coming. But those who piece together the prophecies concerning Him, by mere human intelligence and logic, will suffer from delusion and a final eclipse of faith.

Prayer Thought: Keep me ready for Your coming, Lord, and enable me to heartily work for You until Your coming.

SUGGESTED READING: LUKE 18:1–8

Esteeming the reproach of Christ greater riches than the treasures in Egypt: for he had respect unto the recompence of the reward.

—Hebrews 11:26

WHEREVER ONE'S HOPES ARE FOUNDED, there will that person's idea of prosperity be. And whatever the soul conceives to be prosperity will become that person's measurement of hope.

All of the Christian's hopes spring from being with God; consequently, all prosperity is measured from that Source. The world looks upon what we call prosperity as a way of failure, but we know that any so-called prosperity apart from God would be disastrous.

Jesus Christ prospered in the way of God. As He walked alone with God, He was bruised and despised. Yet the heavenly Father worked out His good pleasure in His own inscrutable way. Now you and I follow in Jesus' steps and the pleasure of the Lord prospers in our hands. What is that pleasure? Making disciples—"seeing His seed" multiplied in His children, through regeneration and entire sanctification.

Eternal prosperity begins in the "innermost of the innermost," as we are alone with God; and it works out to the outermost, as we do God's will each day. It is a spiritual prosperity, realized as we are transfigured into the beauty of holiness.

Prayer Thought: Like Moses and Jesus, I esteem the will of God more than the way of the world.

SUGGESTED READING: HEBREWS 11:23–28

Thou wilt shew me the path of life: in thy presence is fulness of joy; at thy right hand there are pleasures for evermore.

—Psalm 16:11

THE CHRISTIAN'S WALK WITH GOD is a way of inexplicable rapture. All that we Christians call bliss and pleasure in our fellowship with mankind is but the faintest shadow of the unspeakable pleasure of the communion we have with God.

Scripture uses the language of human relationships to suggest the unspeakable pleasure of eternal fellowship with God. Just as the language of lovers, or of a husband and wife, is imponderable to the unloving nature, so the language of the heart in communion with God is imponderable to those who are not in a like relationship.

Jesus said, "And this is life eternal, that they might know thee the only true God, and Jesus Christ, whom thou hast sent" (John 17:3). This is eternal life: increasing knowledge of the unfathomable God and His only begotten Son. What a sharp contrast to our ordinary conception of heaven, with its rewards and crowns! Simply to know Him—this is eternal pleasure!

Prayer Thought: O Lord, the very thought of eternal fellowship with You is beyond my comprehension.

SUGGESTED READING: PSALM 16

To him that overcometh will I give to eat of the tree of life, which is in the midst of the paradise of God.

—Revelation 2:7

PARADISE IS A BEAUTIFUL WORD. It stands for a spiritual reality conveyed by no other word. It refers to a city that "ad no need of the sun, neither of the moon, to shine in it: for the glory of God did lighten it, and the Lamb is the light thereof" (Revelation 21:23).

This eternal Paradise begins even now in those who walk with God. The soul who has personal communion with God knows that a Paradise has begun and will lead to a greater blessedness, more grand than one can imagine. This is not a false dream. The human heart longs for the real and visible paradise of God.

With God we have the glory that Jesus had, here and now—the glory of His holiness. But then we will be changed into His image, following the Lamb "whithersoever he goeth" (Revelation 14:4). How can we conceive what it shall be like?

Prayer Thought: Oh, the bliss and wonder of heaven. I long for it!

SUGGESTED READING: LUKE 23:39–45

He maketh me to lie down in green pastures: he leadeth me beside the still waters.

—Psalm 23:2

DIVINE GUIDANCE IS A SUBJECT as old as the Bible. There is nothing more important to the Christian.

The Bible has made the way of divine guidance so simple that only fools make a mistake in it. Only when we get wise in our own conceits, in our own experiences, or in listening to our own convictions, do we go astray spiritually.

Psalm 23 tells us that "the LORD is my shepherd." He leads us in the right way. It is the way that leads out into the green pastures, beside the still waters, and among the glorious hills of God.

God puts despair along any way that does not lead to Him. Discouragement arises from following self-love, and from nothing else. We get discouraged because we do not get our way.

Isaiah 42:4 tells us that the Lord "shall not fail nor be discouraged," and neither should His saints. For God will always be our Guide!

Prayer Thought: Heavenly Father, be my Guide. Lead me. Take complete control.

SUGGESTED READING: PSALM 23

Howbeit when he, the Spirit of truth, is come, he will guide you into all truth: for he shall not speak of himself; but whatsoever he shall hear, that shall he speak: and he will shew you things to come.

—John 16:13

JESUS DID NOT PROMISE WE would comprehend everything after we are entirely sanctified. He did suggest that the Holy Spirit will lead us into all truth from the point of sanctification, though growing pains will be characteristic of a sanctified life.

Sanctification is the point at which the soul is married to the Lord and the Holy Spirit fills us. God's will is that all of us should be saved (1 Timothy 2:4) and sanctified (1 Thessalonians 4:3). There is no obscurity about these statements of His will. They are clear signposts on our spiritual journey, indicating where we can expect divine guidance to begin.

Prayer Thought: Holy Spirit, guide me in the will of God.

SUGGESTED READING: MATTHEW 7:21–29

For it is God which worketh in you both to will and to do of his good pleasure.

—Philippians 2:13

IF YOU THINK THAT YOUR obedience, your repentance, or your morality is going to get you nearer to Jesus Christ, you are making a mistake. Intimacy with Christ comes only by abandoning yourself to Him.

Your crying to God will not save you. Surrendering your possessions will not save you. You may give God everything you like and still be damned. God never asked you to give Him anything but your will.

The only barrier to your salvation is yourself. The same is true with entire sanctification. God has put salvation and sanctification within your grasp, for Jesus has done everything in your behalf. Yet all depends on whether you submit your will to Him.

Some people are more concerned about being in earnest than they are about being in God's will.

Prayer Thought: Thank You, Lord God, for adequate provisions for my salvation—all for my seeking and asking!

SUGGESTED READING: PHILIPPIANS 2:12–16

Jesus answered and said unto her, If thou knewest the gift of God, and who it is that saith to thee, Give me to drink; thou wouldest have asked of him, and he would have given thee living water.

—John 4:10

TWO FUNDAMENTAL GIFTS OF GOD are provided through the atonement of Jesus Christ—salvation and sanctification. These are for you to take, not for you to gain. Nobody but an abject spiritual pauper can get saved or sanctified. Oh, God, deliver us from thinking that the energy of the flesh can save us!

And may God prevent anyone from being tripped by the profound simplicity of Christ! It is easy to be saved or sanctified. All depends upon our obeying God's will, when it is clearly stated.

Prayer Thought: Heavenly Father, give me faith to fully accept salvation and sanctification as a free gift of Your love to me.

SUGGESTED READING: JOHN 4:1–26

And for this cause God shall send them strong delusion, that they should believe a lie: That they all might be damned who believed not the truth, but had pleasure in unrighteousness.

—2 Thessalonians 2:11–12

M AY GOD GRANT THAT WE may get rooted and grounded in spiritual truth. Of those who will not accept the truth, the Bible says: "God shall send them strong delusion, that they should believe a lie." God has done this very thing. Those who love not the truth as it is in Christ, and everybody who is living for Christ by "experiences," will be void of God's guiding voice.

May God bring us to that glorious rest in Him and to that simplicity of faith. Satan can imitate the Holy Spirit in everything but one. Experiences? The Devil will give you thousands of them. But he can never produce the result the Holy Spirit produces—a holy character that glorifies Jesus.

I have made my choice forever,
I will walk with Christ my Lord;
Naught from Him my soul can sever,
While I'm trusting in His word.
I the lonely way have taken,
Rough and toilsome though it be,
And although despised, forsaken,
Jesus, I'll go through with Thee.

Prayer Thought: Yes, I have made my choice forever. To God be all the praise!

SUGGESTED READING: 2 THESSALONIANS 2:1–12

And he is the propitiation for our sins: and not for ours only, but also for the sins of the whole world.

—1 John 2:2

S IN IS NOT MERELY IMMORALITY. Sin is deeper, more massive, more awful. Sin reflects a disposition that absolutely refuses to let God rule. Sin rules in both the "bad man" and the "good man," until the Holy Spirit has invaded a person with the new disposition of holiness.

Brothers and sisters, we are playing fools around the Cross of Christ to think that Jesus came just to challenge us to set our wrongs right. He did not. He became sin so that He might destroy sin in us.

When a Christian takes on the role of a moral reformer, he is a traitor to the Cross of Jesus Christ, because the Christian's mission is not to change other people's sin. Jesus Christ is the substitute for the sin of the world.

May God the Holy Spirit convict us of sin, and destroy the so-called "Christian experience" some of us have.

Prayer Thought: Spirit of God, rid me of the tendency to be satisfied with less than Your best.

SUGGESTED READING: 1 JOHN 2:1–15

For all have sinned, and come short of the glory of God.

—Romans 3:23

S IN IS UNIVERSAL. YET THE Cross of Jesus can destroy the disposition of sin. The Cross can give us a clean heart; its power can invade and indwell us, making us masters over every thought and desire.

Thus, the salvation of Jesus Christ is not for just "an experience." God save us from this "experience" business! Sin must be eradicated and strangled to death. An absolute surrender must be made to God—we must yield ourselves to a full invasion of God. There is no deliverance from sin until we seek the Cross of Jesus Christ, who became sin for us. Holy character is the result of God's work—a character pure in secret and in public.

We must be leagues above moral integrity. We must be stamped, not only by moral integrity, but by the supernatural character of God, made available to us by the atonement of Jesus Christ.

Prayer Thought: Lord, create true character within me—a character pleasing to You!

SUGGESTED READING: ROMANS 3:19–23

To the end he may stablish your hearts unblameable in holiness before God, even our Father, at the coming of our Lord Jesus Christ with all his saints.

—1 Thessalonians 3:13

S IN IS BLINDNESS. ONE OF the greatest crises of our day is that we are contented with easy satisfaction in our spiritual lives. We are content with moral fastidiousness. If we are to get at the heart of the religion of the Cross, we will have to forget such religious trivialities. We must be "unblamable in holiness before God."

May God stop the preachers with moral measuring rods. Down with them! We need broken-hearted preachers with an awful conviction of sin, preachers who cry, "My God! My God! Against Thee, Thee only have I sinned!"

Christ did not come to put our relationships right with one another; He came to put our relationships right with Him. To accomplish this, He must eradicate the old disposition of sin and fill the cleansed heart with His blazing, incandescent glory.

Prayer Thought: Establish true holiness in my heart and life so that I will be ready for the coming of Christ.

SUGGESTED READING: PSALM 51:1–12

My little children, these things write I unto you, that ye sin not. And if any man sin, we have an advocate with the Father, Jesus Christ the righteous.

—1 John 2:1

WHAT WE NEED TO HEAR is not something new, but the very thing to which we have always listened and yet paid no attention. God wants to stagger our convictions and lead us to a point of spiritual maturity where our convictions will go to the winds. It is Christ, not our convictions, who saves us.

There is nothing grander, nothing more majestic than when the Lord comes into our souls. The gates of hell cannot prevail against us. Nothing can pluck us out of the hand of God. No external power can make us backslide. (We "are more than conquerors," and if we backslide, it is by our own choice.)

John wrote his first epistle to people who say there is no such thing as sin after we are saved. Sin is a persistent danger, even to the Christian.

Sin is anarchy against God's Word. So if you sin, you are a traitor to God—even if you hold very bold convictions. If your "holiness experiences," your "healing," or your "testimony" are not based on the eradication of the old carnal nature, you have nothing to do with Calvary.

Prayer Thought: Lord, let me submit even my convictions to You.

SUGGESTED READING: 1 JOHN 2:1–12.

And he said unto them, Ye are they which justify yourselves before men; but God knoweth your hearts: for that which is highly esteemed among men is abomination in the sight of God.

—Luke 16:15

WHAT IS MOST HIGHLY ESTEEMED among men and women today? The god of this present age is "my mastery over myself."

Many attempt to face our Lord Jesus Christ with moral self-righteousness, proud to think they have subjected themselves to an exacting moral law. But Christ never looks at a person's external life. Christ often treats with a light hand the moral lepers, yet puts the most tremendous denunciations on those who seem to be all right.

Your disposition of "my right to myself" must go. Do not think your salvation consists of your morality, your holiness, your experiences, or anything else based on this disposition of self-rule.

God grant that you may be crucified with Christ. There is no hope anywhere under heaven but in the Cross of Jesus. God made Him to be sin for your sake, because sin is your usual disposition. It must be removed here and now, or you will be damned.

Prayer Thought: To You I cling, Lord Jesus.
You are my only hope of salvation.

SUGGESTED READING: LUKE 16:13–17

MAY

Wherefore come out from among them, and be ye separate, saith the Lord, and touch not the unclean thing; and I will receive you.

—2 Corinthians 6:17

THE LIFE OF FAITH IN Jesus Christ is marked by separation, sacrifice, and satisfaction.

Are you looking to God and His truth for the purpose of your life? Or are you paying more attention to your culture, or your church, or your little circle of friends? You must be willing to separate yourself from all of those and be true to God! You must learn to separate yourself unto God.

Sacrifice does not mean merely giving up what you prize most. Sacrifice means giving yourself to God in perfect surrender, because you can give Him nothing else.

What is the purpose of sacrifice? Let me say it this way: If a consecrated life is one of everlasting giving, I would go straight to ruin; my surrender to God was once and forever, so that I might be filled with God's fullness. Only His fullness satisfies Him!

Prayer Thought: He is Lord of nothing if He is not Lord of all.

SUGGESTED READING: 2 CORINTHIANS 6:14–18

And he removed from thence unto a mountain on the east of Bethel, and pitched his tent, having Bethel on the west, and Hai on the east: and there he builded an altar unto the Lord, and called upon the name of the Lord.

—Genesis 12:8

WHAT IS PRAYER? THE PREPARATION for spiritual battle? Never! Prayer is the battle.

When do you pray? A practice of Jesus' life revealed the secret of prayer. Jesus enjoyed "victorious days" because He spent many nights alone in prayer. And when did His lonely nights of prayer come? Usually after a day of victory. Like Him, we must learn how to cope with victory.

Let me illustrate. One of our younger Scottish peers went to the Alps and climbed a certain peak with a guide. Then he tried one that had not been ascended before. When he came to the pinnacle, he turned aside and began jumping about. His guide told him it was not safe behaving like that and said to get down on his knees.

After reaching a point of spiritual victory, get down on your knees. Pray! Commune with God. Do not shout to others.

Prayer Thought: In these hectic days, enable me to separate myself from others and really pray—as You did, Lord.

SUGGESTED READING: LUKE 6:12–18

My sheep hear my voice, and I know them, and they follow me: And I give unto them eternal life; and they shall never perish, neither shall any man pluck them out of my hand.

—John 10:27–28

HAVE YOU EVER SEEN GOD give someone a tremendous blow for molesting one of His children? Woe to the person who touches or troubles the children of God—the apple of His eye.

Over and over again, the first disciples of Jesus made that blunder. Remember Peter? He once said, "Jesus, what shall this man do?" Jesus told Peter, in effect, "Mind your own business" (John 21:22). Martha said, "I am serving You, Jesus. Make Mary come and help me in the work." Jesus replied, "Martha, Mary has chosen the better way. She has taken orders from Me" (Luke 10:41–42).

We are not to touch God's obedient child. If anyone were to abuse a child of God, Jesus said, "It were better for him that a millstone were hanged about his neck, and that he were drowned in the depth of the sea" (Matthew 18:6).

God blights the hypocrites who pretend to be virtuous and pious, for the purpose of winning favor for themselves, as they correct and chastise other Christians.

Remember, God will condemn everyone who dares to say anything against His children.

Prayer Thought: Father, forgive us for not loving each other as we ought. Help me not to be guilty of deliberately offending another Christian.

SUGGESTED READING: MATTHEW 18:1–6

His lord said unto him, Well done, thou good and faithful servant: thou hast been faithful over a few things, I will make thee ruler over many things: enter thou into the joy of thy lord.

—Matthew 25:21

MANY OF US PLACE TOO much emphasis on our work for God and not enough emphasis on preparation for the work. The Nazarene Carpenter prepared for thirty years in obscurity, to do three years of work. Today the standard is three or four years of preparation for thirty years' work.

May God help us to understand that, before He puts His servants in a place of power, He puts them in a place of preparation. God grant that we will remain where He puts us, and not run before we are sent.

There is loneliness in being faithful to God's will. But we must be faithful!

Prayer Thought: Lord, as You enable and empower, I will be faithful to You.

SUGGESTED READING: MATTHEW 25:14–23

They should not depart from Jerusalem, but wait for the promise of the Father, which, saith he, ye have heard of me.

—Acts 1:4

DID PENTECOST COME BECAUSE THE believers waited for it? Did their waiting produce it? Did God give the Day of Pentecost to them as a reward for their patience? These questions represent a misunderstanding of the ways of God as revealed in the Scriptures. The Day of Pentecost would have come, whether the disciples waited for it or not.

The Day of Pentecost "fully came" twenty centuries ago, and the Holy Spirit has been here on earth ever since. The baptism in the Holy Spirit—when power from on high is manifested in a frail human being—is the infallible sign that Jesus is risen and lives.

Have you been baptized in the Holy Spirit? Some people say, "Oh, I am waiting like the disciples did in the upper room." That is very foolish. The Holy Spirit is here. Now, now, now is the time to receive Him. With singleness of purpose, receive Him now.

Are you and your Christian friends in one accord, one mind, one purpose, in one place? Yes? Then the Holy Spirit will manifest His unspeakable power.

Prayer Thought: Fill me daily, Lord, with the fullness of Your Holy Spirit. May I ever be completely Yours!

SUGGESTED READING: ACTS 2:1–36

In whom ye also trusted, after that ye heard the word of truth, the gospel of your salvation: in whom also after that ye believed, ye were sealed with that holy Spirit of promise.

—Ephesians 1:13

IF YOU SAY YOU ARE entirely sanctified and have never been baptized in the Holy Spirit, you have deluded yourself. You have merely accepted a holiness Shibboleth. The baptism in the Holy Spirit is Jesus Christ's seal on your soul and is your inauguration into service to battle for your King.

Sanctification begins at regeneration and goes on to the second crisis and work of grace—that is, entire sanctification and the baptism in the Holy Spirit.

Are you in one purpose, in one determination? Then receive Him. It is not your waiting, but your wanting; it is not your running, but your receiving that matters in this. You can receive your Pentecost now! If you are born again, it is your birthright.

Prayer Thought: Thank You, Lord, for the sanctifying presence of the Holy Spirit.

SUGGESTED READING: EPHESIANS 1

Knowing this, that our old man is crucified with him, that the body of sin might be destroyed, that henceforth we should not serve sin.

—Romans 6:6

THE IMPORTANT THING IS NOT what I am thought to be, what I would like to be, or what I think I am, but what I really am in the sight of God.

I am ruled by my disposition. Not my human nature nor my personality, but my disposition is the principle that rules my personality. And disposition is what the atonement of Jesus Christ radically alters. That disposition is called "the old man," the "body of sin," or "original sin," and it is something quite apart from human nature. For this reason, the apostle Paul distinguishes emphatically between "the flesh" and "this mortal body."

Sin is not the essence of your mortal body. Sin is the disposition that rules it, and it is what Jesus Christ cleanses through the atonement.

Prayer Thought: Thank You, Lord Jesus, for the grace to be freed from the power and pollution of the carnal nature of sin.

SUGGESTED READING: ROMANS 6:1–18

But if we walk in the light, as he is in the light, we have fellowship one with another, and the blood of Jesus Christ his Son cleanseth us from all sin.

—1 John 1:7

THE BIBLE NEVER CONFUSES SIN and sins. Sins must be forgiven, while sin must be cleansed. The Bible never uses the word *forgive* in connection with sin.

John wrote his first epistle to Christians who say there is no such thing as a disposition of sin. John says that if you think you have no sin, you deceive yourself (1 John 1:8). The disposition of sin "is enmity with God" (James 4:4) and cannot be reconciled to God. There is only one thing to do with it. You must enter into the death of Jesus and have the "old man" of sin crucified with Christ.

First John 1:9 tells us that "if we confess our sins [not sin], he is faithful and just to forgive us our sins [not sin], and to cleanse us from all unrighteousness"—that is, from the disposition to sin. We must deal with this disposition of sin, a principle that rules human nature.

Prayer Thought: Crucify once and for all this disposition of sin within me, dear Father.

SUGGESTED READING: 1 JOHN 1

When a strong man armed keepeth his palace, his goods are in peace:
But when a stronger than he shall come upon him, and overcome
him, he taketh from him all his armour wherein he trusted, and divi-
deth his spoils.

—Luke 11:21–22

SOMETIMES WE FORGET THAT THE carnal heart of man is
at peace. Psalm 73 pictures the wicked person from God's
standpoint. Such a person is happy, peaceful, contented, and not
bothered about the future.

Luke 11 says this world is "the palace" of the Devil. He
lives in his palace. And what are his goods? Men and women.
Undisturbed peace in a person's life may be a sign of Satan's rule
as well as of God's rule. This is but another way in which the
Devil is an imitator of God.

The disposition of darkness (sin) keeps one happy, peaceful, and undisturbed until meeting Jesus Christ. Then one is
pained. A sign of life is pain when you learn you are wrong.

The gospel is hid from those who are lost (2 Corinthians 4:3),
and they feel they are all right. But Jesus Christ is the disturber of
sinful people. When He disturbs us, He offers deliverance from
the dark disposition of sin.

Prayer Thought: Jesus, I appreciate the deliverance
from sin through Your shed blood on Calvary.

SUGGESTED READING: PSALM 73

Now we have received, not the spirit of the world, but the spirit which is of God; that we might know the things that are freely given to us of God.

—1 Corinthians 2:12

THE BIBLE USES SEVERAL PHRASES to describe a person's disposition of sin. First is "the natural man." First Corinthians 2:14 tells us that "the natural man receiveth not the things of the Spirit of God: for they are foolishness unto him."

You can hammer away at someone about spiritual things as long as you like; but until you rely on the Holy Spirit, and realize that only He can convict your friend of sin, you might as well talk to a wooden seat. Jesus Christ can satisfy only those whom the Holy Spirit has convicted of sin.

The Bible also talks about "the rational man," who is highly intelligent. Such a person reasons things out. Paul says that "Christ crucified" is foolishness to the rational person. Preach Jesus Christ to someone who is moral, upright, and well-educated, and he will say, "Why did Jesus want to die for me? I am all right." The disposition of the rational man makes God's truth seem like stupidity. But Paul says, "The foolishness of God is wiser than men" (1 Corinthians 1:25).

Prayer Thought: Open my eyes and enlighten my understanding, O Lord, to a clearer comprehension of spiritual truth.

SUGGESTED READING: 1 CORINTHIANS 2:6–16

Think not that I am come to send peace on earth: I came not to send peace, but a sword. For I am come to set a man at variance against his father, and the daughter against her mother, and the daughter in law against her mother in law.

—Matthew 10:34–35

"THE RATIONAL MAN," UNLESS HE has been disturbed by the Spirit of God, will treat the Bible like any other book. How can such a person do otherwise? Unless one is born again, the Bible seems like any other book.

Criticism of the Bible does not hurt the Bible; it reveals the disposition of the critic. "We are the children of wrath" by nature and are in danger of becoming eternal children of the Devil. But when Christ meets someone who is in peace (because of the natural, dark disposition of sin), there is a disturbance. There is a change in one's view of things—including the Bible.

Jesus Christ will destroy every peace and every love that is not based on the disposition of holiness. Jesus is our enemy before He is our friend.

A cry for peace and unity may be of the Devil, quite as much as of the Lord. Be careful that you do not obtain inner peace and unity at the Devil's price. Obtain them as Christ bestows them, through the alteration of your sinful disposition through the Holy Spirit.

Prayer Thought: Reconcile those who are enemies of the Cross, I pray, O God.

SUGGESTED READING: MATTHEW 10:29–39

Whosoever is born of God doth not commit sin; for his seed re-maineth in him: and he cannot sin, because he is born of God.

—1 John 3:9

WHAT PAUL DESCRIBES IN THE seventh chapter of Romans is a person's human nature in the throes of two alternating dispositions. One disposition wishes to fulfill the lusts of the flesh, while the other disposition longs to obey the Spirit of God in all things.

Too many people think that this struggle is the highest possible experience of grace through the atonement of Jesus Christ. They suppose that all Jesus does is to disturb their natural peace, awaken them, and then taunt them with the consciousness of what they ought to be—without any possibility of being it.

But the regenerated life is not an "up and down" life; it is a life "up and up."

Regeneration divorces the disposition of the flesh and the disposition of the Spirit; and it then can produce a wonderful thing in your nature—a life without sin (1 John 3:9).

This is not sanctification; it is another aspect of salvation. Sanctification makes little difference in your external life, but it makes all the difference inside. Yet even before sanctification, every man or woman who is born again of the Spirit of God has victory over sin!

Prayer Thought: O God, Your grace is sufficient for my needs. Your sanctifying power is adequate!

SUGGESTED READING: ROMANS 7

For the flesh lusteth against the Spirit, and the Spirit against the flesh: and these are contrary the one to the other: so that ye cannot do the things that ye would.

—Galatians 5:17

THERE IS A DUAL NATURE in every regenerated soul. When a soul is born again, and is under the first glorious flush of the regenerated life, one often thinks, What could be more marvelous? But after a while, the regenerated soul becomes conscious of the debating inside his heart. He now has to sign the death warrant of the old disposition of sin.

The first time Christ comes to the natural man as a Disturber, to do the work of conviction. The next time He comes to the awakened man as a Deliverer, in salvation. The third time He comes to the one who has been born again by the Spirit of God as a Disposer, in the work of entire sanctification. That is to say, Christ disposes of the old disposition of sin as soon as a person is willing to sign its death warrant.

We are told in 1 John 3:8, "For this purpose the Son of God was manifested, that he might destroy the works of the devil." What is the work of the Devil? The disposition of sin. And this disposition Jesus Christ destroys in every regenerated soul that will let Him.

Prayer Thought: The warrings in the soul are never too fierce that we cannot conquer, O God, with Your help.

SUGGESTED READING: GALATIANS 5:16–21

Put off concerning the former conversation the old man, which is corrupt according to the deceitful lusts.

—Ephesians 4:22

A DIVINE DISPOSITION CAN TAKE THE place of the dark disposition of sin. This divine disposition is the last and glorious work of Christ to be experienced this side of heaven. This is the work of grace that makes us "more than conquerors."

As Paul says in 2 Corinthians 5:21, Jesus Christ was made to be "sin," not sins. Jesus took up my disposition of sin so that I might be free from sin—not free from my personality or my ruined human nature. Jesus came to dispose of that old monster of sin in human nature that has ruled and ruined it.

When you are born again, the Spirit of God soon brings you to the altar again. For what purpose? To destroy that old disposition of sin. Crucifixion is a cruel, ghastly death; but you and I must be willing to endure it. Our religion is a vain farce unless we have died to the disposition of sin. Our Lord is merciless to sin.

Prayer Thought: Thank You, Lord, for full deliverance from the sinful nature that shadows and threatens my spiritual life.

SUGGESTED READING: EPHESIANS 4:17–24

I can do all things through Christ which strengtheneth me.

—Philippians 4:13

WHEN I HEAR PEOPLE SHOUT, "I have the victory," I feel like saying, "Go further. Let the Victor have you. Let God gain victories through you."

God gains victories through every soul in whom He has gained the victory. There is no such thing as defeat or failure or discouragement in the vocabulary of the sanctified. If you are discouraged, let God search your heart. When the old disposition of sin is gone, God makes us "more than conquerors."

Entire sanctification is an instantaneous, continuous work of grace, wrought by the mighty atonement of Jesus Christ. It is instant cleansing by the crucifixion of the "old man," followed by a life of endless growth and victory.

Prayer Thought: My soul longs for more of You, God. I desire to grow in the grace and knowledge of the Lord Jesus Christ.

SUGGESTED READING: 2 PETER 3:10–18

Salt is good: but if the salt have lost his savour, wherewith shall it be seasoned? It is neither fit for the land, nor yet for the dunghill; but men cast it out. He that hath ears to hear, let him hear.

—Luke 14:34–35

WHEN GOD HAS YOU COMPLETELY, you will never ask anyone if you are sanctified. You will not need to guess whether you are sanctified. It is grander inside than outside.

External sins never bothered me; I was brought up too carefully to be externally sinful. But when God the Holy Spirit convicted me of my disposition of sin, of my pride, and of my self-rule, I experienced such howling wastes of agony on account of the years God was not fully in control!

Fellowship with God grows grander, brighter all the way. No matter what your case is or what your circumstances are, if you go through on God's line, He will save and entirely sanctify you.

Prayer Thought: Increase my faith, O God, that
I may fully accept Your will for my life.

SUGGESTED READING: PSALM 139:14–17

I will behave myself wisely in a perfect way. O when wilt thou come unto me? I will walk within my house with a perfect heart.

—Psalm 101:2

"PRESENT YOUR BODIES A LIVING sacrifice, holy, acceptable unto God, which is your reasonable service" (Romans 12:1). Until you have done this, you may fall at the altar of God again and again, with weeping. There could be two reasons for this habitual feeling of guilt: Your spirit may indeed be wrong, or you may have guilty feelings that you ought not to have.

Feelings are a poor standard by which to measure your relationship with God. The disciple of Jesus is more concerned with doing right than with feeling right.

Show me the person whom Jesus Christ has saved from perdition and sanctified wholly, and about whom Jesus says, "Father, that is My work. I cleaned that life up; I sanctified that life entirely." Show me the man or woman whom God—through the atonement of Jesus—has fully satisfied to the last aching abyss of the human heart, one who is truly in love with Jesus Christ. That person will be living for God, not just feeling favorably about Him.

The test of entire sanctification is not your experience, but your life.

Prayer Thought: May my life, Lord Jesus,
be acceptable in Your sight.

SUGGESTED READING: PSALM 101

Being justified freely by his grace through the redemption that is in Christ Jesus.

—Romans 3:24

I WANT THE HOLINESS THAT IS given to me by God through faith. Holiness by faith lays hold of God and accepts from Him His righteousness. Hundreds fail by striving to give up things to God, striving to become holy by their acts and deeds; this is the righteousness of the law, not the righteousness by faith. The crucial thing is not the righteousness of my faith; it is the righteousness received "through faith." Righteousness is the gift of God to one who knows he is a spiritual pauper.

This is why Jesus Christ would say to someone who came into the presence of the King without a wedding garment, "Friend, how camest thou in hither not having a wedding garment? . . . Bind him hand and foot, and take him away, and cast him into outer darkness, there shall be weeping and gnashing of teeth" (Matthew 22:12–13). Such a person may have gone under the name of one of the Lord's saints, but he is not His handiwork. He is not the handiwork of God Almighty by the power of the Holy Spirit.

Nothing in my hands I bring,
Simply to thy cross I cling.

Prayer Thought: Through faith, O God, I cling to Your Word. Fill me with Your righteousness.

SUGGESTED READING: MATTHEW 22:1–14

Jesus said unto him, If thou wilt be perfect, go and sell that thou hast, and give to the poor, and thou shalt have treasure in heaven: and come and follow me.

—Matthew 19:21

THE LORD JESUS CHRIST EXERCISED a great fascination over people. Multitudes were attracted to Him, until He turned and withered their enthusiasm. The rich young ruler came to Jesus, fascinated; but when Jesus spoke, He said something that withered the young man's enthusiasm. Jesus merely asked him to become totally His!

The Lord Jesus Christ is the enemy of every love, every relationship, and every aim that does not aid the eternal sanctification of the soul. Everything counts as naught until the Lord gets us absolutely remade from the inside—until the disposition of holiness is planted within us.

Prayer Thought: I yearn to be holy. Holiness of heart and life is my inward craving.

SUGGESTED READING: MATHEW 19:16–22

Behold, ye fast for strife and debate, and to smite with the fist of wickedness: ye shall not fast as ye do this day, to make your voice to be heard on high.

—Isaiah 58:4

OUR LORD JESUS CHRIST TOLD His disciples, "But thou, when thou fastest, anoint thine head, and wash thy face; that thou appear not unto men to fast, but unto thy Father which is in secret: and thy Father, which seeth in secret, shall reward thee openly" (Matthew 6:17–18). The true inward significance of fasting is that I have turned to God, either on account of my own sins or others, allowing Him to fulfill His purpose in me.

Isaiah 58 describes a pretentious sort of fasting. What direction will our feet take as soon as the vestments of fasting are taken off? What way will our faces naturally turn? What are our hands going to do? Unless the feet, the hands, and the face are images of the true condition of the heart, our fasting is a deep distress to God. He will not accept hypocritical fasting and praying.

Prayer Thought: Lord, help me to fast in the interests of Your kingdom.

SUGGESTED READING: ISAIAH 58:1–7

But without faith it is impossible to please him: for he that cometh to God must believe that he is, and that he is a rewarder of them that diligently seek him.

—Hebrews 11:6

F AITH IS SOMETHING THAT GOD puts into you. Faith is the gift of God.

Many say, "Have faith!" But how can you have faith on your own initiative? It is impossible. Folks come to the altar and are told to "take God at His Word." But how can you take God's Word on faith until God has given you faith?

To be sure, you must seek God. But when you have done that, the Holy Spirit will make the words of Jesus warm to your heart; and with that will come faith. You then will say, "I never saw it so before! I have been so slow of heart to believe!"

Prayer Thought: Thank You, Lord, for faith.

SUGGESTED READING: HEBREWS 11:1–6

And there was in their synagogue a man with an unclean spirit; and he cried out, saying, Let us alone; what have we to do with thee, thou Jesus of Nazareth? art thou come to destroy us? I know thee who thou art, the Holy One of God.

—Mark 1:23–24

THE FIRST ATTRACTION OF JESUS is on the human basis, not the miraculous. The holiness of Jesus fascinates us because it is a distinctly human holiness.

Yes, Jesus attracts us by His holiness. And then He says, "If you want to be like that, you will have to meet the conditions." This is not a judgment, but a statement of fact. Jesus does not command our allegiance. Yet the heart of every man or woman must confess Him as Lord and Master to obtain the fullness of life.

This idea is reflected in Napoleon's statement at St. Helena: "Jesus has succeeded in making every human soul an appendage of His own." Only in Jesus do we find what our hearts and minds crave.

I wish that everyone would obey this instinct of the heart. To see Jesus and refuse Him is to be condemned, as surely as to accept Him is to be saved.

Prayer Thought: I am human, Lord. Yet I am glad to know that, with my human inadequacies, I am fully able to follow You.

SUGGESTED READING: MARK 1:22–27

Then said I, Woe is me! for I am undone; because I am a man of unclean lips, and I dwell in the midst of a people of unclean lips: for mine eyes have seen the King, the LORD of hosts.

—Isaiah 6:5

GOD, BY THE HOLY SPIRIT, may reveal in trying circumstances that you are not fully His. This revelation may be distressing. Yet it is by infinite mercy that God gives you such experiences. Only then can you be set blazing and passionately on fire as a devoted bond slave of the Lord Jesus Christ.

Regardless of your convictions or testimonies today, you may find yourself lacking when you stand in the presence of God. You may realize suddenly that your own efforts amount to nothing. Then the Lord can become what He should be in your life—absolutely all in all!

Prayer Thought: Possess my mind, my heart, my all, O God!

SUGGESTED READING: ISAIAH 6:1–13

That I may know him, and the power of his resurrection, and the fellowship of his sufferings, being made conformable unto his death.
—Philippians 3:10

L ET THE LORD HAVE HIS way. Beware of the tendency toward a sentimental admiration of Jesus, which withholds the reins of your life from Jesus' hands.

The real enemies of Christ are not the poor fallen people on the streets, but those who profess holiness, yet never let Him eradicate the self-centered disposition inside of them. Oh, may you let God eradicate your self-centeredness today!

Prayer Thought: I fully surrender my life to You, dear Lord.

SUGGESTED READING: JAMES 1:8–12

Finally, brethren, farewell. Be perfect, be of good comfort, be of one mind, live in peace; and the God of love and peace shall be with you.

—2 Corinthians 13:11

WHAT IS DEATH? WHEN JESUS Christ grips my soul, death is a mere episode; death has no sting in it. The saint has a peace as deep as God, as unruffled as God, even in the face of death.

Do you understand that "the joy of the Lord is your strength"? We are so apt to look at the difficulty of the ways we are going; but the saint has God's mighty peace in his heart, and he sees it is all right. Do not let your heart be troubled, for the joy of the Lord is your strength.

Prayer Thought: Oh, the bliss of Your peace!
Your joy, Lord, is my strength.

SUGGESTED READING: PSALM 91:10–16

And the Lord said, Simon, Simon, behold, Satan hath desired to have you, that he may sift you as wheat.

—Luke 22:31

JESUS DEALT TENDERLY WITH THE infirmities of His disciples. He seemed to overlook everything. But He never overlooked the point that He was after—the eradication of their self-centeredness. He brought every one of them to the place where He said, "I count not my life dear unto myself; your life should be for Jesus only."

Every one of His disciples was stamped with the realization of this truth: "I am Christ's." Jesus removed the self-centered principle from their hearts and implanted a personal, passionate devotion to Him.

May God the Holy Spirit drive this home to you as He has to me. We must live only for one thing: Jesus ever, Jesus only, Jesus all in all! That is what the Son of Man desires.

Prayer Thought: Implant within me, dear
Lord, a renewed devotion to You.

SUGGESTED READING: LUKE 22:31–38

And this is the condemnation, that light is come into the world, and men loved darkness rather than light, because their deeds were evil.

—John 3:19

WHAT KIND OF HEART HAVE you? Is it a self-centered heart? There is only one result to that—condemnation. No one is condemned for being bad. No one is condemned for doing wrong. The person condemned is the one who insists on saving himself, instead of trusting Jesus to save him.

Be careful, my friend! You may have a good testimony, a spotless record, and yet be condemned at the end of it all. Like Judas, you may have been with Jesus Christ for three long years, night and day; you may have been used of Him; but you may be exposed, expelled, and condemned by Him.

Judas was "the man with a double mind," who served Jesus on one side but groveled to Jesus' enemies on the other. Have you followed Judas's example? Then confess it to the Lord. It is not a question between you and me, or you and any other human being, but a question between you and God.

Prayer Thought: Father, correct me when I stumble. Cleanse me of any tendency to betray You.

SUGGESTED READING: JOHN 3:18–21

And to know the love of Christ, which passeth knowledge, that ye might be filled with all the fulness of God.

—Ephesians 3:19

A SAINT IS NOT A PERSON "with" a saintly character. A saint is a saintly character. Character, not ecstatic moods, is the essence of saintliness.

By the same token, you cannot have a change of "the will" and be the same person two minutes later. If your will is committed to the Lord Jesus Christ, all is changed.

I feel confident that God is preparing you for that divine stamp of the character of the Lord Jesus Christ. God wants to bring you to the place of being a true servant of His.

Prayer Thought: Heavenly Father, I resolve to allow You to reign supremely in my life.

SUGGESTED READING: EPHESIANS 3:14–21

Beloved, if our heart condemn us not, then have we confidence toward God.

—1 John 3:21

Too many people suppose that if they clean up their dealings with others, they will be right with God! But a reformed person is as much condemned as before. And it is not getting right with men, but with God, that leads to eternal life.

Sin is more than moral irregularity. It is a disposition to follow one's own way rather than God's way.

The Bible says that God condemns those whom the god of this age has blinded so that they do not realize the sinful disposition in their lives. If we deny our sinful disposition, we make God a liar and deceive ourselves.

Prayer Thought: I fully realize the grim consequences of sin. Deliver me, Lord, from my sinfulness.

SUGGESTED READING: 1 JOHN 3:18–24

If the world hate you, ye know that it hated me before it hated you.

—John 15:18

BEARING THE FAMILY LIKENESS OF our Lord will enable others to know beyond doubt that we have been with Jesus. The line of demarcation between the world and the saint is at the line of death—to this world. The saint is spoiled for this world and no longer shares the aims and ambitions of the world.

The saint, in short, bears the marks of unworldliness while in this world. He bears the evidence of a readjusted individuality.

The people who say, "Oh, I am no saint," try to pass as modest, ordinary people among their peers. But such a statement means, "I do not care what Jesus Christ and the atonement can do." To be "no saint" means that one is a proud sinner.

Prayer Thought: O God, I truly desire that Your power will enable others to see Christ in me.

SUGGESTED READING: JOHN 15:18–21

We have sinned, and have committed iniquity, and have done wickedly, and have rebelled, even by departing from thy precepts and from thy judgments.

—Daniel 9:5

WHEN YOU READ DANIEL'S PRAYER, you find there are no excuses made by Daniel, either for himself or his people. One of the hardest things for a person to do is to face oneself with the holiness of God—to face oneself in the pure, unsullied light of God—and let God's Spirit search into the avenues of the mind and the imaginations of the heart, into the purposes of one's life, and to let God see all the wrong, the evil, and the self-seeking that are there.

That is what the Bible means when it challenges me to "set my face toward God" in repentance. Other religions ignore the fact of sin, and they tell us to ignore it. They tell us our only attitude is "to never remember what you have done; never think about it; keep in the sunshine and keep bright." Jesus Christ does exactly the opposite. He brings us, by His Spirit, face to face with the sin in our lives.

The sign that His Spirit is at work is that true remorse begins to show itself. Our faces are set toward God, with no excuses.

Prayer Thought: With Daniel, I seek to be honest with God and true with my fellow man.

SUGGESTED READING: DANIEL 9:1–19

JUNE

Surely every man walketh in a vain shew: surely . . . he heapeth up riches, and knoweth not who shall gather them. And now, Lord, what wait I for? my hope is in thee.

—Psalm 39:6–7

SANCTIFICATION IS (1) THE REMOVAL, by the blood of Jesus, of the evil principle of sin, (2) having the presence of the Holy Spirit, and (3) living a life of praise for the glory of God. This last link of sanctification might be called absolute sanctification.

The life of Godward praise is essential. May God the Holy Spirit sift our testimonies, our experiences, and all the externals of religion until we realize there "is no One but Thee, my God." The stamp of the sanctified life is that we have made our choice forever: We will walk with Christ.

My Lord, I the lonely way have taken,
Rough and toilsome though it be,
And although despised, forsaken,
Jesus, I'll go through with thee.

Prayer Thought: Lord, I want only to praise You today.

SUGGESTED READING: PSALM 39

Jesus answered them, Have not I chosen you twelve, and one of you is a devil?

—John 6:70

L ET ME SAY ONE WORD to conscientious Christians: You cannot judge the faithfulness of other disciples. Peter assumed he was speaking for all of the Twelve when he said, "We believe and are sure that thou art that Christ, the Son of the living God" (John 6:69). Yet Jesus answered, "One of you is a devil" (v. 70). And this was not the last time a Christian presumed faith on behalf of others.

When you speak to the Lord, don't speak of "we," but of "me." "Who art thou that judgest another man's servant? to his own master he standeth or falleth" (Romans 14:4). In fact, the twelve disciples were marked with total ignorance of themselves. Peter said, "This thing will never happen as long as I am with You," and the Lord had to let him go straight over the precipice of denial before he found out who he was. Jesus led Peter into crisis after crisis, until he knew himself.

Prayer Thought: Reveal the "real me" and make me alive to You—pleasing You!

SUGGESTED READING: ACTS 1:19–25

Whosoever therefore shall break one of these least commandments, and shall teach men so, he shall be called the least in the kingdom of heaven: but whosoever shall do and teach them, the same shall be called great in the kingdom of heaven.

—Matthew 5:19

JESUS TAUGHT THAT IF WE are to be spiritual we must sacrifice the natural, or physical and material, life. One of the greatest principles that we do not seem to grasp, but was very evident in our Lord's life, is that the natural life is neither moral nor immoral; we make it moral or immoral.

Jesus says the natural life is meant for sacrifice. We give it as a gift to God. This is the way to become spiritual.

That is where Adam failed. He refused to sacrifice his natural life and make it spiritual by obeying God's voice. Consequently, he sinned by insisting on his right to have his own way.

If we say, "I like this natural life. I do not want to be a saint. I do not want to sacrifice the natural life for the spiritual," then Jesus says we barter the spiritual life we could have had. It is not a punishment. It is an eternal principle.

Spirituality is not a sweet tendency toward piety in bad people who do not have enough life in them to be bad. Spirituality is being possessed by the Holy Spirit of God, who makes the most corrupt and twisted, sin-stained life a truly spiritual life if He is obeyed.

Prayer Thought: I love You, Lord. Fill me with more of Your love.

SUGGESTED READING: MATTHEW 5:18–22

Men and brethren, this scripture must needs have been fulfilled, which the Holy Ghost by the mouth of David spake before concerning Judas, which was guide to them that took Jesus.

—Acts 1:16

IF YOU TAKE TIME TO follow Jesus Christ's contact with His disciples, you will find that He brought each of them to a crisis of decision. For instance, Peter was led to a moral precipice in which he was nearly lost, before he knew that he must forever give up his right to himself and entertain Jesus Christ as his Lord. John the beloved disciple experienced the same thing. The only disciple who failed this test was Judas.

Coming in contact with mighty revivals, being swept by the power of God, having devils cast out while you pray, are no signs that you are saved. God never judges us by what we do or say, or what our reputations happen to be. He judges us where no one else can—by the motives of the heart.

Judas was chosen of God to be an apostle. He followed Christ three years. He was with Him night and day. Following Jesus through the fascination of that marvelous Personality, like the others, he grew to hate Him where the others loved Him. How will you decide, when your hour of testing comes?

Prayer Thought: Lord, take full control of my life.
Cleanse me of all selfishness, for I love You.

SUGGESTED READING: ACTS 1:15–18

Let your light so shine before men, that they may see your good works, and glorify your Father which is in heaven.

—Matthew 5:16

WHAT IS THE STANDARD OF success as a Christian? Do you know what spiritual success is? It is to be the "preserving salt" and "shining light" of the world, not losing your Christlike savor but preserving it in health.

God will continually use you as an exhibition of His way of life, but you will not be conscious of it. You won't make that your conscious motive. You won't be thinking that "I have to walk just that way and look just like this," or show what a magnificent specimen God can make of a man or woman. When you think like that, you are in danger of degeneration.

Do you seek success? Then let God work through you. Allow Him to possess you fully. The advantage is a successful journey to heaven. The light of His Word will show you the way!

Prayer Thought: With You, Lord, I can be successful. Without You, I would be a miserable failure.

SUGGESTED READING: MATTHEW 5:13–16

Searching what, or what manner of time the Spirit of Christ which was in them did signify, when it testified beforehand the sufferings of Christ, and the glory that should follow.

—1 Peter 1:11

THE INTENT OF OUR MOTIVES and the springs of our dreams must be so right that our deeds and actions will naturally follow. Some tell us certain attitudes to suppress and certain rules and regulations to obey. But Jesus Christ never gives us rules and regulations. He gives us His ruling Spirit.

The spiritual truths that Jesus taught require a new heart and a new spirit within us in order for us to obey them. Quite often, the only way in which we know that Jesus has given us a pure heart is through trying circumstances.

This is the way it works: You are brought under difficult circumstances.

People impute wrong motives to you. But, if the Lord Jesus Christ has purified your heart with love for God and others, then instead of feeling resentment, you feel exactly the opposite. There is an amazing difference inside. This is proof that God has indeed altered your heart by His love.

Prayer Thought: My strength comes from You, Lord. Enable me to stand true in the midst of difficulties.

SUGGESTED READING: 1 PETER 1:6–16

Then entered Satan into Judas surnamed Iscariot, being of the number of the twelve.

—Luke 22:3

THE ISRAELITES MIGHT HAVE GREATLY disliked Caleb and Joshua since they were the only ones originally allowed to enter the Promised Land. Why? Because they knew Caleb and Joshua were right and wanted to go the right way, and they did not.

Judas had hatred against Jesus because he was unwilling to do what was right. He refused to have the carnal self-eradicated out of him. And when the time came for the Lord to expose him, Jesus referred to Judas as the "son of perdition."

Judas could have been one of Christ's own, but he chose otherwise. Neither men nor angels nor devils have the slightest bit of power over the soul of man, unless that soul first gives consent.

Prayer Thought: Dear Lord, grant that I will never reject You for temporary satisfactions.

SUGGESTED READING: PSALM 106

So he fed them according to the integrity of his heart; and guided them by the skillfulness of his hands.

—Psalm 78:72

INTEGRITY MEANS THE UNIMPAIRED STATE of a thing. A person of integrity speaks and acts with unimpaired faithfulness to the principles that guide his life—or, in the case of a Christian, faithfulness to his Lord.

We get ourselves into tangles that compromise our integrity by not leaving things alone. If people around you make mistakes, leave them alone. Let them correct their mistakes. Our Lord seldom told His disciples when they made mistakes. They made many blunders in His presence, but He went on quietly planting truth.

It never occurs to a pure and honest heart to back up what it says with evidence; yet even the person of high integrity will be met at times with suspicion. Suspicion is of the Devil. This is why we ought never to treat children with suspicion. Believe in their integrity; they will, in turn, believe in yours.

Prayer Thought: Thank You for really believing in me, Lord, and allowing me the freedom to grow in grace and in the knowledge of Your Word.

SUGGESTED READING: PSALM 78:1–10, 65–72

But godliness with contentment is great gain.

—1 Timothy 6:6

THE ULTIMATE EXPRESSION OF CHRISTIAN character is not doing good, but Godlikeness. If the Spirit of God has transformed you, you will exhibit not only good human characteristics, but good divine characteristics in your life.

It is not sufficient to be good and to do the right thing. You must have goodness stamped upon your life by the superscription of Jesus Christ. The whole secret of a Christian's character is that the supernatural has been made natural in his life, by the grace of God. The supernatural influences natural human life, not just in granting us secret communion with God; it flows out of us in the practical workings of our daily lives.

What results do we see? When problems come, to our great astonishment, we have a power we never had before—a power that keeps us wonderfully poised in the midst of it all. And this is because of the supernatural grace of God, working within us and flowing out of us.

Prayer Thought: God, I need You every moment of this day. Your power and grace are what I need to face the day.

SUGGESTED READING: 1 TIMOTHY 6:1–2

And why take ye thought for raiment? Consider the lilies of the field, how they grow; they toil not, neither do they spin.

—Matthew 6:28

JESUS SAID, "CONSIDER THE LILY." It obeys the laws of its life in the circumstances where it is placed. As a Christian, consider your hidden life with God. Pay attention to the source of your life—God! Realize that He will care for your provision.

The most hard-working creature of our world is a bird, yet it does not toil to stick feathers to itself. It obeys the law of its life and becomes what it is. The same is true for Christians.

You cannot enjoy life by heeding outside pressures to change. Imagine what would happen if a lily did what some of us try to do. We say, "Oh, I must give up this; I must go here and there." Imagine a lily's hauling itself out of a pot and saying, "Well, I don't think I smell nice enough. I don't think I look exactly right. I must change myself!" The lily's duty is to obey the law of its life where it is placed by the gardener.

Watch your life, dear Christian friend, and allow God to be the source of your life. Then you will grow in His grace.

Prayer Thought: Thank You, Lord, for providing all the necessities of my life.

SUGGESTED READING: LUKE 12:22–30

The backslider in heart shall be filled with his own ways: and a good man shall be satisfied from himself.

—Proverbs 14:14

THE BACKSLIDDEN CONDITION IS TWOFOLD—IT is forsaking God and taking up with something else.

Remember Peter. Peter was a man loyal-hearted and true to Jesus, but grossly ignorant about what he was capable of, in the way of sin. Quite loyal but quite ignorant, he got into difficult circumstances and trying crises. Suddenly, to his amazement, he found that he was capable of evil that horrified him.

Satan is after you. He wants to entice you away from Christ. Beware of his allurements.

Prayer Thought: Heavenly Father, may I never forget my human weakness and vulnerability.

SUGGESTED READING: PROVERBS 14:9–14

Then took they him, and led him, and brought him into the high priest's house. And Peter followed afar off.

—Luke 22:54

WHAT WERE THE CONDITIONS THAT led Peter to his fall? He had followed Jesus Christ out of true loyalty of heart and genuine devotion. He had pictured a great many things that might happen. But he never imagined, in his wildest moments, that Jesus Christ was going to give Himself right over to His captors. When that occurred, all Peter's thoughts were turned into confusion. His heart was in despair. He followed in that condition "afar off." And when he was tormented by stinging questions from serving women in the courtyard, he answered with oaths and curses that he never knew Jesus Christ.

That is the condition of a backslider—one who is fully awake to the possibility of carnality within him, who knows what God's grace is, what sin is, and what deliverance is. A backslider knows the danger of denying the Lord Jesus, but has deliberately forsaken Him because he loved something else better.

Prayer Thought: O God, I understand Peter's problem of denying his Lord at a time when He needed him. Make me fully aware of a similar temptation in my own life.

SUGGESTED READING: LUKE 22:54–62

Forsake me not, O Lord: O my God, be not far from me. Make haste to help me, O Lord my salvation.

—Psalm 38:21–22

THE QUESTION IS OFTEN ASKED, "Can a Christian commit a sin?" He certainly can. I mean it is possible. But the sin must be immediately confessed and forgiven; for if a Christian allows that act of sin to remain unresolved, it will lead to the condition of backsliding. An unrepentant Christian perverts all the ways of God and hews out a way for himself. The backslider must have his backslidings healed and be restored, or else he will be lost.

Only those who have the indwelling Spirit of God, who have had the disposition of sin removed and the disposition of holiness implanted, can discern the perfect will of God. As we discover and do God's will, we are able steadfastly to serve Him until He has finished His purpose in our lives.

Prayer Thought: I need You, Lord, to overcome
the temptations that confront me each day. Thank
You for sufficient grace and spiritual power!

SUGGESTED READING: PSALM 109

And the L{.sc ord} God formed man of the dust of the ground, and breathed into his nostrils the breath of life; and man became a living soul.

—Genesis 2:7

E{.sc very corpuscle of blood, every} nerve, every sinew, and every muscle of Adam's body became the temple that could manifest an exact harmony with God and manifest the image of God in perfect faith and love. Angels can manifest the image of God only in what we call "bodiless spirits." There is only one creature who can manifest the life of God on this earth, and that is man.

Satan attempted to thwart that purpose, and then laughed his devilish laugh against God. But the Bible says that God will laugh last. God is on His throne. He rules the universe. He is almighty. He is God! Put your trust in Him.

Prayer Thought: I adore and worship You, O God.

SUGGESTED READING: GENESIS 2:1–17

Which have forsaken the right way, and are gone astray, follow-ing the way of Balaam the son of Bosor, who loved the wages of unrighteousness.

—2 Peter 2:15

THE NEW TESTAMENT SPEAKS IN three different contexts about Balaam. Peter talks about the "way of Balaam," Jude (v. 11) talks about the "error of Balaam," and Revelation (2:14) talks about the "doctrine of Balaam."

The "way of Balaam" is to make a market of one's gift. A Christian who does this begins to put himself into the "show" business.

The "error of Balaam" is seeing only the standard of natural morality and never discerning God's ways. When a Christian follows his own common sense morally, rather than the dictates of the Word of God, he falls into this error.

The "doctrine of Balaam" is teaching the corruption of God's people. Balaam taught Balak to corrupt the Israelite people by enticing them to marry the women of Moab. In mod-ern terms, the "doctrine of Balaam" is any teaching that tries to strike a compromise between corrupt worldliness and Christian profession.

After God has entirely sanctified you, everything is against you to put you to death. Heed the disastrous example of Balaam, and stay true to your Lord.

Prayer Thought: Oh, deliver me from making gross perversions of Your will, Lord!

SUGGESTED READING: JUDE 1–13

Ah sinful nation, a people laden with iniquity, a seed of evildoers, children that are corrupters: they have forsaken the LORD, they have provoked the Holy One of Israel unto anger, they are gone away backward.

—Isaiah 1:4

B E CAREFUL ABOUT HOW YOU guide your Christian life. You must do more than follow the ordinary standards of the world.

It is very tempting to follow the world's standards in your business and to say, "Oh, well, they all do it. I must do the same." But if that standard conflicts in the tiniest degree with the clear standard of God, beware! It is an attempt to make a judicious blend of corrupting worldliness and godliness.

Compromising Christians spread their disease quicker than any other kind. One backslider exerts an influence over the community that is tenfold worse than the influence of a hundred sinners who have never been saved.

Prayer Thought: If my conduct has provoked You, Lord, I pray that You will reveal my fault and forgive me.

SUGGESTED READING: EPHESIANS 5:1–15

I will heal their backsliding, I will love them freely: for mine anger is turned away from him.

—Hosea 14:4

GOD IS FORGIVING, GRACIOUS, AND merciful to the backslider. Let me take as an illustration the fifteenth chapter of Luke. I know that parable is used in ever so many ways; but I want to use it as a picture of the backslider. It might be called the Parable of Two Sons.

One went away and spent his substance in riotous living, and the other stayed at home. Each of them is as bad as the other; in fact, the spirit of the stay-at-home was every bit as bad as the wild rioting of the younger boy who went away.

Did the father send any message to the boy in the far country? There is no record of any message being sent. But what did that boy have to do? Exactly what was recorded in Hosea 14, ages before that parable was spoken by our Lord: He had to return!

The backslider had to get up, leave the pigs and what pigs eat, and go back from whence he came. Was help granted him? None whatever. Messages from the home country? Not one. Were there tender touches of God's grace on his life? Not one.

Is there a backslider reading this? Then rouse yourself and go back to God. Are you tempted to say, "But I feel no drawing"? You will feel none, dear friend. I do not find one instance in the Bible in which God drew a backslider in the same way that He draws a sinner. The word to the backslider is, "Return unto the LORD thy God; for thou hast fallen by thine iniquity" (Hosea 14:1).

Prayer Thought: God, I pray for the backsliders. Help them, like the prodigal son, to confess their sins and return to their Father.

SUGGESTED READING: HOSEA 14:1–9

And I, if I be lifted up from the earth, will draw all men unto me.

—John 12:32

IT IS SO EASY TO persuade myself that my convictions are the standards of Christ. When I succumb to such thinking, I condemn to perdition everyone who does not agree with me, because my convictions have taken the place of Jesus Christ.

Take heed that you do not let such carnal suspicion take the place of the discernment of God's own Spirit. Spiritual fruit, not your personal fancies, are the real test of your faithfulness to Christ. Wait for that fruit to manifest itself in your life, and don't trust the apparent confirmation of your own ideals.

The character of God, the love of Christ, and the indwelling fullness of the Holy Spirit are the crowning evidences of Christ's presence in our lives.

Prayer Thought: Lord Jesus, convince me of my wrong when I attempt to force my own convictions on others. Remind me that You are the standard for my life.

SUGGESTED READING: 2 CORINTHIANS 4:1–6

But brother goeth to law with brother, and that before the unbelievers. . . . Why do ye not rather take wrong? why do ye not rather suffer yourselves to be defrauded?

—1 Corinthians 6:6–7

I HOPE EVERY CHRISTIAN WORKER WILL listen carefully when I say that in dealing with a backslider you will be exhausted to the last drop of your energy. When we work with other cases, God seems to supply grace at the very moment we need Him. But we need to remember that, if we need to rely on the Holy Spirit in the other cases of dealing with sinners, we need Him ten thousand times more to deal with backsliders.

Intercessory prayer for a backslider is a most instructive, but a most trying, act. It teaches a Christian that prayer is not only making petitions, but is breathing a holy atmosphere. The two must go together. You need to be bathed moment by moment in the limpid life of God as you pray for a backslider.

If ever you need "the wisdom that cometh from above," it is in the moment of dealing with a backslider. You will wonder, How am I going to awaken this soul? How am I going to sting into action this backslidden heart? How am I going to make this person go back to God? You cannot. But the Spirit of God is ready to accomplish the miracle, if you will open the way for Him.

Prayer Thought: Dear Lord, teach me how to deal with a backslider. Help me to be alert to the spiritual needs of the wayward soul.

SUGGESTED READING: 1 CORINTHIANS 6:1–10

Follow peace with all men, and holiness, without which no man shall see the Lord.

—Hebrews 12:14

THE CHRISTIAN LIFE IS A holy life. Do not substitute the word *happy*; happiness is a consequence of holiness.

So many good people are caught up in what we may call "the gospel of temperament." In other words, they subscribe to the belief that they must be happy and bright. But these moods are consequences, and not causes, of the Christian's relationship with God.

Our Lord insists that we keep our eyes fixed on "the strait gate and the narrow way" which, in essence, is pure love and holy living in every area of our lives. Happiness is not to be our primary aim. Our aim is to please the Lord Jesus Christ, to serve Him in the beauty of holiness, in love, and in humility. Is this your aim?

Prayer Thought: Holiness and happiness come from You, O Lord. Without a holy life, my happiness is not fully possible.

SUGGESTED READING: ROMANS 6:15–23

Not every one that saith unto me, Lord, Lord, shall enter into the kingdom of heaven; but he that doeth the will of my Father which is in heaven.

—Matthew 7:21

HUMAN NATURE IS VERY FOND of labels. It is so easy to be branded with labels, and easy to give other people labels they do not deserve.

Our Lord said that the test of goodness was doing the will of God. That is how we are to discern between the man labeled as being "good" and the man with "the goods." Christian discipleship will reveal itself in character and behavior. The ultimate test of a person's Christian faith is a right relationship to Jesus Christ, unsullied in every detail, privately and publicly.

Prayer Thought: Search my motives, Holy Spirit, and empower me to be wholly the Lord's in every thought and deed.

SUGGESTED READING: GALATIANS 5:22–26

And he said unto her, Daughter, thy faith hath made thee whole; go in peace, and be whole of thy plague.

—Mark 5:34

If our religion is only one of sunshine for the healthy-minded, it is no good, because many people throughout the world are not capable of enjoying sunshine. Their lives are so twisted and tortured that exactly the opposite seems to be their portion. All of our talking about healthy-mindedness, about cheering up and living in sunshine, will never touch that crowd.

If all Jesus Christ can do is tell someone to be better when he is poorly, if all the Christian worker can do is tell someone he has no business feeling miserable, then I say the Christian religion is a failure.

But the wonder of our Lord Jesus Christ is just this: You can confront Him with any kind of person you like—no matter how wan and dejected—and He can put that person into a right relationship with God.

Prayer Thought: I praise You, Lord, for Your power to overcome all the trials and troubles of life.

SUGGESTED READING: MARK 5:25–34

When Jesus heard that, he said, This sickness is not unto death, but for the glory of God, that the Son of God might be glorified thereby.

—John 11:4

THE NEW TESTAMENT MENTIONS QUITE a few sick souls. Take Thomas for example.

Why do I mention Thomas? Because he was very loyal to Jesus Christ, but he was very gloomy. He took the sick view of life. He always thought the worst was going to happen—and the worst always did happen! There was no use going to Thomas and saying, "Cheer up." He knew you could not alter facts by saying that.

Every time you hear from Thomas, he says something about death or disease. When Lazarus died, and Jesus said He was going to the place where Lazarus was buried, Thomas said, "Let us also go, that we may die with him."

Are you like Thomas? Then keep your eyes upon Jesus. Watch Him turn death into life, sadness into gladness, failure into success, defeat into victory.

Prayer Thought: Unlike Thomas, I want to view life as victory. Like Thomas, I need You to help me believe the power of God.

SUGGESTED READING: JOHN 11:1–17

Then they went out to see what was done; and came to Jesus, and found the man, out of whom the devils were departed, sitting at the feet of Jesus, clothed, and in his right mind: and they were afraid.

—Luke 8:35

MARY MAGDALENE WAS POSSESSED OF seven demons. She is a type of the tortured and afflicted sick soul. There was no use going to Mary and telling her to take healthy exercises, or to believe there is no such thing as the Devil or sin. She would have been absolutely incapable of taking the first step.

What did Jesus Christ do for Thomas? He brought Himself into personal contact with him and altered him entirely. What did Jesus Christ do for Mary Magdalene? He cast out the demons and healed her. Completely!

Jesus wants to cure our sick bodies, but He also wants to heal our sick souls and minds. Will you let Him do that for you?

Prayer Thought: Heal me, dear Lord, of my lack of faith.

SUGGESTED READING: LUKE 8:1–3, 26–36

But I will hope continually, and will yet praise thee more and more.

—Psalm 71:14

THERE IS A THRESHOLD TO our nerves. By that I mean there is a point at which our nerves begin to be affected. Some people's nerves are not affected as quickly as others, while some seem to live in constant misery. One person can sleep in a tremendous racket, while another would be kept awake by the slightest noise.

Take sound alone. The ears gather up vibrations, and only when those vibrations are quick enough do I hear. If my threshold of hearing were a little lower, I could hear many other disturbing noises; but as it is, I can go through my normal activities without being the least bothered by them.

Get a nervous system whose threshold is very low, and you have a person whose life is abject torture wherever he goes. What is the purpose of telling that person to cheer up? He is tortured by things we never hear, discomforted by things we never feel. He cannot help being nervous.

Shall we preach our temperament of cheerfulness to such a person? The doctrine of cheerfulness is all very well among people who are cheerful; but what about the folks who cannot be cheerful—who, through no fault of their own, have a nervous threshold so low that life is a misery?

Prayer Thought: O God, I want to be considerate of people who have nervous problems. Forgive me when I get impatient with them.

SUGGESTED READING: PSALM 71:14–24

Then Peter opened his mouth, and said, Of a truth I perceive that God
is no respecter of persons.

—Acts 10:34

IN ACTS 10, PETER SAYS a wonderful thing about Jesus
Christ. Peter has just awakened to the fact that God is no
respecter of persons, and so he resolved to preach Jesus to all
sorts of people.

You will always find in the New Testament that, when
people are being led by the Spirit of God, they never preach their
own convictions. They preach Jesus Christ and Him crucified!
Peter had never preached like that before. He had always talked
to the Jews about Jesus Christ. As soon as he came into contact
with people who were not Jews, and who were not religious, the
Spirit of God made him present Jesus to them as well.

All people need to know Jesus as the One who suffered for
them. He is no respecter of persons.

Prayer Thought: I praise You, Lord, for the
love You have shown toward all people.

SUGGESTED READING: ACTS 10:34–48

These things I have spoken unto you, that in me ye might have peace. In the world ye shall have tribulation: but be of good cheer; I have overcome the world.

—John 16:33

I WANT TO GIVE YOU A strange warning: Beware of the "gospel of cheerfulness." Many well-meaning people tell us to ignore sin and to ignore gloomy people; yet more than half of the human race is gloomy.

Sum up your own circle of acquaintances, and then draw your inference. Go over the list, and before long you will come across one who is gloomy. How are you going to get that person's oppression taken off? By telling him to "cheer up"? No! By urging him to spend several weeks by the seaside? No! By giving him iron pills? No!

Living in the joy of God's forgiveness and favor is the only thing that will bring cheerfulness to such a person. God's healing of a sick soul is complete.

Prayer Thought: Dear Lord, in You is joy and happiness. May my life reflect this joy to others.

SUGGESTED READING: JOHN 16:17–33

I will say of the LORD, He is my refuge and my fortress: my God; in him will I trust.

—Psalm 91:2

I
F YOU ARE A WORKER for Jesus Christ, open your eyes wide to the fact that sin and misery and anguish are not imaginary. They are real. Jangled and tortured nerves are as real as healthy nerves. Listen to this, taken from the life of Martin Luther:

"I am utterly weary of life. I pray the Lord will come forthwith and carry me hence. Let him come, above all, with his last Judgment: I will stretch out my neck, the thunder will burst forth and I shall be at rest."—And having a necklace of white agates in his hand at the time he added: "O God, grant that it may come without delay. I would readily eat up this necklace today for the Judgment to come tomorrow." The Electress Dowager, one day when Luther was dining with her, said to him, "Doctor, I wish you may live forty years to come." "Madam," replied he, "rather than live forty years more, I would give up my chance of Paradise."

That was Luther at the end of his life. What produced it in him? He saw the Reformation wreak havoc, not good; he was too near it. He was too enmeshed with his responsibilities to enjoy the fruit of his labor.

Prayer Thought: Keep me balanced, O Lord, in my outlook on life.

SUGGESTED READING: PSALM 91

Howbeit this kind goeth not out but by prayer and fasting.

—Matthew 17:21

ROBERT LOUIS STEVENSON SAID THAT three hours out of every five he was insane with misery. John Stuart Mill said that life was not worth living after he was a boy.

These are not fictitious statements, but facts. Christian Science ignores them! The New Thought cult ignores them! The Mind Cure cult ignores them! But Jesus Christ opens our eyes to the fact of depression and despair.

How are we going to get those dark souls in contact with Jesus Christ? In the first place, we should realize that we do not know how to do it. I want to lay that one principle down very strongly: If you think you know how to present Jesus Christ to a depressed soul, you will never be able to do it. But if you will learn how to rely on the Holy Spirit, believing that Jesus Christ can do it, then I am bold enough to state that He will.

If you get your little lists of Scripture texts and search them out and say, "I know how to deal with this soul," you will never be able to help. But if you realize your absolute helplessness, saying, "My God, I cannot touch this case. I do not know where to begin. But I believe that Thou canst do it," then you can do something.

Prayer Thought: I will depend upon You, Lord, in dealing with needy people today.

SUGGESTED READING: MATTHEW 17:14–21

Jesus saith unto him, Thomas, because thou hast seen me, thou hast believed: blessed are they that have not seen, and yet have believed.

—John 20:29

IT IS WONDERFUL TO SEE Jesus Christ slip His balm through tired and jangled nerves, turning out demons, altering the whole outlook, and lifting the whole life into a totally new relationship with Him. Have you ever seen Him do that?

I have seen it twice in my life, and I will never forget it. While I watched the marvelous work of God in those gloomy, tortured lives, it was as if I were bathed in the sunlight of the presence of God. It made me realize my own utter helplessness and the power of Jesus Christ.

Jesus Christ had to come into contact with Thomas to alter his gloom. The disciples' testimony could not do it. They told Thomas, "We have seen the LORD!" And out of the agony of his sick soul, Thomas said, "I cannot, I dare not, believe. Except I see in His hands and feet the wound-prints, I will not believe" (John 20:25). The testimony of the disciples was not the slightest bit of use; but when Jesus Christ came into contact with Thomas, He made the difference.

Prayer Thought: I praise Your name, Lord, for the healing balm of Your presence.

SUGGESTED READING: JOHN 20:24–29

JULY

And Jesus went about all the cities and villages, teaching in their synagogues, and preaching the gospel of the kingdom, and healing every sickness and every disease among the people.

—Matthew 9:35

WHAT IS A MIRACLE? THERE is no such thing as a miracle to the soul who belongs to Jesus Christ. There is nothing unusual in the work that the Holy Spirit does, even though it seems out of the ordinary course of nature to our finite sense and judgment.

Jesus Christ can heal the body. He can deliver the tortured mind. God grant us the grace to know our ignorance and to get out of the way with our limited knowledge, so that we will let the Holy Spirit bring our majestic Christ face to face with the diseased, sick folk we have to face!

Prayer Thought: Holy Spirit of God, reveal the beauty of Christ to me and through me.

SUGGESTED READING: MATTHEW 9:35–38

And they were astonished at his doctrine: for his word was with power.

—Luke 4:32

THE MAJORITY OF CHRISTIAN WORKERS are trying to serve the Lord with their own convictions about how God ought to work. Too often we do not have real reliance on the Holy Spirit. God grant that we may learn to allow the Holy Spirit to introduce, through the agony of our intercession, the living Christ!

Are you willing to allow Jesus Christ to tramp on your life on His way to another sick soul? Do you know anything about giving one costly drop of blood for intercession? There are no lasting results in answer to prayer, unless that prayer costs somebody something. And though we are intent upon helping the lost, I fear that the Lord would say, "Ye have not yet resisted unto blood, striving against sin" (Hebrews 12:4).

When you discover a sin-sick soul, do you cry awhile and then go home and sleep? Instead take that soul before God and vicariously intercede until, by reliance on the Spirit of God, Jesus Christ is presented to that darkened, difficult life. There is no case too hard for Jesus Christ!

Prayer Thought: I believe in the power of the Lord Jesus Christ and His redemptive provisions to save.

SUGGESTED READING: LUKE 4:16–32

Help us, O God of our salvation, for the glory of thy name: and deliver us, and purge away our sins, for thy name's sake.

—Psalm 79:9

Y OU HAVE SOME THINGS AT home that are of no use to anybody on earth, but to you they are enormously valuable. Your emotions are like that: They may seem pointless to anyone else, but you know they are associated with something quite meaningful.

Let an experience derange your emotions, and what kind of world are you in? It would be a world from which suicide would seem the only escape.

Recall the anguished emotions of the Prodigal Son. Try to fathom one phrase of the Prodigal's cry: "I have sinned against heaven" (Luke 15:21). Oh, the agony he must have felt! The gloom! The darkness! The shadow! No preaching of the "gospel of good cheer" will touch that. Only the great life-giving, life-imparting Christ can touch those pained emotions.

Prayer Thought: Dear Lord, bring healing
to my wounded emotions.

SUGGESTED READING: PSALM 79

Take heed unto thyself, and unto the doctrine; continue in them: for in doing this thou shalt both save thyself, and them that hear thee.

—1 Timothy 4:16

IN THIS VERSE, THE WORD *heed* means "to hold up, to concentrate, screw your mind down, fix it, limit it, curb it, confine it, and rivet it" on yourself and your teaching. It is a strong word, a powerful word, a rousing word, a word that grips us—body, mind, and spirit. We are to concentrate on God's work, stick at it, fix the mind, be careful of our self-preparation, and take heed to reading. That is what we have to do if we are going to be workers approved unto God.

Notice who is talking and to whom he is talking. The apostle Paul is writing to Timothy; and notice that the apostle's method was like the journeyman's method with an apprentice. That is the method of God always.

Let me explain what I mean. A journeyman's apprentice is a boy put in the charge of a skilled worker in order to learn a trade. That was God's method of teaching this young man. Timothy had a good mother, and a godly grandmother, and then he had the apostle Paul. He was brought up in the journeyman apprentice's style, spiritually.

God does not use anyone who is undisciplined. If you are a worker for the spiritual welfare of souls, God will help you to grow spiritually under masters, teachers, and other workers. Thank God for every worker who was ever placed under the apprentice!

Prayer Thought: Teach me to learn from the examples of others.

SUGGESTED READING: 1 TIMOTHY 4:12–16

Study to shew thyself approved unto God, a workman that needeth
not to be ashamed, rightly dividing the word of truth.

—2 Timothy 2:15

WHEN JESUS CHRIST SAID, "THOU shalt love the Lord thy God with all thy heart," He did not stop there. He said, "And with all thy soul, and with all thy mind, and with all thy strength" (Mark 12:30). Oh, I wish I could kindle you to learn how some folks have lifted themselves out of the very gutter of ignominy and ignorance by sheer grind, in the secular callings of life! Would to God we had the same stick-to-it energy in God's line!

Many a lad in Scotland has worked hard, day and night, to attain a scholarship in secular callings. Are we to be less disciplined in God's calling?

Prayer Thought: Discipline my mind and body, Lord,
so I can effectively serve You and the church.

SUGGESTED READING: 2 TIMOTHY 2:15–18

But shun profane and vain babblings: for they will increase unto more ungodliness.

—2 Timothy 2:16

PAUL TOLD TIMOTHY NOT TO enter into controversy. And Paul was the arch-controversialist himself! Paul spent many of his days in controversy. Two solid years of his life were spent in the school of Tyrannus, controverting and arguing; and yet he says to Timothy, "The servant of the Lord must not strive" (2 Timothy 2:24).

Have you read of Paul's method of arguing? Paul could put himself with amazing tenderness into the place of the person he was disputing. The reason Paul tells Timothy not to argue—and the reason he tells us not to argue—is that we tend to argue from our own point of view. We argue, not for the truth's sake, but to prove we are right.

God grant that we may learn to take heed, lest we get switched off onto arguing instead of teaching the truth. Are you a worker for God who is likely turned aside by battling for the faith? Then let me read you some words that I have jotted down in my Bible beside this text: "Oh, the unmitigated curse of controversy!"

Prayer Thought: Deliver me, dear Lord, from arguing the gospel. Help me to share Your truth, not my opinions.

SUGGESTED READING: 2 TIMOTHY 2:19–22

But foolish and unlearned questions avoid, knowing that they do gender strifes.

—2 Timothy 2:23

CORRECTIONS AND CONTRADICTIONS KINDLE FURY in the proud heart! So avoid controversy, my friend, as you would avoid the entrance to hell itself.

Let others have it their way. Let them talk. Let them write. Let them correct you. Let them traduce you. Let them judge and condemn you. Let them slay you. Let the truth of God suffer rather than let His love suffer. You do not have enough of the divine nature in you to be a controversialist.

"He was oppressed, and he was afflicted, yet he opened not his mouth: he is brought as a lamb to the slaughter, and as a sheep before her shearers is dumb, so he openeth not his mouth" (Isaiah 53:7).

"Heal me," prays Augustine, "of this lust of always vindicating myself." Take heed that you are not wheedled into controversy.

Prayer Thought: Oh, Lord, give me forbearance
to avoid needless controversy!

SUGGESTED READING: 2 TIMOTHY 2:23–26

But continue thou in the things which thou hast learned and hast been assured of, knowing of whom thou hast learned them.

—2 Timothy 3:14

LET THE SPIRIT OF GOD wrestle with your dissenters.

One of my greatest weaknesses, ever since I was a Christian, has been the tendency to argue with others. I know the galling humiliation and agony of wanting intensely to argue a point. But I have learned that when any soul begins to discuss the baptism with the Holy Spirit, it is time I got out of the way. That person has a controversy with the Holy Spirit, not with me. Sanctification is not my term; baptism with the Holy Spirit is not my concept, it is God's. When people begin to argue on that line, I must remember it is the Holy Spirit they are arguing with and the Word of God they are haggling with.

God grant that we may not hinder those who are battling their way slowly into spiritual light.

Prayer Thought: Bless those dear souls who are seeking the way into a clearer comprehension of You and Your Word.

SUGGESTED READING: 2 TIMOTHY 3:10–17

Woe to them that are at ease in Zion.

—Amos 6:1

TIMOTHY WAS A FEEBLE YOUNG man, physically; Paul was continually telling him how to take care of his body. Yet, the apostle told Timothy to preach the Word "in season and out." What did he mean? To take every opportunity? No, I believe Paul meant he should preach in season or out of season, regarding himself. He seemed to say, "Never let your bodily condition hinder you, but preach in season or out of season."

If you do not believe that is the correct reading, read it again. The apostle Paul is aiming his word at laziness.

Physical laziness and spiritual sloth are all too common among Christians. May God rouse you up to get you reading! And praying! And witnessing!

Prayer Thought: Awake us, O God, and strengthen us to be alert and active in Your kingdom.

SUGGESTED READING: 2 TIMOTHY 4:1–5

Let no man despise thy youth; but be thou an example of the believers, in word, in conversation, in charity, in spirit, in faith, in purity.

—1 Timothy 4:12

WHEN PAUL SAID, "LET NO man despise thy youth," he meant that Timothy should be an example to all who believe—in word, in manner of life, in love, in faith, and in purity. God grant that we too may be the pattern of what we teach!

The only way we can be saved from being despised is if our life is in keeping with the gospel and backed by our conversation, manner of life, purity, and upright behavior. The baptism with the Holy Spirit made the disciples the incarnation of what they taught. God grant that we may be the same—Christian workers "approved unto God . . . rightly dividing the word of truth" (2 Timothy 2:15).

Prayer Thought: I want to be helpful, not hurtful, to those who look to my life as an example of godliness.

SUGGESTED READING: PSALM 71:1–12

But he giveth more grace. Wherefore he saith, God resisteth the proud, but giveth grace unto the humble.

—James 4:6

IT IS WRONG TO THINK that we must help only the people who deserve it. Sometimes I can almost hear the Spirit of God shout, "Who are you? Did you deserve the salvation of God? Did you deserve the sanctification that God has given you? Did you deserve to be filled with the Holy Spirit?" The answers are obvious. The work of God within our lives is done out of the sheer mercy of God.

For this reason, kindness and holiness always go together. Whenever harshness begins to creep into our actions toward one another, we may be certain that we are swerving from the light of the gospel of Jesus Christ. If we stand in the fullness of God's blessing, we stand there by the sheer grace of God. So let us have a spirit of humility in our dealings with one another.

Prayer Thought: I give You praise and glory, O God, for the mercy you have shown me. Let me express that mercy in my dealings with others.

SUGGESTED READING: PSALM 142

By faith Abel offered unto God a more excellent sacrifice than Cain, by which he obtained witness that he was righteous, God testifying of his gifts: and by it he being dead yet speaketh.

—Hebrews 11:4

A POINT OF SPECIAL NOTE ABOUT the sacrifice we make to the Lord: We must bind the sacrifice to the horns of the altar; we cannot place it on the altar. God does that. As soon as the sacrifice is presented to the altar and bound with cords of faith, God places the offering on the altar, so to speak. And then His own song begins.

No individual can be placed on the altar of self-sacrifice except he has been divinely born again of the Spirit of God. Yet many people are pleading, praying, and asking God to baptize them with the Holy Spirit and fire, who really need to be born again. The burnt offering—in the Old Testament figure and in the New Testament application—must have no disease about it.

The act of sacrifice simply changes the identity of the offering, from physical to spiritual. And when the burnt offering is reduced to ashes, God gives beauty for ashes!

Prayer Thought: I surrender all, Lord, to You and Your holy will.

SUGGESTED READING: GENESIS 4:1–16

And the ransomed of the Lord shall return, and come to Zion with songs and everlasting joy upon their heads: they shall obtain joy and gladness, and sorrow and sighing shall flee away.

—Isaiah 35:10

In Galatians 2:20, Paul states, "I am crucified with Christ: nevertheless I live; yet not I, but Christ liveth in me: and the life which I now live in the flesh I live by the faith of the Son of God, who loved me, and gave himself for me." Paul is referring to a changed identity—or, more strictly speaking, to a changed disposition ruling in his human nature.

When I consecrate myself with an unreserved surrender to God, having made the moral decision that I shall no longer live for myself or for the pleasure of my own spiritual experience, God will share His beauty and joy in me forever. This martyr spirit is the only spirit the Lord Jesus Christ recognizes in a fully mature Christian.

Prayer Thought: Thank You, Lord, for the beauty of Your holy love and the thrill of Your joy.

SUGGESTED READING: ISAIAH 35

For the kingdom of God is not meat and drink; but righteousness, and peace, and joy in the Holy Ghost.

—Romans 14:17

THE ONLY ABIDING FRUIT OF entire sanctification is not my joy in God, but God's joy in me.

The psalmist says in Psalm 43:4: "Then will I go unto the altar of God, unto God my exceeding joy." Note that the emphasis is not on the joy we have as we come to God, which is a much shallower thing, but on God Himself as the mainspring of joy.

The consciousness of the Christian after entire sanctification is not simply one of blessing and benediction; that is characteristic of all those who are born again. But the sanctified believer has a consciousness of the inner presence of God and a complete absorption into God's purposes, God's plans, and God's ideas.

Prayer Thought: Share with me, Father, the consciousness of Your joy within my life.

SUGGESTED READING: ROMANS 14:17–23

I must work the works of him that sent me.

—John 9:4

OUR LORD SAID THAT HE never worked from His own initiative. He let God the Father do His work through Him, and He obeyed Him. Has your life been thoroughly given over to God? Or are you still striving to create joy and peace and happiness? If so, turn to God, and let Him do His work.

The joy of the Lord is not dependent on our feelings or our circumstances. It is dependent entirely on God's acceptance of us as burnt offerings, wholly consecrated to Him.

Jesus mentions in John 15:16, "Ye have not chosen me, but I have chosen you, and ordained you, that ye should go and bring forth fruit, and that your fruit should remain: that whatsoever ye shall ask of the Father in my name, he may give it you." May God grant it!

The lives of the saints are songs for God, composed and rendered by the indwelling Holy Spirit.

Prayer Thought: Have Your own way, Lord Jesus, and direct my pathways.

SUGGESTED READING: PHILIPPIANS 3:13–21

And the Word was made flesh, and dwelt among us, (and we beheld his glory, the glory as of the only begotten of the Father,) full of grace and truth.

—John 1:14

Have you ever paused and thought about this astonishing revelation of our Lord? It would be well if you made an opportunity to get alone with God and reverently asked Him to take you to the threshold of understanding this declaration. It is a great moment when you stand, as it were, before Christ, saying by your very attitude,

I cannot soar into the heights you show,
Nor dive among the deeps that you reveal;
But it is much that high things are to know,
That deep things are to feel!

This spirit is quite in contrast to the one that petulantly says, "Oh, I can't know! Why does God make it so difficult to understand?" It is equally in contrast with the flippant impudence in which too many Christians say, "Oh, there is no mystery that I cannot understand."

Jesus is truth—the truth—and we cannot know the truth apart from Him. To believe so is to experience a radical change in our lives.

Prayer Thought: I long to know the truth of God's Word, the way of God's will, and the completeness of life in Christ.

SUGGESTED READING: JOHN 1:1–14

What is truth?

—John 18:38

OUR LORD MADE NO ATTEMPT to proclaim all truth so that we could go to His statements, as to a textbook, and verify things. Our Lord said nothing about what we call science, or art, or history; these are distinctly in the domain of human study. God never encourages laziness in the pursuit of such knowledge.

The boundaries of our knowledge must continually enlarge and alter. That is why no intelligent person would ever ask, "Does the Bible agree with the findings of modern science?" The question all enlightened persons should ask is, "Do the findings of modern science give us a better understanding of the scheme of things revealed in the Bible?"

Knowledge, for us, is difficult to gain—
Is difficult to gain, and hard to keep,
As Virtue's self; like Virtue is beset,
With snares; tried, emptied, subject to decay.

Prayer Thought: Spirit of God, create within me a heart full of grace and a mind full of knowledge.

SUGGESTED READING: JOHN 18:28–40

Speak every man truth with his neighbor.

—Ephesians 4:25

W E SHOULD REPORT THINGS THAT happen in words as exact as we can find. But, even then, we should bear in mind that the human heart is subtle and deceitful. We do well to remember William Blake's quaint words:

A truth that's told with bad intent
Beats all the lies you can invent.

Scripture says that "Lying lips are abomination to the LORD" (Proverbs 12:22). Even with good intentions to tell the truth, we shall grieve God if our motives distort the tenor of what we say.

Words are mighty, words are living—
Serpents with their venomous stings,
Or bright angels crowding round us,
With heaven's light upon their wings:
Every word has its own spirit,
True or false, that never dies:
Every word man's lips have uttered,
Echoes in God's skies.

Prayer Thought: Lord, deliver me from speaking falsely, either consciously or subconsciously.

SUGGESTED READING: EPHESIANS 4:25–32

Thou knowest my downsitting and mine uprising, thou understandest my thought afar off. Thou compassest my path and my lying down, and art acquainted with all my ways.

—Psalm 139:2–3

ALWAYS REMEMBER THAT GOD'S CONTROL is behind everything. His care encircles every incident and event of our lives. This means that we can maintain an attitude of perfect trust in Him and an eagerness to ask God for aid in our daily living.

If our minds are conditioned to think in this manner, when we are in difficulty it is easy to remember, "My Father knows all about it." We need not exert an effort to do so; such a thought will come naturally. Rather than rushing to ask someone else what we should do about our problems, we realize the nearness of God and simply take the matter to Him.

Who is the first person you consult when you have a problem? What is the first thing you do?

Remember, nothing happens unless God's will is behind it. Therefore, you can rest confident in the midst of your situation. Also remember that prayer is more than asking; it is an attitude of trust—an attitude that produces an atmosphere in which asking God for help is perfectly natural.

Prayer Thought: The comfort of Your nearness
is my strength today, dear Lord.

SUGGESTED READING: PSALM 139:1–10

Ye shall know the truth, and the truth shall make you free.

—John 8:32

GOD CALLS EVERY CHRISTIAN TO be made part and parcel of the nature of our Lord Jesus Christ, being born of the Spirit and baptized into the mystical body of that new humanity, which are "in Christ." This stands in contrast to the tragic condition of many Christians, who see the truth with the mind, while life and character lag woefully behind.

Who among us has not met with clearness—almost dictatorial clearness—wrong attitudes and actions in some Christians? This dichotomy was clearly manifested in the lives of Jesus' disciples in the days of His flesh, when they forbade others' doing good deeds because they did not follow Jesus with them. They wanted to call fire down from heaven to consume the inhabitants of some Samaritan villages that had a hostile attitude to Jesus because of racial prejudice.

Are you consistent in your attitudes and actions? If not, being "in the truth" can set you free from your old ways!

Prayer Thought: Free me from bondage to prejudice and fear.

SUGGESTED READING: JOHN 8:12–32

That he might present it to himself a glorious church, not having spot, or wrinkle, or any such thing; but that it should be holy and without blemish.

—Ephesians 5:27

O<small>UR</small> L<small>ORD</small> <small>IS</small> G<small>OD'S</small> <small>TRUTH</small> incarnate, God's ideal in the flesh. God gave His final revelation in Christ and then set processes at work to make His ideal a reality in the lives of many more people—in the character of Christians, who are His truth incorporated in flesh and blood.

You see, in pursuits such as art, music, and literature, the ideal is a great vague end toward which all the artisans evolve their work more or less blindly. But in spiritual pursuits, we have the ideal manifested in flesh and blood; and we can measure certainly our growing up into Him in all things (Ephesians 4:12–13).

Being "in Christ" does not mean that somehow God pretends we are all right. It means that we are recreated by the Spirit of God, in regeneration and the mighty baptism with the Holy Spirit. In this way that glorious Spirit-baptized community is created, which is often called "the church."

I believe, however, that such a usage of the term *church* is a misleading limitation of our Lord's meaning. When He refers to the church in Matthew 16:18, for instance, we would be much nearer His meaning if we translated *ekklçsia* as "my new humanity," against which death and time have no power.

Being "in Christ" means proclaiming, by my bodily life, what is easily discerned to be the life of Jesus. It means that I am undeserving of censure before God. It means that I am part of an innumerable host of the *ekklçsia*, the new people in Christ (Ephesians 5:25–27).

Prayer Thought: Jesus, I am determined to live each day in Your fullness.

SUGGESTED READING: [25]Husbands, love your wives, even as Christ also loved the church, and gave himself for it; [26]That he might sanctify and cleanse it with the washing of water by the word, [27]That he might present it to himself a glorious church, not having spot, or wrinkle, or any such thing; but that it should be holy and without blemish. [28]So ought men to love their wives as their own bodies. He that loveth his wife loveth himself. [29]For no man ever yet hated his own flesh; but nourisheth and cherisheth it, even as the Lord the church: [30]For we are members of his body, of his flesh, and of his bones. [31]For this cause shall a man leave his father and mother, and shall be joined unto his wife, and they two shall be one flesh. [32]This is a great mystery: but I speak concerning Christ and the church. [33]Nevertheless let every one of you in particular so love his wife even as himself; and the wife see that she reverence her husband.

—EPHESIANS 5:25–33

While he yet spake, behold, a bright cloud overshadowed them: and behold a voice out of the cloud, which said, This is my beloved Son, in whom I am well pleased; hear ye him.

—Matthew 17:5

WE MUST NOT SUPPOSE THAT we are left with the great revelation of our Lord and the powerful presence of the Holy Spirit, without any interpretation of what they mean for our lives. The Bible is the interpretation, and our Lord's work is never understood apart from the Bible.

A final court of appeal, in matters of the spirit, is given us in the Bible. It is not a question of the infallibility of the Bible; that is a side issue. What matters is the finality of the Bible.

Just as our Lord is the final revelation of God incarnate, so the Bible is the final revelation that interprets the meaning of God incarnate. I can understand the two by the gift of the Holy Spirit, who identifies me with both.

Such a revelation as our Lord Jesus Christ ought to have a corresponding revelation to interpret Him. In the Bible we have that corresponding revelation, and it is final.

Prayer Thought: I affirm my belief in the Bible as the Word of God.

SUGGESTED READING: MATTHEW 17:1–13

All scripture is given by inspiration of God, and is profitable for doctrine, for reproof, for correction, for instruction in righteousness.

—2 Timothy 3:16

EVERY CRITICISM THAT IS BROUGHT against the Bible has been brought against our Lord Jesus Christ. The two cannot be parted.

"The truth" is our Lord Himself. "The whole truth" is the inspired Scripture, interpreting our Lord to us. And "nothing but the truth" is the gracious Holy Spirit, efficaciously regenerating and identifying us with our Lord in heaven. We cannot be parted from Him, either.

Ye wish, I know, we could as one unite,
And have a Church as ample as the sky,
Whence every Church might draw its whole of light,
And not divide—but only multiply.
Good is your purpose! but, ye English youth,
Mistake ye not the symbol for the truth?

Prayer Thought: Instruct me, Holy Spirit, in the way of righteousness as I read and study the Scriptures.

SUGGESTED READING: 2 TIMOTHY 3:14–17

Sanctify them through thy truth: thy word is truth.

—John 17:17

THE WORK OF OUR LORD Jesus Christ in the world is twofold. First, it is a work accomplished in our behalf, a reconciliation with God (Romans 5:6, 8; Hebrews 2:17). Second, it is a work accomplished in us, our entire sanctification (John 14:12, 17).

The first establishes a right relationship between God and us. The second is the fruit of that relationship (James 2:17–20; 1 John 5:1–5). The first work introduces the condemned sinner into a state of grace (Ephesians 1:7). By the second work, the pardoned sinner is associated with the life and purposes of God (Galatians 2:20).

The first work is the means by which the latter is obtained; the second work is the Lord's aim for our lives. The object of Christ's work is to make us holy (1 Corinthians 1:30).

Jesus Christ baptizes us with the Holy Spirit and fire (Matthew 3:11); this is His pronouncement that His work is finished. He did this for the world at Pentecost (Acts 1:8; 2:1–4); and this He does personally for every man, woman, and child who enters by faith into His finished work (Acts 15:8–11).

Prayer Thought: Perfect Your work of grace in our hearts and lives, O Lord, according to the will of God.

SUGGESTED READING: JOHN 17:1–17

Neither by the blood of goats and calves, but by his own blood he entered in once into the holy place, having obtained eternal redemption for us.

—Hebrews 9:12

THE NEW TESTAMENT USES INTERCHANGEABLY the phrases "sanctified by the Spirit," "sanctified by the blood," and "sanctified by the Word." Also, "being baptized with the Holy Spirit (and fire)," "receiving the Holy Spirit," and "being filled with the Spirit" are used as interchangeable terms. Why? Because they all mean one thing—i.e., entire sanctification.

Entire sanctification is not primarily for service, but for the "praise of his glory" (Ephesians 1:12). Our Lord told His disciples to rejoice, not over the fact that they had gifts to heal and to cast out demons or to do many wonderful things, but over the fact that "your names are written in heaven" (Luke 10:20).

Seek this marvelous work of grace, not for what the Spirit will enable you to do, but for the glory that your transformed nature can reflect to the Lord.

Prayer Thought: Holy Spirit of God, guide me into all Your holy ways.

SUGGESTED READING: HEBREWS 9:11–28

A good tree cannot bring forth evil fruit, neither can a corrupt tree bring forth good fruit.

—Matthew 7:18

THE RESULTS OF THE BAPTISM with the Holy Spirit are not that you are gifted, but that you bear fruit (John 15:2, 8). The fruit of the Spirit become clearly manifested in your daily life. Love, joy, peace, longsuffering, gentleness, goodness, faith, meekness, and temperance—these spring from one source, the indwelling presence of the Holy Spirit (Galatians 5:22–23).

The gifts of the Spirit are very diverse and are not necessarily the result of the indwelling Spirit. Paul distinctly says that a person may have gifts without having been entirely sanctified, without the fruit of the Spirit being there (1 Corinthians 13:1–8). Such a person's exercise of spiritual gifts amounts to nothing more than the clashing of a tambourine (1 Corinthians 13:1)!

"Every good gift cometh from above," but at times the Devil seems to use it. God's Holy Spirit may give power for service, even to unsanctified souls. God may use as His instrument a person who is not His servant. This reminds us again of the importance of recognizing a person's spiritual fruit.

Remember that our Lord told us to judge prophets, not by their words or works, but by their fruit.

Prayer Thought: Enable me, Lord Jesus, to manifest the beauty of holiness through the fruit of the Spirit.

SUGGESTED READING: MATTHEW 7:15–23

The wind bloweth where it listeth, and thou hearest the sound there-of, but canst not tell whence it cometh, and whither it goeth: so is every one that is born of the Spirit.

—John 3:8

ANOTHER IMPORTANT FACTOR IN OUR study of the Holy Spirit is the cosmic side of the Holy Spirit's work. By that I mean the fact that the Holy Spirit may influence entire districts, as in the great revivals of John Wesley, Charles Finney, D. L. Moody, and the Welsh Revival.

This does not mean that those districts are sanctified, any more than the individuals in those districts (unless they definitely enter into a personal transaction with God). But it does mean that it is graciously easy, at those times, to enter into such transactions with God; and the souls who do not are more likely to increase their chances of being lost.

Cosmic visitations are all of the sovereignty of God. Nearly always, before one of these great "coming down" seasons of the Holy Spirit, God will burden His own sanctified and faithful ones to pray for souls. Of course, there are natural marvels in connection with the Lord's mighty presence. But widespread prayer is the greatest marvel of all.

Prayer Thought: Spirit of God, hover over our community and nation until You pour out a revival of divine power.

SUGGESTED READING: 1 CORINTHIANS 12

For the commandment is a lamp; and the law is light; and reproofs of instruction are the way of life.

—Proverbs 6:23

So MANY NOWADAYS WILL STUDY the Bible only insofar as it illustrates a special doctrine they are fond of. But that is not reading the Word of God distinctly. That is distorting the whole truth of God for only one aspect of the truth.

It must ever be borne in mind by Scripture readers that no "scripture is of any private interpretation" (2 Peter 1:20). And if we twist Scripture to suit one particular doctrine at the expense of others, we will not have God's approval, because this does not enable us to understand properly the Word of God.

Satan does not switch Christians onto a sidetrack that is wrong; he switches them onto a track that is one-railed. Numbers of people today are enamored with one special doctrine, such as healing or holiness or the Second Coming (all magnificently glorious truths of God, when viewed in their proper setting in the full law of God). These hobbied Christians distort God's truth so that His law is not distinctly understood.

Our Lord insisted that the only thing that would draw all people to Him was the uplifting of Himself. This should be our supreme spiritual attraction.

Prayer Thought: Forgive me, Lord, if I have tried to twist the meaning of Scripture to suit my selfish interpretations.

SUGGESTED READING: PROVERBS 6:20–35

And all the people went their way to eat, and to drink, and to send portions, and to make great mirth, because they had understood the words that were declared unto them.

—Nehemiah 8:12

THIS IS ALWAYS THE RESULT of rightly understanding the Word of God. Understanding the Bible makes us better fathers and mothers, better husbands and wives, better sons and daughters, better citizens, and better human beings.

One reason why the Bible is not read clearly is because we have the habit of teaching from isolated texts, and the teacher too often takes the text as a title. The way to get back to reading the whole Word of God, and to reading it with understanding, is to live in Bible territory—to regulate one's life and experience in every detail by God's revealed law.

We must rely on His Holy Spirit to interpret the Bible, of course, so that the commonplace moods are stripped from us as we listen.

Prayer Thought: As I understand the Word of God, help me to grow in personal holiness.

SUGGESTED READING: NEHEMIAH 8:9–18

Incline your ear, and come unto me: hear, and your soul shall live; and I will make an everlasting covenant with you, even the sure mercies of David.

—Isaiah 55:3

AFTER A TIME OF DROUGHT, we are refreshed to hear the rain pattering through the leaves of the trees, to see it being drunk in by the thirsty earth, and to feel the whole air laden with the sweet moist aroma as earth rejoices at the downfalling rain. This has its spiritual counterpart in a time of spiritual awakening. When God's Word is received, there is a melting of the whole life; the bands around the heart go; the spirit expands; and the whole grace and beauty of God come into sharp focus.

When Elijah was praying for rain, he told Ahab to get up and go, for there was the sound of an "abundance of rain." But Elijah went to the top of Carmel, buried his face in his hands, and prayed. Likewise, when the abundance of the blessing of God comes, some people rise up to eat, drink, and be merry because of the blessing. Others get alone with God, to pray that the blessings of God may flow into the right channels.

How do you react?

Prayer Thought: Lord of the harvest, may the seed of Your Word blossom in the lives of the people around me.

SUGGESTED READING: ISAIAH 55:1–5

That ye may be the children of your Father which is in heaven: for he maketh his sun to rise on the evil and on the good, and sendeth rain on the just and on the unjust.

—Matthew 5:45

D URING A RAINY SEASON, IT is not only the flowers and the trees and the sweet-smelling grass and the wholesome vegetables and fruit that are watered, but also the noxious weeds, spiteful animals, vicious insects, and reptiles, which endanger human beings.

During every religious awakening, the good and the bad, the right and the wrong, the false and the true are prospered. This is an aspect of God's truth that we ought to remember.

We cannot guide God's blessings so that they fall on our plot and leave our neighbor's alone. That is the essence of the denominational spirit, and there is a denominational spirit in us all. (The person who says he belongs to no denomination is a denomination of one.) We tend to build up walls around ourselves and imagine that God's blessings will only fall inside our plot and not on our brother's; but that is not so.

Great freedom comes to the person who realizes that God sends His rain on the good and bad!

Prayer Thought: I praise You, Lord, for the sunshine and rain of Your blessing.

SUGGESTED READING: ISAIAH 55:6–13

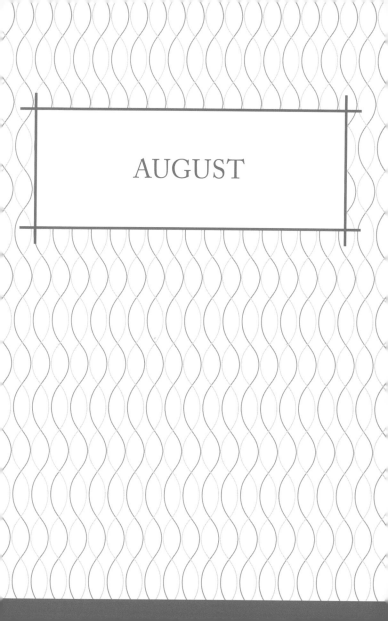

AUGUST

But whosoever drinketh of the water that I shall give him shall never thirst; but the water that I shall give him shall be in him a well of water springing up into everlasting life.

—John 4:14

RAIN COMES FROM HEAVEN, BUT it does not return. The Word of God comes from heaven, but it does not return in the same form.

The Word of God (to change the figure) comes like seed. Our Lord Jesus Christ planted the seed thought of truth and then left it to develop. No one can be the same after hearing the Word of God. He may object to it; he may revolt against it; but God has given that person a standard of conduct whereby he will judge himself in his best moments.

Jesus Christ preached His greatest discourses to the smallest audiences. His great discourse on the fountain of water, springing up within us unto eternal life, was given to a lone woman at the well of Samaria. He knew that the planting of that seed with one person would lead to a great harvest.

Seed evangelism is an idea that we modern preachers should adopt. So many of us suppose that we have to plow the field, sow the seed, reap the grain, bind it into sheaves, put it through the threshing machine, and make bread of it—all in one discourse. When we get back to the evangelistic method of the New Testament, we find that one may sow and another reap.

Let every Christian remain true to the calling God has given him.

Prayer Thought: Enable me, O God, to remain faithful to my calling.

SUGGESTED READING: JOHN 4:7–26

O how love I thy law! it is my meditation all the day.

—Psalm 119:97

Iᶠ ᴡᴇ ʜᴀᴠᴇ ᴘʀᴇsᴇɴᴛᴇᴅ ᴛʜᴇ Word of God, it is not our business to apply it, for the Spirit of God will do that. Our hearers may seem to subside to their old level of living and forget what has been said. But they cannot forget all about it, because God says, "My word . . . shall not return unto me void, but it shall accomplish that which I please, and it shall prosper in the thing whereto I sent it" (Isaiah 55:11). That does not mean the Word will produce what we want. But it will produce what God wants. We must sow the Word. Then, God says, "It shall accomplish that which I please."

In some cases, the Word of God will be a "savour of life unto life"; in other cases, it will be a "savour of death unto death." But rest assured, no individual who believingly receives the Word of God can ever be the same again. It profoundly alters life! The force and power of the new idea that is planted by the Word of God will certainly bring forth fruit after many days—either in damnation or in salvation!

Prayer Thought: Have Your way, according to Your will, in the lives of those with whom I share God's Word.

SUGGESTED READING: PSALM 119:97–104

For ye shall go out with joy, and be led forth with peace: the mountains and the hills shall break forth before you into singing, and all the trees of the field shall clap their hands.

—Isaiah 55:12

N O SHOWER OF RAIN EVER fell near human habitations without producing mud; and mud spatters on people's clothes, and people who have mud on their clothes complain. By the same token, there never was a religious awakening that did not produce some elements that disgusted certain folks.

When the woman lost her coin, Jesus said she swept the house. What dust and what a turmoil that sweeping must have caused! If she had any friends in her house, they might well have protested at the dust; but she would not have stopped. She cared for nothing but the lost coin.

When God is at work, He produces all kinds of turmoil, all kinds of things that people object to; but it makes no difference to our heavenly Father. He goes on just the same, for He has His own ends to serve. And He will serve them, no matter what we feel like. God help us to understand this lesson!

Prayer Thought: O God, help me not to complain when the truth of Your Word disturbs or destroys my habits or ideas.

SUGGESTED READING: LUKE 15:8–10

And the Lord said unto Satan, Hast thou considered my servant Job, that there is none like him in the earth, a perfect and an upright man, one that feareth God, and escheweth evil?

—Job 1:8

THE AWFUL PROBLEM OF SUFFERING appears often in the Scriptures and in our own lives. There remains a mystery, though, about suffering.

After the noisy clamor of the novice in suffering and the weighty words of the veteran in suffering, after the sarcasm and cynicism and bitterness of those in pain, after the slander of Satan against God, the voice of the Spirit sounds clear, "Hast thou considered my servant Job?" (Job 2:3).

Perhaps a person's ability to explain suffering is the clearest indication of never having suffered. Sin, suffering, and sanctification are not problems of the mind, but facts of life—mysteries that awaken all other mysteries, till the heart and life rest in God and, waiting patiently, know that "He doeth all things well."

Oh, the unspeakable comfort of knowing "God reigns," that God is "our Father," and that "the clouds are the dust of his feet."

Prayer Thought: When I do not understand why I must suffer, help me to trust in Your tender care and love.

SUGGESTED READING: JOB 1:1–12

God is our refuge and strength, a very present help in trouble.

—Psalm 46:1

RELIGIOUS LIFE IS BASED AND matured on implicit trust and then transfigured by love. That life can be simply described only by the spectator, not by the saint.

The wife of a murdered missionary in China told me of the blank, amazed agony of those excruciating days. "We did not pray, we did not feel. We were dazed with sorrow," she said.

The townspeople showed this woman a golden lock of her little child's hair. She was told that both husband and child were discovered murdered—beheaded and naked—in that godless Chinese town. Shattered and undone, the widow returned with her other little ones to Britain. She did not doubt God, but, she said, "He didn't answer prayer. Oh, how many thousands prayed for my husband, that good, valued servant of God, but all to no avail."

In those days of dull amazement, the people who drove her nearly wild with distress were those who knew the Scriptures well and went to great lengths to explain the "why" and "wherefore" of her troubles and suffering and grief. She said, "Oh, how I used to beat a tattoo on the floor with my foot while they chattered, crying in my heart, How long, O Lord, how long?

"Once, as I lay prostrate on the sofa, an elderly minister entered the room softly. The old minister, who knew my husband in the other glad days, did not speak, but he came gently over to me and, kissing me on the forehead, and went out. He never spoke. From that moment, my heart began to heal."

Trust and love are the twin habits of victorious Christian living.

Prayer Thought: When I tend to dominate another Christian with my personal viewpoints, forgive me, Lord.

SUGGESTED READING: ¹God is our refuge and strength, a very present help in trouble. ²Therefore will not we fear, though the earth be removed, and though the mountains be carried into the midst of the sea;³Though the waters thereof roar and be troubled, though the mountains shake with the swelling thereof. Selah.⁴There is a river, the streams whereof shall make glad the city of God, the holy place of the tabernacles of the most High. ⁵God is in the midst of her; she shall not be moved: God shall help her, and that right early. ⁶The heathen raged, the kingdoms were moved: he uttered his voice, the earth melted. ⁷The LORD of hosts is with us; the God of Jacob is our refuge. Selah. ⁸Come, behold the works of the LORD, what desolations he hath made in the earth. ⁹He maketh wars to cease unto the end of the earth; he breaketh the bow, and cutteth the spear in sunder; he burneth the chariot in the fire. ¹⁰Be still, and know that I am God: I will be exalted among the heathen, I will be exalted in the earth. ¹¹The LORD of hosts is with us; the God of Jacob is our refuge. Selah.

—PSALM 46

Beloved, think it not strange concerning the fiery trial which is to try you, as though some strange thing happened unto you.

—1 Peter 4:12

THE UNEXPLAINED THINGS IN LIFE are more than the explained. God seems careless whether mankind understands Him or not. He scarcely vindicates His saints to the world.

People told Jesus of the sickness of Lazarus. "He whom thou lovest is sick," they cried. But Jesus went on His way. He did not send any words of hope, nor did He even go. Lazarus died, was buried, and four days afterwards Jesus appeared. Perhaps you can understand Martha, as she exclaimed, "Lord, if thou hadst been here, my brother had not died" (John 11:21).

If you do not understand that, you are unaware of the real nature of suffering. You are unaware of the poignant agony of God's silences.

Have you read 1 Peter 4:12–19? An informal consideration of those verses will serve to knot into some kind of order what the Bible indicates, states, and implies regarding suffering.

Prayer Thought: Suffering is a mystery. Yet I commit my suffering to Your providential care.

SUGGESTED READING: 1 PETER 4:12–15

But let none of you suffer as a murderer, or as a thief, or as an evildoer, or as a busybody in other men's matters.

—1 Peter 4:15

THE SPRINGS OF SUFFERING, FROM a biblical point of view, are twofold: wrongdoing and wrong temper.

Wrongdoing is identified by Peter as he writes, "Let none of you suffer as a murderer, or as a thief, or as an evildoer." Wrongdoing finds expression in the literature of all ages. It works a suffering as cruel as that of the grave. Myers accurately describes the suffering of wrongdoing in his poem "Ammergau":

> *When this man's best desire and highest aim*
> *Had ended in the deed of traitorous shame;*
> *When to his blood-shot eyes grew wild and dim,*
> *The stony faces of the Sanhedrin,—*
> *When in his rage he could not longer bear*
> *Men's voices nor the sunlight nor the air,*
> . . . .
> *Nor God in Heaven, nor anything but death.*
> *I bowed my head, and through my fingers ran*
> *Tears for the end of that Iscariot man,*
> *Lost in the hopeless struggle of the soul*
> *To make the done, undone; the broken whole.*

Prayer Thought: God forbid that I allow personal wrongdoing to create pain for others.

SUGGESTED READING: 1 PETER 4:15–19

Whosoever therefore shall humble himself as this little child, the same is greatest in the kingdom of heaven.

—Matthew 18:4

HUMILITY IS NOT AN IDEAL; it is the unconscious result of living in right relationship to God, centered in Him. The conscious eye of a humble person is not on his service, but on his Savior.

There is nothing more awful than conscious humility; it is the most satanic type of pride. A person who consciously serves you is worse than the Pharisee eaten up with conceit.

We will be humble if the center of our affection is God's honor. Our humility will never be understood by someone who is not Christ-centered; but Christ will know the source of our attitude.

Jesus Christ did not lift up humility as an ideal. He lived it. When we serve others only for the sake of Christ's glory, and not for the purpose of being appreciated by them, we will be humble as He is.

Prayer Thought: Purge all pride, O God, from my heart and mind. Fill me with the humility of Your holiness.

SUGGESTED READING: PHILIPPIANS 2:1–4

And that ye study to be quiet, and to do your own business, and to work with your own hands, as we commanded you.

—1 Thessalonians 4:11

FIRST PETER 4:15 SPEAKS OF the suffering that springs from the wrong temper: "Let none of you suffer . . . as a busybody in other men's matters." From talking in the wrong mood there springs a suffering so keen, so stinging, so belittling, so hopeless, that it debases and drives still lower the suffering one. An old song from the ancient pilgrim's songbook, Psalm 120, has this thorn at the heart of its suffering. Read it carefully, dear friend.

It is humiliating to suffer from being a "busybody" or a meddler "in other men's matters."

The suffering that arises from a wrong temper has no refining quality, only a humiliating aspect. Peter, as a meddler in other men's matters, got a rebuke from our Lord (John 21:21–22). Surely the rebuke contained in our Lord's answer to Martha, who complained that Mary did not serve Him as she did, is similar (Luke 10:42). The wrecks of many severed friendships began in that mutiny and final abandonment of busybody meddlesomeness.

> How will sad memory point where here and there,
> Friend after friend, by falsehood or by fate,
> From him or from each other parted were,
> And love sometimes becomes the nurse of hate!
> Rather, he thinks he held not duly dear
> Love, the best gift that man on man bestows,
> While round his downward path, recluse and drear,
> He feels the chill, indifferent shadows close.

. . . .

"Why did I not," his spirit murmurs deep,
"At every cost of momentary pride,
Preserve the love for which in vain I weep;
Why had I wish, or hope, or sense beside?"
O cruel issue of some selfish thought!
O fruitless lesson, mercilessly taught,
Oh long, long echo of some angry tone!
Alone to linger—and to die alone!

Prayer Thought: Lord, enable me to resist the
temptation to pry into other people's affairs.

SUGGESTED READING: PSALM 69:1–19

Blessed are ye, when men shall hate you, and when they shall separate you from their company, and shall reproach you, and cast out
your name as evil, for the Son of man's sake.

—Luke 6:22

OUR DESIGNATION AS CHRISTIANS IS of divine appoint-
ment, no matter whether it comes from the versatile wit of
Antioch or the reverent respect of the Gentile. To live worthy of
the name of Christian is to suffer persecution. And mark you
this, mark it well—to suffer as a Christian is a shameful thing
in the eyes of this world.

Your friends who, in your hour of trial and slander, gather
around you to support and stand with you, are first amazed,
then dazed, then disgusted, that you really mean not to stand
up for yourself but to submit meekly. They do not understand
that it is a great honor to suffer on Christ's behalf.

But in that hour, that hour when your friends pity you,
Jesus Himself will come and whisper to your spirit, " Blessed
are ye, when men shall hate you, and when they shall separate
you from their company, and shall reproach you, and cast out
your name as evil, for the Son of man's sake. Rejoice ye in that
day . . . leap for joy: for, behold, your reward is great in heaven"
(Luke 6:22–23).

To suffer for your Christian meekness is an ennobling,
exalting, refining, and God-glorifying form of suffering.

Prayer Thought: Jesus, You suffered for me. Enable
me to suffer for You without complaining.

SUGGESTED READING: LUKE 6:20–36

Yet if any man suffer as a Christian, let him not be ashamed; but let him glorify God on this behalf.

—1 Peter 4:16

To suffer as a Christian is not the same as being marked as peculiar because of your views or because you will not bend to conventionality. These causes of suffering are not uniquely Christian; they are things from which all people suffer, irrespective of creed or religion, or no religion. But to suffer as a Christian stems from an essential difference, which rouses the contempt of the world.

You will suffer as a Christian because you have no answer when the world's satire is turned on you, as it was on Jesus while He hung on the Cross. There Jesus' enemies turned His words into a jesting and a jeering, and they will do the same to you. He gave no answer, nor can you.

It was in the throes of that blinding problem that Peter staggered. He meant to go with His Lord to death, and he did, but never had he imagined that he would have to go without Him. To see Jesus, His Lord, taken by the power of the world as meek as a lamb to the slaughter, making no answer, performing no work to explain it—this froze Peter to the soul!

That is what it means to suffer as a Christian. To hear people taunt and tear His promises to you in pieces, and know you cannot answer, or to smart under the merciless, pitying sarcasms of belonging to the contemptible sect of "Christians"—that is Christian suffering.

Prayer Thought: Glorify Yourself, O God, through my sufferings.

SUGGESTED READING: PHILIPPIANS 4:10–19

Now no chastening for the present seemeth to be joyous, but grievous: nevertheless afterward it yieldeth the peaceable fruit of righteousness unto them which are exercised thereby.

—Hebrews 12:11

WHEN MY HEART IS STUNG in the first moment of suffering, and when His "rod and staff have comforted me," I count it all joy to suffer for the glory of God.

> *How very hard it is to be*
> *A Christian! Hard for you and me.*
> . . . .
> *And the sole thing that I remark*
> *Upon this difficulty, this;*
> *We do not see it where it is,*
> *At the beginning of the race:*
> *As we proceed, it shifts its place,*
> *And where we looked for crowns to fall,*
> *We find the tug's to come—that's all.*
> . . . .
> *And I find it hard*
> *To be a Christian, as I said!*
> *Still every now and then my head*
> *Raised glad, sinks mournful—all grows*
> *drear*
> *Spite of the sunshine.*
> . . . .
> *But Easter-Day breaks! But*
> *Christ rises! Mercy every way*
> *Is infinite—and who can say? (Robert Browning)*

"Yet if any man suffer as a Christian, let him not be ashamed; but let him glorify God on this behalf." Be willing to suffer as a Christian!

Prayer Thought: Help me to have patience in suffering, O Lord, knowing that "all things work together" according to Your will and wishes.

Suggested Reading: [1]Wherefore seeing we also are compassed about with so great a cloud of witnesses, let us lay aside every weight, and the sin which doth so easily beset us, and let us run with patience the race that is set before us, [2]Looking unto Jesus the author and finisher of our faith; who for the joy that was set before him endured the cross, despising the shame, and is set down at the right hand of the throne of God. [3]For consider him that endured such contradiction of sinners against himself, lest ye be wearied and faint in your minds. [4]Ye have not yet resisted unto blood, striving against sin. [5]And ye have forgotten the exhortation which speaketh unto you as unto children, My son, despise not thou the chastening of the Lord, nor faint when thou art rebuked of him: [6]For whom the Lord loveth he chasteneth, and scourgeth every son whom he receiveth. [7]If ye endure chastening, God dealeth with you as with sons; for what son is he whom the father chasteneth not? [8]But if ye be without chastisement, whereof all are partakers, then are ye bastards, and not sons. [9]Furthermore we have had fathers of our flesh which corrected us, and we gave them reverence: shall we not much rather be in subjection unto the Father of spirits, and live? ¹⁰For they verily for a few days chastened us after their own pleasure; but he for our profit, that we might be partakers of his holiness. ¹¹Now no chastening for the present seemeth to be joyous, but grievous: nevertheless afterward it yieldeth the peaceable fruit of righteousness unto them which are exercised thereby. ¹²Wherefore lift up the hands which hang down, and the feeble knees; ¹³And make straight paths for your feet, lest that which is lame be turned out of the way; but let it rather be healed. ¹⁴Follow peace with all men, and holiness, without which no man shall see the Lord.

—HEBREWS 12:1–14

Wherefore let them that suffer according to the will of God commit the keeping of their souls to him in well doing, as unto a faithful Creator.

—1 Peter 4:19

THE SPLENDID SOLITUDE OF GOD's purpose transfigures agony into redemption, and the baffling hurricanes speed the soul like a "flaming arrow" into God's great day. G. K. Chesterton, writing on the experience of Job, says, "But God comforts Job with indecipherable mystery, and for the first time Job is comforted. Eliphaz gives one answer, Job gives another answer, and the question still remains an open wound. God simply refuses to answer, and somehow the question is answered. Job flings at God one riddle, God flings back at Job a hundred riddles, and Job is at peace. He is comforted with conundrums."

When the petty things, the trite things, the sentimental things, the poetic and the explainable things have been said about suffering, the still small voice of the Spirit puts the perpetual conundrum, "Hast thou considered my servant Job?" When our commonplace shoes are off our feet, and we stand before His cross, we hear the muddling conundrum still deeper and more perplexing, "This is my beloved Son, hear him." "Yet it pleased the LORD to bruise him; he hath put him to grief."

We bow our heads, our spirits murmuring, "Who hath believed our report? and to whom is the arm of the LORD revealed?" (Isaiah 53:1).

Prayer Thought: Lord, I commit my present sufferings and future problems into Your hands.

SUGGESTED READING: JOB 1:13–22

Wherefore is light given to him that is in misery, and life unto the bitter in soul.

—Job 3:20

JOB DID NOT KNOW THE preface to his own story, and neither does any man. He was never told that God and the Devil had made a battleground of his soul. His suffering was not for his sake, or his perfecting, or his purifying—these were all incidental. No! It was simply the will of God.

In the midst of suffering, the word sounds with deeper, truer significance: " If any man will come after me, let him deny himself, and take up his cross, and follow me" (Matthew 16:24). The true disciple learns the meaning of "follow me" in the hour when the dilemma perplexes him, the billows overwhelm him, and the noise of God's water spouts deafen him.

Doing God's will according to my will—surely that is the very essence of Satan's temptation of our Lord and of every sanctified soul. Some are tempted to take back their right to themselves and do God's will according to their own sanctified understanding. "Never!" said Jesus. " For I came down from heaven, not to do mine own will, but the will of him that sent me."

Prayer Thought: Lord, teach me to follow You, even when I do not understand the circumstances.

SUGGESTED READING: JOB 3

And he spake many things unto them in parables.

—Matthew 13:3

A MYSTERY, IN THE BIBLICAL SENSE, is simply a truth that has not yet been revealed. The only way to understand it rightly is through the interpretation of the Spirit of God.

Some people think that Jesus uttered some hard words in the thirteenth chapter of Matthew. They think He said, "I will talk to you in parables, because I do not want you to understand." But by examining the Scriptures, we find an altogether different meaning. The real interpretation is this: "I am going to talk to you in parables, because many of you have dull ears and hard hearts and blind eyes and cannot understand My voice. And if you will only open your ears and hear, you will understand through these parables."

Many have dull ears and are unable to hear the voice of God. When God spoke to Jesus, the people said it thundered. But Jesus declared, "Father spoke to me." He knew His Father's voice. The ears of the people were stopped, but His ears were opened and could hear the message.

Think of a telegraph operator. He listens to the clicking of his instrument and takes down the message, while I might listen and listen, and yet I can make nothing of it. I do not know the voice of the telegraph instrument.

I wonder how many of us are so dull of hearing that we cannot understand when Jesus talks to us through the parables. Many people, to whom the Word of God comes in this present generation, will not listen.

Prayer Thought: Reveal to me, O Lord, the truth of Your Word. Guide me.

SUGGESTED READING: MATTHEW 13:1–6

Who hath ears to hear, let him hear.

—Matthew 13:9

IN THE PARABLE OF THE sower, Jesus said there were spiritually shallow people in every place where His Word is known; and every worker of God will find this is a fact. I am not referring to natural stupidity. God will not hold people accountable for that. I am referring to spiritual stupidity, the very kind that David meant when he said, "I was a brute before God."

Soil in a pathway across a field is no doubt as good as any other soil, but it has been crushed down and become hard and compact. The only way to make it become fruitful is to break it up with a plow. If we do not watch and pray, we will let the cares of this life and the lust of other things harden our hearts until we will be in no condition, after a time, to hear what God says. This is exactly the condition that Jesus predicted for this present generation.

Prayer Thought: Father, as I watch and pray, keep my conscience tender, my heart pure, and my whole life spiritually productive.

SUGGESTED READING: MATTHEW 13:7–9

For whosoever hath, to him shall be given, and he shall have more abundance: but whosoever hath not, from him shall be taken away even that he hath.

—Matthew 13:12

T HOSE WHO HEAR THE WORD of God and do not understand it are like the wayside ground, so hard that the seed does not penetrate it. Then the Devil comes along and snatches the Word away.

By getting into a state where you do not listen to what Jesus says, you give free course to the entrance of Satan into your life. The only thing that God can do with spiritually shallow people is to permit tribulation, adversity, conviction, and sickness. When such problems come, your ears are opened and you receive a new word from God. I am not surprised that Jesus says, "In the world ye shall have tribulation." Tribulation is God's plow to keep the ground of the heart broken up and ready for His truth.

Prayer Thought: Oh, deliver me from the snares of Satan's subtle attacks. I am listening, Lord, to Your voice.

SUGGESTED READING: MATTHEW 13:10–12

For this people's heart is waxed gross, and their ears are dull of hearing, and their eyes they have closed; lest at any time they should see with their eyes and hear with their ears, and should understand with their heart, and should be converted, and I should heal them.

—Matthew 13:15

SOME PEOPLE CLAIM TO GET converted and entirely sanctified at every camp meeting or revival meeting. They receive the Word of God with great joy, but they soon fall back into their old way of living. They are spiritually shallow because they have never had their selfish wills broken.

Stony ground is a layer of rock, covered with only a thin soil of earth. There are many people like this.

What's the trouble? They have never had the soil of their wills broken; they have not gone to the bottom of their spirits. Jesus says many people will bless God for the truth and receive it with gladness; but when persecution arises, they are offended.

Prayer Thought: Break my stubborn will, Lord Jesus, and have Your holy way in all I do and say.

SUGGESTED READING: MATTHEW 13:13–17

But he that received seed into the good ground is he that heareth the word, and understandeth it; which also beareth fruit, and bringeth forth, some an hundredfold, some sixty, some thirty.

—Matthew 13:23

MANY FOLKS HAVE ONLY THEIR emotions stirred when they hear the Word of God. You may have your emotions stirred every day of every year, and yet be the same old crooked, twisted, bent man or woman. You may have the affections of your heart stirred every day, and yet be good for nothing.

If you imagine that the world is going to be saved in this generation, you are mistaken. If we were to take literally the parable of the sower, we would realize that only one fourth of those to whom the Word is preached will prove to be good ground. And this one fourth He is using in the uttermost parts of the earth. Some are being sown in the foreign fields, some in the home fields.

Prayer Thought: I praise You, Lord, for the inner transformation of my heart and life!

SUGGESTED READING: MATTHEW 13:18–23

And some fell on stony ground, where it had not much earth; and immediately it sprang up, because it had no depth of earth.

—Mark 4:5

SOME PEOPLE RECEIVE THE WORD of God and run well for a time, but they permit something to hinder them—usually the cares of this world. They will tell you, "If you only knew what I have to contend with" or, "If you only knew my peculiar situation, my trials, my difficulties."

This kind of self-sympathy, arising from the cares of this life, is carnal. It will kill the Spirit of God within you.

Jesus said, "If you look at your problems instead of Me, the Word will be choked in your heart." Satan will try his best to have you look at the difficulties of your life. He knows that if he can get your eyes off of Jesus and onto these, he will be able to choke your spiritual life.

Have you ever noticed how many times Scripture warns us not to be anxious, not to worry? He tells us to cast our cares upon Him, to trust Him, to wait on Him, and to fret not. May God help us to keep the thorns from growing up in our hearts and choking the Word of God in us!

Prayer Thought: Forgive me when I cease to trust You, Lord, and begin to worry selfishly.

SUGGESTED READING: MARK 4:1–5

And other fell on good ground, and did yield fruit that sprang up and increased.

—Mark 4:8

WHAT IS THE GOOD GROUND in the parable of the sower? This good ground is the heart that is ready to receive the Word of God. Paul told King Agrippa that Jesus sent him to the Gentiles to "open their eyes, and to turn them from darkness to light, and from the power of Satan unto God" (Acts 26:18). But this alone was not salvation; their salvation came when they accepted Paul's message and received the forgiveness of sins.

I wonder how many who shall read these lines have really proven "good ground" to God! The question of whether your spiritual yield will be one hundredfold, sixtyfold, or thirtyfold has nothing to do with it. Christ puts His Word into us, and we bring forth His fruit; and then He takes us and plants us and makes us what He pleases in this world.

The measure of my growth in grace is my growth in God's sight, not in man's sight. I wonder, do we listen to God's Word and allow it to bear fruit?

Prayer Thought: Take my life, Lord, and make it what You want it to be.

SUGGESTED READING: MARK 4:6–13

And the cares of this world, and the deceitfulness of riches, and the lusts of other things entering in, choke the word, and it becometh unfruitful.

—Mark 4:19

Many people are trying to live the life of a Christian, who have not been born again by the Spirit of God. My friend, if you are in this class, your difficulties will drive you insane. You cannot possibly live the Christian life unless you have received the strength of the Lord in the new birth. The thorns of life will choke you.

In the parable of the sower, thorns represent the cares of this life or anything that will hinder you spiritually. Remember, if you determine to go with God, you will have difficulties.

Paul did not say, "A great and effectual door is opened unto me, and there is nothing to hinder"; but he said, "There are many adversaries" (1 Corinthians 16:9). Jesus says the cares of this world and the deceitfulness of riches are hindering many. In this sense, "riches" refers not to money alone, but to anything you treasure above the presence of the Son of God.

Oh, may the Lord help us to understand His truth!

Prayer Thought: Discipline my walk with You, Jesus, so that I can effectively overcome setbacks in life.

SUGGESTED READING: MARK 4:14–20

But straightway Jesus spake unto them, saying, Be of good cheer; it is I; be not afraid.

—Matthew 14:27

JESUS KNOWS EVERYTHING ABOUT US. He knows about our surroundings and our conditions. He knows better than we how to manage our daily affairs, such as how to manage a fish boat. Peter, with his experience along this line, had to acknowledge that Jesus knew more than he. Jesus sees the typewriting, the shorthand, the cleaning, the scrubbing, the preaching, and the praying that we do.

Moreover, Jesus experiences all of these things with you. You cannot get hold of God unless you realize the glorious fact that Christ lives in you and is working through you by the indwelling power of the Holy Spirit.

Prayer Thought: Thank You, Lord, for Your comforting presence.

SUGGESTED READING: MATTHEW 14:22–33

But that on the good ground are they, which in an honest and good heart, having heard the word, keep it, and bring forth fruit with patience.

—Luke 8:15

HAVE WE LET JESUS CHRIST have His way with us in all things?

Many will pay attention to what God says until it gets to one certain thing, and then they refuse to listen. Herod, you will remember, listened to John's preaching until that preacher declared, "It is not lawful for thee to have her" (Matthew 14:4). Instantly, Herod would hear no more.

I pray that we may indeed listen and be "good ground" to the Son of God. Then can He truly work out His plans, His will, and His way through us. Then can He truly make of us broken bread and poured out wine to needy people.

Oh, have you received the Word of God in salvation? In entire sanctification? In the daily leadings of your life? Have you the Word dwelling richly in your heart? If not, will you not meet God's conditions and become "good ground" to the Son of God?

Prayer Thought: O God, lead me correctly
in the way of righteousness.

SUGGESTED READING: LUKE 8:4–15

It is vain for you to rise up early, to sit up late, to eat the bread of sorrows: for so he giveth his beloved sleep.

—Psalm 127:2

How many of us have considered the spiritual implications of sleep? When one considers the enormous proportion of human life that is spent in sleep, the question arises, "Why?" The usual answer is, "For physical recuperation." But surely much less time than that would serve the physical purpose.

We read in Genesis 2:21 that God caused a deep sleep to fall on Adam, and again in Genesis 15:12 that a deep sleep fell on Abraham. Marvelous new revelations were the outcome. In fact, all the dreams in the Bible sprang from a deeper center than common dreams; dreams are really the sign that we are awakening. But in the slumber of the body, God seems to take the souls of His servants into deeper communion.

Whether the dispensation of dreams and their ministry in this respect is past or not, I do not know. But I would like to suggest that God does great things for us and in us during our moments of sleep.

Prayer Thought: While I rest, Lord, keep
Your protective hand upon me.

SUGGESTED READING: PSALM 127

Likewise the Spirit also helpeth our infirmities: for we know not what we should pray for as we ought: but the Spirit itself maketh intercession for us with groanings which cannot be uttered.

—Romans 8:26

WHEN A PROBLEM OR PERPLEXITY harasses the mind and there seems no solution, how often, after a night's rest, the solution is easy and the problem has no further terror. When some communication causes the heart to beat unnaturally with excitement or dread, a night's sleep has such a wonderful effect that the pulse is quiet and the mind is clear. The answer to the communication becomes unmistakable.

We are not any different when we are born again of the Spirit of God. Our human nature remains the same, although its mainspring is altered. And in the deep subconscious realm of our soul's life, I believe, the Spirit of God not only carries on profound prayers (Romans 8:26), but profoundly develops our spiritual capacities. When the crises of life are reached, we are astonished at the sudden power within us to meet the new set of circumstances. And in looking back, the soul is amazed in gratitude to God as to how His grace performs.

Praise the Lord!

Prayer Thought: Thank You, Lord, for enabling me to rest in You—physically and spiritually.

SUGGESTED READING: ROMANS 8:26–30

Therefore my heart is glad, and my glory rejoiceth: my flesh also shall rest in hope.

—Psalm 16:9

IN MODERN PSYCHOLOGY THERE IS a great deal of talk about the subconscious mind or the subliminal consciousness. It is in this realm of our souls, beyond our conscious life, that God surely works during our hours of sleep as well as during our hours of waking.

A very important period in a saint's life is the hour before sleep, to which few of us pay sufficient attention. The old heathen philosopher Plato said that he used to quiet his mind by devout and blessed thoughts before he slept. If we saints hurry to bed from work or from conversation, without having the "swelling emptiness" crushed from our lives by a time of communion with God, we deserve the horror of darkness and the unrefreshing slumber that awaits our subsequent hours. The instinct that made our parents teach us to pray each night before going to bed is a more profound one, I am sure, than can be stated. These sorts of habits can give a deeper capacity to our souls.

Prayer Thought: O God, I desire to slow down and prepare myself to be in Your presence as I sleep each night.

SUGGESTED READING: EPHESIANS 6:10–20

I will both lay me down in peace, and sleep: for thou, Lord, only makest me dwell in safety.

—Psalm 4:8

WHEN WE HAVE A BURDEN of prayer for someone, we pray earnestly and strongly, and then comes a sense of answered prayer. We communicate with our friend and tell him that, at the time of prayer, we had the sense of relief. Was he conscious of any deliverance? He may answer no.

There is no need for misgiving, for dangers may have beset his soul in the regions in which he could not be conscious, in the regions which God alone guards. The Spirit of God led us to intercede for him, and God can minister to him, even during hours of sleep. If this points out the profound mystery of our individual souls, it points out on the other hand the marvelous security of our great God. These words are true:

Safe in the arms of Jesus,
Safe on His gentle breast,
There by His love o'ershadowed,
Sweetly my soul shall rest.

Prayer Thought: I am safe in God's providential care. To Him be praise and thanksgiving!

SUGGESTED READING: PSALM 8

The angel of the Lord encampeth round about them that fear him, and delivereth them.

—Psalm 34:7

IN THE SUBCONSCIOUS REALM OF our lives, embraced by our sleep, is the ministry of angels. As so often is the case, our children's hymns are nearer the truth than the speculations of philosophers. When we were taught that angels guarded our beds and watched over us and ministered to us, we were not being told a fairy story; we were being told a fact that has been revealed in the Bible: "Are they not all ministering spirits, sent forth to minister for them who shall be heirs of salvation?" (Hebrews 1:14).

Angels nowadays rarely materialize; therefore, we do not see them with our bodily eyes or feel them with our bodily consciousness. But the ineffable refreshing and intuitive sense of security that merges around our lives at times surely rises from these garrison soldiers of God.

Can you imagine the unspeakable danger of a soul unguarded by God, to whom the unconscious hours of sleep are open to the subtle onslaught of Satan? Being guarded within and without by the Spirit of God, the terrors by night and the destruction that wasteth at noonday have no part in the life of the saint. The ungodly are not shielded from them by their unconsciousness, except by the prayers of their godly friends. This ought to awaken terror in the hearts of those who are living a self-satisfied life, unyielded to God.

Prayer Thought: Lord, I appreciate the ministry of Your angels and the protective care they are to Christians.

SUGGESTED READING: PSALM 34:1–8

When thou liest down, thou shalt not be afraid: yea, thou shalt lie down, and thy sleep shall be sweet.

—Proverbs 3:24

No SPIRITUALIST MEDIUM, NO FORTUNE teller, no mesmerist, or practitioner of the occult can have any effect over the soul of a Christian; because the marvelous mighty power of the Spirit of God within, and the garrison of God's angels without, strike terror into the Devil. We are totally unconscious of anything which attempts to merge into the fringe of our consciousness by such things as spiritualism and theosophies.

Reader, as you retire to rest tonight, give your soul and God a time together; meditate on these things and commit with a conscious peace your life to God during the hours of sleep. Deep and profound alterations will occur in your spirit, soul, and body by the creative hand of our God. May God write over your heart and life tonight, "So he giveth his beloved sleep."

Sleep is God's celestial nurse that croons the consciousness away and deals with the unconscious life of the soul in places where only God and His angels have charge.

Prayer Thought: Minister to my inner spiritual needs tonight, Lord, and may Your peace invade my heart and soul.

SUGGESTED READING: PROVERBS 3:21–26

Keep thy heart with all diligence; for out of it are the issues of life.

—Proverbs 4:23

WE MUST LEARN TO HARNESS our impulses. Thank God, we have the power to do this. We have the ability to fix the form of our choices either for good or bad.

Impulsiveness brings no glory to God. If you suddenly feel you ought to give money to a poor man, and do it, what credit does that give to God? Much of that sort of giving is done to relieve our feelings, not to indicate real generosity. So God does not value our gifts of impulsiveness.

More meaningful are the gifts we offer because we have determined in our heart what to do. Giving that is governed by a fixed determination is blessed and approved by God. He holds us responsible for using or not using the power to choose voluntarily what we shall do.

Prayer Thought: Father, captivate my thoughts and motives. Make them acceptable in Your sight, I pray.

SUGGESTED READING: PROVERBS 4:23–27

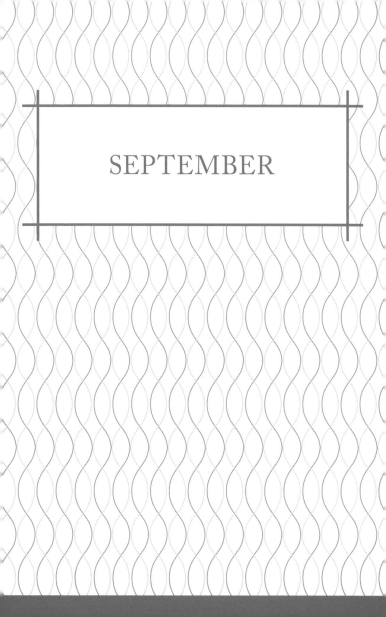

SEPTEMBER

Jesus answered and said unto her, Whosoever drinketh of this water shall thirst again.

—John 4:13

IN THE DAYS OF HIS flesh, our Lord worked nearly exclusively with Jews. But occasionally a Gentile burst through the crowd; and when that happened, Jesus Christ dealt with that person in a totally different manner. In every case of our Lord's dealings with a religious Jew, there is a sort of serious solemnity about the Jew and about our Lord. But when He came in contact with a Greek, He seems to embrace the sharp wit of the Greek and deals with that person accordingly.

The account of the Syrophoenician woman in Matthew 15 is a good example. As the incident begins, the Lord wanted to be alone. He had a lot of publicity, and He was trying to get His disciples away when this Gentile woman burst through the crowd with a request. Jesus paid no attention to her. The reason was quite obvious—He wanted to be quiet.

Watch how our Lord dealt with her. He gave her a proverb and she gave Him a proverb back: "It is not meet to fling the meat to very little dogs." The woman replied, "But it is quite legitimate for the dogs to catch the crumbs that fall from the master's table."

We Christian workers wonder how we are to get these irreligious, yet healthy-minded people to the place where they will want Jesus as their Lord and Savior. Many people seem to be happy without Him. They are moral and upright. But our Lord describes them as lost.

Prayer Thought: O God, help me to help patiently those who say they are "happy and content without Jesus."

SUGGESTED READING: ²⁴And from thence he arose, and went into the borders of Tyre and Sidon, and entered into an house, and would have no man know it: but he could not be hid. ²⁵For a certain woman, whose young daughter had an unclean spirit, heard of him, and came and fell at his feet: ²⁶The woman was a Greek, a Syrophenician by nation; and she besought him that he would cast forth the devil out of her daughter. ²⁷But Jesus said unto her, Let the children first be filled: for it is not meet to take the children's bread, and to cast it unto the dogs. ²⁸And she answered and said unto him, Yes, Lord: yet the dogs under the table eat of the children's crumbs. ²⁹And he said unto her, For this saying go thy way; the devil is gone out of thy daughter. ³⁰And when she was come to her house, she found the devil gone out, and her daughter laid upon the bed.

—MARK 7:24–30

Being justified freely by his grace through the redemption that is in Christ Jesus.

—Romans 3:24

JUST AS THE SYROPHOENICIAN CAME to our Lord at the end of a busy day, you will find that healthy-minded folks often come to you when you are worn out. They will want to ask you all kinds of questions.

They did of the apostle Paul. They asked, "What will this babbler say? What is he talking about? He is evidently talking about some new religion." Paul preached to them Jesus Christ and His marvelous resurrection from the dead. But some of them ridiculed him. When Paul wrote his Epistle to the Corinthians, he said, "But we preach Christ crucified, unto the Jews a stumbling block, and unto the Greeks foolishness" (1 Corinthians 1:23).

Every worker for God has surely come across the type of person who makes him feel foolish. Such a person's external life is quite upright and sterling, and he puts questions to you that bring you to a complete standstill. You cannot answer such a person, and thus he succeeds in making you feel amazingly foolish.

For instance, you preach that Jesus Christ lived and died and rose again to save us from our sins and put us right with God. But some people will tell you quite honestly that they have no sin of which they are conscious. And you cannot point to a spot in their whole lives. So they say, "What is the good in Jesus Christ dying for me? I am all right; I do exactly what I ought to do. I am not a thief. I am not a sinner. Why did Jesus Christ want to die for me?"

That line of reasoning, when you are not used to it, produces a sense of unutterable foolishness on your part. But you must continue to tell those people the truth.

Prayer Thought: I confess, Lord, that all of us are sinners. Only through grace and mercy do we have hope of redemption.

SUGGESTED READING: [24]Being justified freely by his grace through the redemption that is in Christ Jesus: [25]Whom God hath set forth to be a propitiation through faith in his blood, to declare his righteousness for the remission of sins that are past, through the forbearance of God; [26]To declare, I say, at this time his righteousness: that he might be just, and the justifier of him which believeth in Jesus. [27]Where is boasting then? It is excluded. By what law? of works? Nay: but by the law of faith. [28]Therefore we conclude that a man is justified by faith without the deeds of the law. [29]Is he the God of the Jews only? is he not also of the Gentiles? Yes, of the Gentiles also: [30]Seeing it is one God, which shall justify the circumcision by faith, and uncircumcision through faith. [31]Do we then make void the law through faith? God forbid: yea, we establish the law.

—ROMANS 3:24–31

And I, if I be lifted up from the earth, will draw all men unto me.

—John 12:32

GALLIO WAS AN ORDINARY PAGAN—UPRIGHT, sterling, and just—and when they brought Paul before him he did not care for any of these things the apostle was saying. Gallio did not care for the apostle Paul either. He said, in effect, "If it is a question of justice or injustice, I am here to decide it. But do not come here with your religious quarrels; I have nothing whatever to do with them."

We shall have opponents who ignore us. When they do, we should examine the kind of Lord Jesus we are erecting for them to observe. If we are teaching before the kind of pagan I have described—a person upright, righteous, and just, but without a spark of religion—and if we are only teaching that Jesus Christ can save sinners, that is not the Jesus Christ that person needs. We have to preach every aspect of the gospel of the Lord Jesus Christ, revealed in God's Word.

We must not teach only one phase of Christ's work. Have I a pet doctrine I am working? Then those healthy-minded folks will simply heap ridicule on me. But when I share the whole gospel of Christ, something else happens. The Spirit of God begins to work where I cannot touch.

We must offer Christ as our hearers need Him. We must present Jesus Christ to their need!

Prayer Thought: O Lord, help me to present Your truth in all its glory.

SUGGESTED READING: 1 CORINTHIANS 1:17–31

But ye shall receive power, after that the Holy Ghost is come upon you: and ye shall be witnesses unto me both in Jerusalem, and in all Judaea, and in Samaria, and unto the uttermost part of the earth.

—Acts 1:8

PAUL WAS ABLE TO WITHSTAND the cultured ridicule of wicked philosophers. He still declared Jesus to them as the greatest, grandest, and most worthy Being who had ever come on this earth.

The Lord Jesus Christ must be presented to sinners. The Spirit of God will guide you, as you rely on Him, to the presentation of Him that is required for each sinner. But if you attempt to enclose Jesus Christ into neat little doctrinal packets, one marked "salvation," another marked "sanctification," another marked "the baptism in the Holy Ghost," you will fail to convince sinners that they need Him.

In every case, we need to rely on the Holy Spirit. Often we pray, "Lord, I cannot deal with that man; his life is healthy, his sense of justice is clear, his record clean, and he cares for none of these things." But we must present Jesus Christ in all His power, and rely on the Holy Spirit to deal with each sinner.

Prayer Thought: Spirit of God, deal with sinners. Guide my thoughts and words when I converse with them.

SUGGESTED READING: ACTS 19:1–12

At that time Jesus answered and said, I thank thee, O Father, Lord of heaven and earth, because thou hast hid these things from the wise and prudent, and hast revealed them unto babes.

—Matthew 11:25

JESUS CHRIST IS NOT INTERESTED in simply hearing us testify that we are pure in heart, or full of love for God and our fellow man. He wants us to prove it in our attitudes and actions. He looks at our minds, not at the mannerisms of our speech. We may say wonderfully truthful things, but what we think is the thing that counts with Him. Our Lord makes us real, not just sincere. Are you truly honest with God—enough to allow Him to rule in your heart, mind, and life? That is the way to full victory in Christ.

Prayer Thought: O God, create in me the right attitudes, pleasing to You and helpful to others.

SUGGESTED READING: MATTHEW 5:23–26

Happy is the man that feareth alway: but he that hardeneth his heart shall fall into mischief.

—Proverbs 28:14

IF GOD HAS EVER POINTED out to you the one thing that is wrong in your life—as He did with that vigorous pagan called Herod—you are to blame if you did not listen. Too many of us once listened gladly to the things God said, but have now grown "dull of hearing."

There is coming a time when God will not speak to you, if you insist in your disobedience. Truth will become a farce and all of the truth of God will become a farce likewise. God forbid that any man or woman who reads this should ever stand face to face with the son of perdition! Yet that is the fate of anyone who turns away from God's voice.

When a person has this immoral fixity of character, his waywardness will be arrested by God, not by the Devil. This is an awful and terrible truth, one to which many people will not readily listen.

Prayer Thought: May I never cease to obey You, O God.

SUGGESTED READING: PROVERBS 28:13–28

And so Pilate, willing to content the people, released Barabbas unto them, and delivered Jesus, when he had scourged him, to be crucified.

—Mark 15:15

PILATE ALWAYS SOUGHT HIS OWN interests. That type of person is known to us even today. People belong to certain churches because it is better for their business. This sort of unsaved person acts from this point of view: "If it is Jesus Christ's gospel that is rising in power, then I will use it to serve my own needs." But bring that person face to face with Christ, and he will be unable to ignore the fact that Christ would make certain claims upon his life.

False teachers of religion are deceiving thousands of people by bending the gospel to suit their own purposes. And in this regard, the human mind is ready to be deceived. If you can teach someone how to ignore sin, he will listen to you. If you can tell him how to ignore the possibility of judgment for his wrongdoing, he will listen to you. This is why the cults of deception are so popular—not because they are true, but because they alter the truth to suit the carnal desires of mankind.

May God have mercy on the deceived and on the deceivers!

Prayer Thought: Enable me, Lord; to bring others face to face with the realities of Your gospel.

SUGGESTED READING: MARK 15:1–15

Say not thou, I will recompense evil; but wait on the Lord, and he shall save thee.

—Proverbs 20:22

IF YOU CAN SHOW SOMEONE how to be delivered from the torture of sin, or healed of a pain-stricken body, or loosened from a terrible past, then you have that person as your friend. Yet the "prince of this world" would convince us that we can have these benefits of the gospel without having to surrender ourselves to the Lord Jesus.

Watch how people will take all His blessings, but will not relate rightly to Him. Our challenge is to present them with Christ apart from what Christ can do.

Perhaps you have lately been brought face to face with someone who was experiencing much anxiety, and you said, "This person is under conviction of sin." But you learned that was not so. You tried every scriptural teaching you knew, applied in big and little measure, and yet had no result. You tried to preach temperament, explaining that the person felt anxious by nature. You tried to advocate this and that and the other spiritual discipline. Still there have been no results. You have been humiliated to the dust before God.

You have been trying to find out what is wrong. And that is where you are mistaken. God will never show you what is wrong with someone else; that is not your business. He wants you to bring the case to Him.

God grant that you may get so centered in Him that He can use you in that wonderful way!

Prayer Thought: Let me never forget the primary importance of bringing others to You, Lord.

SUGGESTED READING: PROVERBS 24:1–16

If any man serve me, let him follow me; and where I am, there shall also my servant be: if any man serve me, him will my Father honour.

—John 12:26

THE SYROPHOENICIAN WOMAN WANTED JESUS Christ. She did not care one iota about the disciples or any of their teaching; she wanted the Lord Jesus Christ.

In John 12, we read that certain Greeks came and said to the disciples, "We want to see Jesus." What did those disciples do? They went to Jesus and told Him so. When anyone says, "We wish to see Jesus," what do you do about their request? Try and persuade them to accept certain teachings first? You never will. Remember what Philip and Andrew did; they went and told Jesus.

Whenever people ask you to help them find Jesus, do not begin with "firstly, secondly, and thirdly." Go to Jesus and say, "Lord, these people want to see you." Rely on the Holy Spirit to help you. Live among the facts of God's Word, and among human facts, so that people will recognize Jesus Christ through you. Remember that the only One who will touch sinners is the Lord Jesus Christ Himself!

Christians say that it is so hard to present Jesus Christ to sinners today. Of course it is! So hard that it is impossible, except by the power of the indwelling Holy Spirit.

Prayer Thought: I desire that others will see Christ through my attitudes and actions.

SUGGESTED READING: JOHN 12:20–36

Oh that men would praise the LORD for his goodness, and for his wonderful works to the children of men!

—Psalm 107:31

PSALM 107 CONTAINS AN ACCOUNT of people who would not come to God until they got to their wit's end. Then they cried to God and He heard them. But people who are filled with the Holy Spirit are ready to give praise to God at all times; praise flows naturally from their hearts. Our Lord said that the Holy Spirit would not do anything but the following:

1. He will glorify Me.

2. He will bring to your remembrance what I have said and lead you into all truth about that.

3. He will not speak of Himself.

In analyzing God's marvelous work of entire sanctification, we find a natural fascination with the purifying and cleansing side of sanctification; indeed, the Bible refers often to this aspect of the Spirit's work (John 17:17; Hebrews 13:12; Acts 15:8–9). Yet there is more. The Holy Spirit is the presence of God in the heart of man. The Holy Spirit is the gift of Jesus Christ to mankind. And when He dwells within us, we want only to praise our God.

Prayer Thought: I praise Your name, O God, for Your goodness and wonderful works on my behalf!

SUGGESTED READING: PSALM 107

God is faithful, by whom ye were called unto the fellowship of his Son Jesus Christ our Lord.

—1 Corinthians 1:9

OH, UNSPEAKABLY BLESSED IS THE believer's fellowship with God! "In thy presence is fulness of joy; at thy right hand there are pleasures for evermore" (Psalm 16:11).

This fellowship is ours by the sheer might of the atonement of Jesus, who gave Himself for us. The Christian soul, incandescent with the Holy Spirit, walks and talks with God as friend with friend, and lets God do as He will with him.

My goal is God Himself, not joy, nor peace,
Nor even blessing, but Himself, my God;
'Tis His to lead me there, not mine, but His—
"At any cost, dear Lord, by any road."

Prayer Thought: Father, I am grateful for the privilege of living for You.

SUGGESTED READING: 1 CORINTHIANS 1:1–9

To the weak became I as weak, that I might gain the weak: I am made all things to all men, that I might by all means save some.

—1 Corinthians 9:22

P AUL DID NOT SAY, "I became all things to all men that I might show what a wonderful being I am." That is the modern interpretation of it. I hear people say that Paul showed his wonderful breadth of mind, his wonderful culture and generosity, his gentleness and patience by becoming all things to all men. He did nothing of the sort. He said he became all things to all men for one purpose only—that he might save some. There was no thought about himself in the whole matter.

This attitude of Paul sheds light on the phrase, "passion for souls." A passion for souls may either be a diseased lust or a divine love. Let me give you a specimen of it as a diseased lust: " Woe unto you, scribes and Pharisees, hypocrites! for ye compass sea and land to make one proselyte, and when he is made, ye make him twofold more the child of hell than yourselves" (Matthew 23:15). *Proselyte* is a technical word for "convert." By saying this, our Lord showed that the Pharisees' great passion for souls bore the stamp of the Devil. If you read Acts 13:43–50, you will find that the proselytes became exactly what Jesus Christ said they would be: twofold more the children of hell than the Jews. They became superstitious and even more fanatical.

I wonder whether we understand what a "passion for souls" really is.

Prayer Thought: Lord, increase my vision and passion for lost souls. Help me to love as You love!

SUGGESTED READING: 1 CORINTHIANS 9:16–22

Know ye not that they which run in a race run all, but one receiveth the prize? So run, that ye may obtain.

—1 Corinthians 9:24

A PASSION FOR SOULS WILL COMPRESS all the energy of a Christian's heart and brain and body into one consuming drive, night and day. It is a fiery, burning passion, as was characteristic of our Lord's life, lives of the disciples, and the apostle Paul's life.

"Ye are our reward," Paul told the new converts. In that matchless apostle's life, the consuming passion was for the converts, not the crowd! All the desire of Paul's life was that Jesus Christ might have His way through them.

Discipling converts for Jesus Christ is the chief characteristic of a mature Christian!

Prayer Thought: O God, teach me how to be a "fisher of men," not for vainglory, but for Your glory and their spiritual good.

SUGGESTED READING: 1 CORINTHIANS 9:23–27

The fruit of the righteous is a tree of life; and he that winneth souls is wise.

—Proverbs 11:30

Do you know what it is like to fish all night? I do. About three or four in the morning, before the early dawn, you feel so cold that you do not care about anything.

There is an exact counterpart in the work for God. Do you have a passionate devotion to Jesus Christ, so powerful that you stand steady and faithful through every cold night, watching and waiting to win men and women for God? Those cold nights of waiting, fishing, praying, and preaching are the test of your commitment.

Unless we have a divine passion for souls burning in us, we will quit the work of God. Soul winning requires patience, gentleness, and endurance. Nothing else will do it! A sense that people are perishing won't do it; a sense that they are going down to hell won't do it. Only one thing will do it—a blazing, passionate devotion to the Lord Jesus Christ, an all-consuming passion!

Prayer Thought: Oh, for a consuming devotion to Jesus Christ!

SUGGESTED READING: LUKE 5:1–11

Therefore said he unto them, The harvest truly is great, but the labourers are few: pray ye therefore the Lord of the harvest, that he would send forth labourers into his harvest.

—Luke 10:2

BEWARE OF PEOPLE WHO TELL you how to fish! I know a good many people who have tried to learn how to fish from books; but they never did learn. The only way to learn how to fish is to fish!

An old captain, whom I know very well, has been a fisherman all his days. He told me about a man who published a book on how to catch fish. The captain took him out in his boat; but, by the time he got four miles out to sea, the captain saw him looking like a corpse. They stayed out for hours, and he didn't have enough strength to put his line over the side of the boat. He was too seasick. So much for the instructor of how to catch fish!

Beware of any book that tells you how to catch men for Christ. Go to Calvary and let God deal with you until you understand the meaning of the tremendous cost to Jesus Christ, and then begin fishing for souls.

God grant that we may get out from under the instructors of how to catch fish and get into the fishing business!

Prayer Thought: Grant me, O Lord, the wisdom
to be a true fisherman of souls!

SUGGESTED READING: JOHN 4:31–38

So when they had dined, Jesus saith to Simon Peter, Simon, son of Jonas, lovest thou me more than these? He saith unto him, Yea, Lord; thou knowest that I love thee. He saith unto him, Feed my lambs.

—John 21:15

I THANK GOD THAT IN MY boyhood and early manhood I had to work hard at so many things. I did not like it at the time, but I am very thankful I had to do some shepherding in the highlands of Scotland. When you have to carry across your shoulders a dirty old ram and bring it down the mountainside, you will know whether shepherding is poetry or not. You will know that it is the most taxing, the most exhausting, and the most exasperating thing you can do.

Jesus Christ uses shepherding to illustrate our passion for souls. A quiet, judicious knowing how to do it won't do it. Only an indefatigable passion will do it.

To whom did Jesus say, "Feed My lambs"? To Peter. Who was Peter? A very wayward sheep. Peter had not only forsaken Jesus Christ; he denied he ever knew Him, with oaths and curses. Do you think, after he received the Spirit of God and was personally, passionately devoted to Jesus Christ, that anybody would have such patience with young converts as Peter? Who else could have written, "Feed the flock . . . taking the oversight . . . not for filthy lucre"? (1 Peter 5:2). Peter had learned through his own experience how to be patient, how to be tender, and how to be full of grateful watchfulness over all the Lord's sheep.

Prayer Thought: With joy and delight I will "feed your lambs," Lord Jesus, and do so out of real love for them.

SUGGESTED READING: JOHN 21:15–19

Jesus saith unto him, If I will that he tarry till I come, what is that to thee? follow thou me.

—John 21:22

Y OU CANNOT NOURISH THE SHEEP of God unless you are rightly related to the Shepherd. You may be a mouthpiece for God's truth; but you cannot nourish the sheep of God unless you are willing to let God use you as broken bread and poured-out wine to feed His sheep.

Sunday school teacher, perhaps Jesus Christ is teaching you how He is going to make you broken bread and poured-out wine. Christian worker, maybe you are not understanding what God is putting you through; but perhaps He is teaching you how to feed God's sheep and tend the flock of God.

Take some time to see what God has to say about shepherds. This feeding and tending of sheep is an arduous job, and affection for the sheep will not do it. You must have a deeper love than that. You must have a consuming love for the Great Shepherd, the Lord Jesus Christ.

Love for men, as men, will never stand the strain of Christian work. In order to catch men for the Lord Jesus Christ, you must love Jesus Christ beyond all others. Have a consuming passion for Him, and then He will flow through you in a yearning to draw men to Himself.

Prayer Thought: Fill me, O Lord, with Your passion for the souls of men.

SUGGESTED READING: JOHN 21:20–25

Go ye therefore, and teach all nations, baptizing them in the name of the Father, and of the Son, and of the Holy Ghost.

—Matthew 28:19

WHAT DOES THE BIBLE MEAN when it says to be an example to the flock of God? You must be a walking example of what you believe, in every moment of your life, known and unknown. You must bear the scrutiny of God until you prove that you are indeed a specimen of what He can do. Then He will send you out to disciple all nations.

When souls are born again into the kingdom of God, the church of Christ makes a tremendous rejoicing, as it ought to make. But then what does it do? When God brings souls to you, what have you to do? Disciple them. And the only way you can disciple them is, not by making them proselytes of your views, but by teaching them to do what Jesus commanded you.

Do you say, "Do as I say, but not as I do"? To disciple people for God, we must become what other people should be.

Prayer Thought: I resolve to be a true example of the transforming grace of God.

SUGGESTED READING: MATTHEW 28:16–20

Wherefore if ye be dead with Christ from the rudiments of the world, why, as though living in the world, are ye subject to ordinances?

—Colossians 2:20

EVERYONE ATTEMPTS TO COMMUNICATE DIRECTLY with God. This is why mysticism is a natural ingredient in everybody's makeup, whether he calls himself "atheist," "agnostic," or "Christian."

Jesus Christ reveals that we come into communion with God only through Him. If we refuse Him, we probably will be deluded by supernatural forces stronger than we are. We are deluded into thinking that we can have communion with God through self-denial or, as the apostle Paul puts it, "will worship and . . . neglecting of the body." People can be so wonderfully devout in their mistaken ways of dealing with God!

But when Jesus Christ brings us into communion with God, He does not give us a set of rules and prohibitions. He does not call us to make ourselves nothing. Rather, He transforms our bodies, our relationships, our possessions, and every aspect of our lives as He reconciles us to God.

Prayer Thought: I praise Your name, O Jesus, for redeeming me from a life of confusion.

SUGGESTED READING: COLOSSIANS 2:20–23

The sorrows of death compassed me, and the pains of hell gat hold upon me: I found trouble and sorrow.

—Psalm 116:3

GOD WILL PUT YOU THROUGH many trials to make you "good bread" for the little ones to eat. He wants to bake you well enough to be His standard bread; then He can break you for the little ones, for the feeble amongst the flock.

The apostle Paul said, "I am willing to be accursed from God if Israel my kinsmen could be saved that way. I am willing to spend and be spent, though the more I love, the less I be loved" (2 Corinthians 12:15). What was the ruling passion in that man's life? His devotion to the Lord Jesus Christ.

Have you lost that consuming passion? Remember the Lord Jesus Christ's death and resurrection, and ask the Spirit of God to give you a full insight into that. Ask Him that you may understand it again, and understand it in a new way. Then go forth and "measure thy life by loss, instead of gain; / Not by the wine drunk, but the wine poured forth."

Prayer Thought: O God, make me a blessing to others.

SUGGESTED READING: PSALM 116

For verily I say unto you, Till heaven and earth pass, one jot or one tittle shall in no wise pass from the law, till all be fulfilled.

—Matthew 5:18

THE BIBLE IS A UNIVERSE of revelatory facts, not known to unregenerated common sense, and the only exegete of these words is the Holy Spirit. Understanding comes only to the degree of the individual's reception, recognition, and reliance on the Holy Spirit. Just as facts in the natural world have to be accepted, so facts in the biblical world of God's will have to be accepted. Our explanation of the facts may be more or less open to dispute. But we can never alter the facts.

The Bible is God's revelation of Himself in the interest of grace. Only as we are the recipients of the grace of God will the Bible be opened for us. This Bible is not a book containing communications about God; it is God's giving of Himself, in the limitation of words, in the interests of grace.

The Bible is not a fairy tale to beguile us for a few moments from the sordid realities of life in the natural world. It is the divine complement of the laws of nature, conscience, and humanity.

Prayer Thought: Lord Jesus, Your Word is a lamp unto my feet, and a light unto my path.

SUGGESTED READING: MATTHEW 5:17–20

Therefore shall ye lay up these my words in your heart and in your soul, and bind them for a sign upon your hand, that they may be as frontlets between your eyes.

—Deuteronomy 11:18

IN DEALING WITH BIBLICAL FACTS, our aim is not just to produce "specialists," but to make healthy, practical workers in the work of our Lord. Bible specialists have their counterpart in the natural world in scientists such as astronomers, biologists, geologists, and others. The research systems of these specialists are of the very greatest value to us. We will consult them from time to time; yet their findings have value only as they aid our daily experience. The same is true of the findings of our Bible specialists.

I believe it to be essential to be born of the Spirit of God before we can enter into Bible study. I believe that the only meaningful method of Bible study is to "prove all things" (1 Thessalonians 5:21), not by brain only, but by personal experience. That is the only way to understand spiritual matters.

Prayer Thought: Reading Your Word, O God, is a blessing.

SUGGESTED READING: DEUTERONOMY 11:16–23

Knowing this first, that no prophecy of the scripture is of any private interpretation. For the prophecy came not in old time by the will of man: but holy men of God spake as they were moved by the Holy Ghost.

—2 Peter 1:20–21

THE BIBLE, IT WILL BE found, not only explains the greatest number of facts; it is the only ground for explaining all the facts.

The Bible contains the regions for the loftiest exercise of our regenerated intelligence. It puts in the hands of the Spirit-born the key to the explanation of all mysteries. The Bible does not contradict reason; it introduces a new universe of facts to reason, which demands its loftiest exercise.

The falling of rain from heaven after a time of drought would defy any poet to describe its beauties. Likewise, no tongue can tell the refreshing insight of the Word of God, coming to a soul after a time of difficulty and perplexity.

Prayer Thought: Your Word, Lord, helps life to make sense and gives me hope for the future—the hope of eternal life in heaven!

SUGGESTED READING: 2 PETER 1:16–21

Beware of false prophets, which come to you in sheep's clothing, but inwardly they are ravening wolves.

—Matthew 7:15

"TWO-FACED" IS A FIGURE OF speech used to describe someone's double dealing and falsehood. Probably the hardest and most cruel class of people is those who come under that heading.

When we study the life of King David, we are appalled to learn that for a time he was a double-dealing, two-faced fellow. This mighty man of God committed the wickedest sin possible. I do not refer to adultery or murder, but to something infinitely worse—a deep, subtle, inward hypocrisy, tremendous and profound. David lived a two-faced life for a year. He administered justice to others, while he was a whited sepulcher underneath.

If you want to know how it is possible for a man like David to have done this, you must allow God to reveal the possibilities of your own nature.

Prayer Thought: Lord, forgive me when
I am tempted to be two-faced.

SUGGESTED READING: MATTHEW 7:15–23

And Nathan said to David, Thou art the man. Thus saith the LORD God of Israel, I anointed thee king over Israel, and I delivered thee out of the hand of Saul.

—2 Samuel 12:7

FOR SUBTLETY, FOR AMAZING INSIGHT, and for sublime courage, Nathan is unequaled. What a soul for God to have in His list! Would to God there were more preachers and Christian workers like Nathan!

King David did not even begin to realize, after a year of the grossest and most dastardly hypocrisy, that Nathan was brandishing the sword straight into his conscience. But after David gave his answer, Nathan thrust straight home, "Thou art the man!" David replied, "I have sinned against the LORD!" There was no bungling about Nathan's work.

How do you suppose Nathan prepared himself for this moment of confrontation?

Prayer Thought: Search me, O God, and reveal any spiritual weakness that would make me vulnerable in the hour of trial.

SUGGESTED READING: 2 SAMUEL 12:1–14

And David said unto Nathan, I have sinned against the Lord. And Nathan said unto David, The Lord also hath put away thy sin; thou shalt not die.

—2 Samuel 12:13

ANY WORKER WHO HAS STOOD before God's all-searching eye for five minutes is not surprised by David's fall. Any sin which is recorded in God's Word is possible for any human heart.

If you and I are to press for the salvation of souls, we must allow God to reveal the possibilities of our own nature. That is why God will take you through disciplines and experiences that are not meant for your particular case; they are meant to make you capable of being sent, as God sent Nathan. Only then can you be as "wise as serpents, and harmless as doves."

After a time of hypocrisy in King David's life, he was suddenly faced by Nathan. Notice how Nathan dealt with it. He used a parable with God-given insight. Because David was blind to its meaning, the sword went straight into David's conscience. I believe Nathan confronted David with such compassion only because he was aware of his own vulnerability to sin.

Before you go among the infirm, the sick, the subtle, and the hypocritical, let God deal with you.

Prayer Thought: O God, make me aware of my own human weakness, so that I might deal lovingly with the weakness of others.

SUGGESTED READING: 2 SAMUEL 12:7–23

And that because of false brethren unawares brought in, who came in privily to spy out our liberty which we have in Christ Jesus, that they might bring us into bondage.

—Galatians 2:4

WHAT ARE WE TO DO with false accusers? The Bible comments, "Let brotherly love continue" (Hebrews 13:1). There is a time to smite and a time to smile. There is a time to slay and thrust straight home to the heart of the wrongdoers, "to whom we gave place by subjection, no, not for an hour." Why? That our views might be expounded? No. That they might be detected as hypocrites? No. So that the true gospel might continue within us!

Do you remember what the apostle Paul said to the Ephesians, when he mentioned their godly "conversation"? "See that it is good building-up stuff" is the literal translation of what he said (Ephesians 4:29). Not sanctimonious talk, but solid truth makes people stronger—stronger in the Word of God, stronger in character, and stronger in practical life. Yet even the truth should be spoken in love.

Prayer Thought: Lord, give me grace to show love toward nitpickers and false accusers.

SUGGESTED READING: GALATIANS 2:1–9

And when Jesus came to the place, he looked up, and saw him, and said unto him, Zacchaeus, make haste, and come down; for to day I must abide at thy house.

—Luke 19:5

EARLIER I SAID THAT THE Christian worker has to live in the facts of the Bible and the facts of human life. What are the facts of human life, as God reveals them? God's Word says that the majority of the human race is abnormal. Jesus Christ sees that all men are lost; and the Christian worker must get the same outlook if he is going to work for the cure for souls.

Notice a very important distinction between the lost and the doomed: Jesus Christ is seeking the lost. The doomed are those who rebel against the seeking Savior.

Many Christian workers today are not taking the standpoint of the Lord Jesus Christ; they do not understand why some souls fail to respond to their message. We need to view people as Christ sees them. We must love people as God does. Otherwise we will become loveless, passionless, and totally ineffective as workers of God.

Prayer Thought: Help me, O Lord of mercy, to talk to people as precious souls destined for eternity.

SUGGESTED READING: LUKE 19:1–5

And when they saw it, they all murmured, saying, That he was gone to be guest with a man that is a sinner.

—Luke 19:7

ZACCHAEUS WAS RICH AND A chief publican. He must have possessed many ill-gotten gains if he was a publican (tax collector) in the Lord Jesus Christ's day. Yet, throughout most of his career, he was not troubled in the tiniest degree. His whole nature toward God was frozen. There was not any sign of life in his relation to God.

In the far North, the thermometer freezes and can record nothing. It will remain frozen until the temperature alters. Immediately when the temperature alters, the thermometer works. Likewise, this man Zacchaeus was frozen toward God; and he was lost, his conscience did not bother him. He was quite contented and quite happy. He was also quite curious about Jesus. Whenever Jesus Christ came that way, the "freezing" left his nature, and something began to work at once.

Zacchaeus represents the type of person whose conscience toward God is frozen. He was a man in a wealthy position—a dishonorable man, but perfectly contented with his dishonor. You will meet persons similar to Zacchaeus as you labor for the Lord.

Prayer Thought: When I encounter individuals who are cold and indifferent, may Your love work through me, Lord, to warm their hearts and melt their spiritual stubbornness.

SUGGESTED READING: LUKE 19:6–9

For the Son of man is come to seek and to save that which was lost.

—Luke 19:10

THE FIRST THING THE CHRISTIAN worker has to learn is how to bring the Lord Jesus Christ in contact with those whose souls are perfectly dead toward God, whose consciences are not the slightest bit disturbed. How are we to bring the Lord Jesus Christ to lives that are dead in trespasses and sins and do not know it? By the Holy Spirit and personal experience alone.

By personal experience I mean that I must know what God has done in my soul through Jesus Christ. I must know Jesus Christ personally before I can help someone else to know Him. Furthermore, I must learn to rely on the Holy Spirit, because the Holy Spirit makes the Lord present to all kinds of people.

Whenever Jesus Christ encountered sinners in His day, they either rebelled or followed Him. They either "went away exceedingly sorrowful," or they turned with their whole nature toward Him. We can expect the same thing to happen today.

Prayer Thought: O Lord, help me bring some lost wanderer into contact with You today.

SUGGESTED READING: LUKE 19:10–17

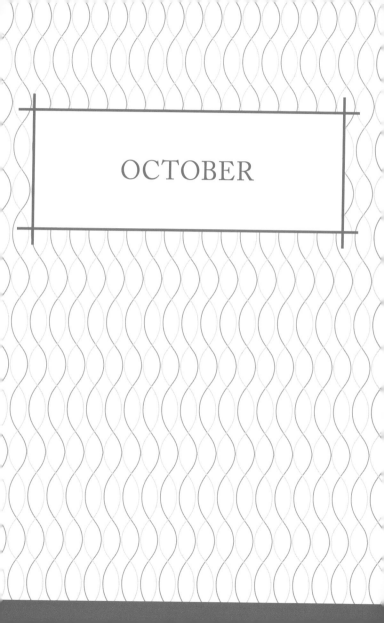

OCTOBER

And Jesus said unto him, This day is salvation come to this house, forsomuch as he also is a son of Abraham.

—Luke 19:9

IF WE ARE TO REACH the lost, we must have the boundless confidence of the Lord Jesus Christ about us. We must know that He can save anybody and everybody. There is a great deal of importance to be attached to this point.

Think for a moment about some "frozen types" of people you know. They have no conviction of sin. They are off the main track altogether and are not a bit troubled about it. Talk to them about their wrongdoing and they are totally indifferent to it. You have to learn how to introduce them to the atmosphere of the Lord Jesus Christ. As soon as you do, something dynamic will happen.

Look what happened to Zacchaeus when he encountered the presence of the Lord: "Zacchaeus stood, and said unto the Lord: Behold, Lord, the half of my goods I give to the poor; and if I have taken any thing from any man by false accusation, I restore him fourfold" (Luke 19:8). Who had been talking to him about his public relations? Not a soul. Jesus had not said a word about his evil dealings. What awakened him? What suddenly made him know where he was? The presence of Jesus!

Prayer Thought: I am glad that salvation will radically change us. Thank You, Lord.

SUGGESTED READING: LUKE 19:18–27

Through God we shall do valiantly: for he it is that shall tread down our enemies.

—Psalm 108:13

IF THE SPIRIT OF GOD is having His way in your life, the presence of God will be felt wherever you go. Sinners will feel convicted of their wrong, and they will not like you. Until they learn the reason, they will say you are always criticizing; but you are perfectly conscious that you are not criticizing. What has happened? The Holy Spirit's presence through you has brought the very atmosphere of Jesus Christ to them; He has thawed the ice around their mind and their conscience, and they are being convicted.

How does Jesus Christ teach us to deal with sin? By forgiving us. How does a pagan world teach us to deal with sin? By telling us to forget it, ignore it, and think no more about it. Can that be done? Of course it can. But one who has forgotten his wrong must still face Jesus Christ; and as soon as he sees Him, the first thing that will flash through his mind and soul is his past wrong!

You must know how to bring Jesus Christ in contact with every kind of person. The only way to do that is by the Holy Spirit and personal experience. If you are trying to work for God with no definite spiritual experience of your own and without knowing how to rely on the Holy Spirit, I pray that God will answer your needs.

Prayer Thought: Lord Jesus, I acknowledge that I cannot effectively labor for You without grace and strength every day. I rejoice in Your power!

SUGGESTED READING: PSALM 108

For Christ is the end of the law for righteousness to every one that believeth.

—Romans 10:4

JESUS CHRIST IS INCARNATE REASON. There is something in Jesus Christ that appeals to everyone, no matter what his condition. If anyone seems dead and indifferent and destitute of goodness, love, or rational behavior, let him come in contact with Jesus Christ. You will instantly see that that person can grasp something about Jesus Christ which he could not understand unless he knew the Holy Spirit.

Jesus Christ is incarnate righteousness. So many people try to explain moral things about Jesus Christ; but no Christian worker need ever try that method. Rely on the Holy Spirit, and He will explain Jesus to the seeking soul.

Have this boundless confidence in Jesus Christ's power the next time you go about working for God. You must!

Prayer Thought: Lord, I cannot share spiritual knowledge from my own understanding. In all of my dealings with the lost, I must acknowledge that Jesus is "the way, the truth, and the life."

SUGGESTED READING: ROMANS 10:1–9

And call upon me in the day of trouble: I will deliver thee, and thou shalt glorify me.

—Psalm 50:15

ARE YOU IN CONSTANT CONTACT with someone—in your family, in your own business, or in a friendship—who is indifferent to Jesus Christ? Have you talked with that person about Jesus, prayed with him, and done everything you know how, but there has not been the slightest sign that he is thinking about a change?

Then get alone with the Lord Jesus Christ and pray, "Lord, do I believe that Thou cannot thaw that man's or woman's nature, until the Holy Spirit has a chance of saving this person?" Ask Him, "What is the state of my own faith in You?"

Then say to yourself, Do I believe that the Lord Jesus Christ can take that selfish, sensual, twisted, satisfied nature and make it perfect in the sight of God? Do I have confidence in the Lord's power?

We must believe in the power of Jesus to wash away the sins of the world. Do we? As Christian workers, we are wasting our time if we do not.

Prayer Thought: Your power is great, Lord. Flow through me!

SUGGESTED READING: PSALM 50

What man of you, having an hundred sheep, if he lose one of them, doth not leave the ninety and nine in the wilderness, and go after that which is lost, until he find it?

—Luke 15:4

THE FIFTEENTH CHAPTER OF LUKE, in which our Lord talks about the joy of finding things lost, has revealed these questions to me: The Lord wants my eyes to look through; is He looking through them? The Lord wants my brain to think through; is He thinking through it? The Lord wants my hands to work with; is He working with them? The Lord wants my body to walk and to live in for one purpose—to go after the lost from His standpoint; am I letting Him walk and live in me?

The Christian must allow Jesus Christ to have His right of way in each particular area of life. Thousands of Christian men and women today are seeking to train their minds and bodies—for what purpose? To help them "realize themselves"! But Jesus Christ wants our bodies so that He can work through them to find those who are lost.

Prayer Thought: Take my mind, my hands, my whole being and make me a blessing for Your glory.

SUGGESTED READING: LUKE 15:1–7

Likewise, I say unto you, there is joy in the presence of the angels of God over one sinner that repenteth.

—Luke 15:10

I F YOU ARE A CHRISTIAN worker, beware of putting anything first in your mind, but Jesus Christ. If you put the needs of your people first, you will have something between you and the power of God. Face Jesus Christ steadily, and allow nothing to come between you and Him. Why? So that the Holy Spirit may flow through your preaching and teaching to the needs of the people. You will find that people will always distinguish between that kind of a message and the message that is spoken out of mere sympathy for them.

Only one Person understands us all, and that is the Holy Spirit. He understands the Lord Jesus Christ too; and if I keep my soul's avenues open to Him and get my message from Him—not allowing anything to obscure it—He will locate the needs of people.

God will give you people who have been convicted by what you say. You will have to deal with them, whether you like it or not, and you will have to take these cases on your heart before God. God will help you!

God grant that, as we go forth in our varied works, we may fill our souls with Christ and then patiently seek souls for Him.

Prayer Thought: Spirit of God, fill my soul with Christ's love of the lost.

SUGGESTED READING: LUKE 15:8–10

Then Philip opened his mouth, and began at the same scripture, and preached unto him Jesus.

—Acts 8:35

G OD WILL HOLD TO OUR account the souls that have gone uncured, unhealed, and untouched by Jesus Christ because we have refused to keep our souls open to Him. He will reprove us for the times we were not ready to present the Lord Jesus Christ to them by the power of the Holy Spirit. Yet, we deal with some people at great length without seeing any results; and we are tempted to quit trying.

Let us never despair of any soul under heaven. If you have a chronic case (by "a chronic case," I mean someone who is always coming to the same place spiritually and never getting anywhere—always coming forward at the altar call but getting nowhere), thank God for that one.

I have found out that God uses those chronic seekers to educate me. If they will keep chronic long enough, the Lord will be able to manifest His patience through me as He never could otherwise. And, all of a sudden, those souls come into the light. Praise the Lord!

Prayer Thought: Give me wisdom to be patient with those individuals who never seem able to surrender all to the Lord Jesus Christ.

SUGGESTED READING: ACTS 8:26–40

Behold, I have set the land before you: go in and possess the land which the LORD sware unto your fathers, Abraham, Isaac, and Jacob, to give unto them and to their seed after them.

—Deuteronomy 1:8

DAVID SERVES AS A BIBLICAL type of what the Christian worker should be, especially in the way he wielded the giant's sword to slay the enemies of his kingdom (1 Samuel 22). David used Goliath's sword much like the Christian must use the sword of God's Word. Hebrews 4:12 says, " For the word of God is quick, and powerful, and sharper than any twoedged sword, piercing even to the dividing asunder of soul and spirit, and of the joints and marrow, and is a discerner of the thoughts and intents of the heart."

Now it is quite obvious that if anyone except David had tried to use Goliath's sword, God would not have blessed him. Likewise, if you are not a spiritual David and you try to use the sword, you will do far more harm to yourself than damage to the cause of the enemy.

When the saints use the Word of God, they do not damage themselves, nor hurt other souls; but they do great damage to the kingdom of the Devil and great benefit to the souls of men.

Prayer Thought: I need wisdom from You, O God, as I labor in the interest of winning souls for Christ.

SUGGESTED READING: DEUTERONOMY 1:1–8

Behold, I send you forth as sheep in the midst of wolves: be ye therefore wise as serpents, and harmless as doves.

—Matthew 10:16

WE CANNOT DEAL WITH AILMENTS of the spirit as we deal with ailments of the body. If we could, ministers would be trained to apply a few curative principles to our various spiritual problems.

But the ailments of the human soul cannot be healed according to any simple principle whatever. We cannot quote certain verses of Scripture and apply them to those who are seeking the new birth, and certain other verses to those who are seeking entire sanctification. That will lead to confusion, because God's Spirit does not work in such a prescribed manner.

Anytime we try to take a shortcut in dealing with souls, God leaves us alone!

Prayer Thought: I know, Lord, that dealing with human souls is an important task. I need Your daily strength and guidance to do it.

SUGGESTED READING: DEUTERONOMY 1:9–18

Behold, the LORD thy God hath set the land before thee: go up and possess it, as the LORD God of thy fathers hath said unto thee; fear not, neither be discouraged.

—Deuteronomy 1:21

RELY ON THE SPIRIT OF God to tell you what to say when you are talking with an unbeliever. Do not rely on your memory. Do not try to remember how you dealt with other cases. Recognize and rely on the Holy Spirit. He will bring to your remembrance what you should say.

You will find, over and over again, that God will bring confusion to your preconceived methods of soul winning. He will make you apply a Scripture text that is quite inappropriate to the problem at hand—yet it will prove to be exactly what the other person needed to hear.

If you are not careful to heed the guidance of the Spirit of God, you will make incessant blunders in your work for God. Remember that the Christian worker must rely on the Holy Spirit for guidance in each individual case.

Prayer Thought: Teach me, Master, not to rely on my soul-winning methods, but on Your example and wisdom.

SUGGESTED READING: DEUTERONOMY 1:19–21

Ye shall not respect persons in judgment; but ye shall hear the small as well as the great; ye shall not be afraid of the face of man; for the judgment is God's. . . . Bring it unto me, and I will hear it.

—Deuteronomy 1:17

JUST AS IN THE MEDICAL profession there are quack doctors and quack prescriptions and quack chemists, there are the very same things in the spiritual domain. You will encounter plenty of "experts," so called, who claim to know the best way to witness and work for Jesus Christ. But beware of anyone who does not lead you to be reliant on the Holy Spirit in the work you are called to do. And beware of anyone who tries to beguile you away from your God-given calling.

One of the greatest difficulties in our colleges for training ministers is that they are never taught how to deal with souls. Ministers who have been serving on the field will confirm this. Everything they know about soul winning has been learned red-handed, right out of their own experience. They are trained in everything but the work they have been called to do.

Let's prepare ourselves to work with souls. The Holy Spirit will aid us.

Prayer Thought: Lord, fill me with Your Spirit, so that I might do the work You have called me to do.

SUGGESTED READING: DEUTERONOMY 1:22–29

Be of the same mind one toward another. Mind not high things, but condescend to men of low estate. Be not wise in your own conceits.

—Romans 12:16

WE MUST KEEP OURSELVES IN touch, not with theories, but with people. We must never get out of touch with them if we are going to use the Word of God skillfully amongst them and if the Holy Spirit is to apply the Word of God through us.

If you are a Christian worker, God will constantly put you to school amongst the facts of human living; He will keep you in contact with "human stuff." Human stuff is very sordid. Why? Because other human beings are made of the same stuff as you and I. Do not shut yourself away from their problems. Beware of the tendency to live apart from them. Get amongst the common people, for that is where you can reap a great harvest for the Lord.

Jesus prayed, "I pray not that thou shouldest take them out of the world, but that thou shouldest keep them from the evil" (John 17:15).

Prayer Thought: Thank You, Lord, for the opportunity to live among needy people.

SUGGESTED READING: DEUTERONOMY 1:30–39

To the weak became I as weak, that I might gain the weak: I am made all things to all men, that I might by all means save some.

—1 Corinthians 9:22

LET ME EMPHASIZE AGAIN THESE three things about doing Christian work:

First, the Christian worker must rely every moment on the Holy Spirit when dealing with another soul.

Second, the Christian worker must live among human men and women, not theories.

And, third, ransack the Bible from cover to cover, in the most practical way you know.

Use the concordance or any other practical tool or method. But by all means, study!

It is easy to ridicule a Christian who begins Bible study by praying, "Lord, direct me to a passage. I am just going to shut my eyes and open the Bible and put my finger on a passage." Yes, it is very easy to ridicule that method. But it is perfectly absurd to say that God has not led people that way. He has.

You cannot put God in a straitjacket. God uses His own extraordinary methods in teaching His people. Get to know the way God is going to deal through you, in the most practical way.

Prayer Thought: Like Paul, I want to reach people in every way possible. And I am willing to be taught in whatever way You deem best, Lord.

SUGGESTED READING: DEUTERONOMY 1:40–46

For of this sort are they which creep into houses, and lead captive silly women laden with sins, led away with divers lusts, ever learning, and never able to come to the knowledge of the truth.

—2 Timothy 3:6–7

HAVE YOU EVER NOTICED THAT the Bible requires men and women to read it? There are things in the Bible that will stagger you, things that will amaze, things that will affright—just as there are things in everyday life that amaze and terrify. But we dare not ignore the Bible, simply because we are perplexed by what we read there.

Too many Christians are "ever learning, and never able to come to the knowledge of the truth." True knowledge is to be found in God's Word.

Prayer Thought: Guide me, Lord, in the ways of righteousness as I study Your Word today.

SUGGESTED READING: 1 SAMUEL 24:1–22

And it was so, that when he had turned his back to go from Samuel, God gave him another heart: and all those signs came to pass that day.

—1 Samuel 10:9

THE READER OF GOD'S WORD often encounters examples of gross stupidity. Note that stupidity is not the same as ignorance: A stupid act is anything done without reason or judgment, while an ignorant act is something done without knowledge.

I think King Saul is the greatest example of stupidity in the Bible. Saul's physique was magnificent, his bodily presence wonderful, but he was amazingly stupid. An indication of his stupidity is the proverb that was based on him: "Is Saul also among the prophets?" It was an expression of scorn, spoken by people who were amused to see that a herder of asses could think himself transformed into a prophet of God.

Indeed, God had given him another heart, but it was not for the purpose of making Saul a prophet. Even though he started out as a cattle manager, he was to become a statesman and a king. But Saul was so carried away by the exultation of the moment that he thought he was supposed to prophesy.

If Saul had gone on in obedience to God's work, his heart would have been right and Saul's life would have fulfilled God's intention. Instead of that, he became a sad example of a stupid soul.

Prayer Thought: Lord, all of us have done unreasonable things— even stupid things. I thank You for having mercy upon us.

SUGGESTED READING: 1 SAMUEL 10:1–16

Wherefore then didst thou not obey the voice of the LORD, but didst fly upon the spoil, and didst evil in the sight of the LORD?

—1 Samuel 15:19

How are we to deal with someone who is floundering in spiritual stupidity? Ignorant souls only need knowledge. But the stupid already know what they should do; they lack the discretion to do it. How are we to respond to such a person?

Every case of stupidity recorded in the Bible is punished by God, so this is a serious matter. Notice how Samuel dealt with Saul. He said, "Wherefore then didst thou not obey the voice of the Lord?" (v. 19). He acknowledged the fact that Saul knew what to do; so he held Saul accountable for it.

Disobedient individuals must be held accountable. God will reprove them. God will not tolerate sin!

Prayer Thought: O God, there are unreasonable souls in the church today. Help me to deal with them as You do.

SUGGESTED READING: 1 SAMUEL 15:1–23

Now therefore, I pray thee, pardon my sin, and turn again with me, that I may worship the LORD.

—1 Samuel 15:25

N O OTHER CLASS OF PEOPLE will drive the Christian closer to God than the stupid. They will tax every bit of patience and endurance you have. These dear people always pretend to want to do something for God. Yet they are "ever learning and never able to come to a knowledge of the truth." Why? Because they do not wish to obey the Word of God they have heard!

Pretending to do right is another characteristic of a stupid soul. Samuel asked Saul if he had fulfilled the word of God with regard to the Amalekites, and Saul said he had. "What meaneth then this bleating of the sheep in mine ears?" (v. 14). Saul said, "I haveobeyed, but . . . took of the spoil." That was the beginning of his stupidity, which would lead him to consult spiritualistic medium and openly defy the Word of God.

Do you know someone who is feverishly studying the Word of God to avoid doing what he already knows of God's will? Or someone who is pretending to obey Him, when secretly he is going his own way? Plead with that person to turn back from his foolish ways.

Prayer Thought: Help me, O Lord, to call people to full obedience.

SUGGESTED READING: 1 SAMUEL 15:24–35

The LORD forbid that I should stretch forth mine hand against the LORD'S anointed: but, I pray thee, take thou now the spear that is at his bolster, and the cruse of water, and let us go.

—1 Samuel 26:11.

HAVE YOU EVER NOTICED HOW some Christians, after they hear the Word of God too much, will turn and trample on the Word?

A man who ultimately became a great power for God said that the center of his life was full of this kind of stupidity. He was a so-called worker for God for several years, until he came across this verse: "You are not your own, you are bought with a price." Everywhere he went, this verse kept chiding him. Whenever he read a book, he would come across that verse. Whenever he heard a sermon, it was from that text. He said, "At last I took my penknife and cut it out of every Bible I had." Then the Spirit of God awakened him to what he had done. He confessed the whole thing before God, and God forgave him the stupidity of his sins.

Christian worker, when God calls you to counsel a soul who is stupid, keep at it. Share the Word of God every time you meet him, every time you write to him, every time you talk to him. The only way you will stir that person out of his stupidity is by driving home the Word of God.

Prayer Thought: Help me to be bold enough to pursue the disobedient person, Lord. Bring to my mind the Word of God as I deal with these needy souls.

SUGGESTED READING: 1 SAMUEL 26:1–12

Then said Saul, I have sinned: return, my son David: for I will no more do thee harm, because my soul was precious in thine eyes this day: behold, I have played the fool, and have erred exceedingly.

—1 Samuel 26:21

If you are apt to make a rash statement or judgment, then beware that it does not become a boomerang. God's Word is always a boomerang to the worker who uses it, if the worker is not right.

Are you quite sure there is no strand of rebellion or stupidity in you? Are you quite sure you are not in the category of those who "ever learn and never come to a knowledge of the truth"? Otherwise, then the Word of God, when you try to deal with another soul, will come straight back to you.

If you are in the center of God's will, then press the Bible home.

Prayer Thought: As I use the Word of God, Lord, help me to understand its far-reaching consequences for my life as well as for those I am trying to help.

SUGGESTED READING: 1 SAMUEL 26:13–25

For when for the time ye ought to be teachers, ye have need that one teach you again which be the first principles of the oracles of God; and are become such as have need of milk, and not of strong meat.

—Hebrews 5:12

A RE YOU GLOSSING OVER THE counsel God gave you for someone else? Hammer at it morning, noon, and night.

If you know someone who says he received the Spirit of God, and yet there are signs he has not gone on with God, you will find a corresponding word of Scripture to tell him why. You will be a persistent thorn, annoyance, and aggravation to that person whenever you share a word from God; but he will ultimately thank God and praise you for the annoyance.

Prayer Thought: Convict those dear souls who are shunning You, Lord, and give me courage to keep pursuing them.

SUGGESTED READING: HEBREWS 5

And it came to pass, that, while they communed together and reasoned, Jesus himself drew near, and went with them.

—Luke 24:15

How did Jesus Christ deal with the foolishness of the two disciples on the road to Emmaus? This is stupidity on another line: a stupidity of simple souls, honest and true, who had become blinded by their own grief and their own point of view.

Jesus said to them: "O fools, and slow of heart to believe all that the prophets have spoken!" (Luke 24:25). Here the word *fools* might be translated, "My little children, when will you believe what the prophets have written?" This is stupidity of a totally different order—a stupidity that Jesus deals with very pointedly, but very patiently. It is a stupidity that obliterates one's understanding of the Word of God because of personal grief, sorrow, or perplexity.

Is Jesus Christ saying to you, "My child, when will you believe what I say?" Is there a particular problem in your life that has made you become slow of heart to believe? Do not let the stupidity grow. Seek what the Word of God has to say about it.

Oh, there is such a need for people who will search the Bible and learn what God is saying to them!

Prayer Thought: Forgive me, Lord, when I am slow to fully believe. Increase my faith in You.

SUGGESTED READING: LUKE 24:13–23

And they said one to another, Did not our heart burn within us, while he talked with us by the way, and while he opened to us the scriptures?

—Luke 24:32

D O NOT PARE DOWN THE Word of God to suit your understanding. Never drag the Word of God down to anybody's understanding. Keep digging into the Word until it drives all laziness out of your life and you are willing to face what the Bible says about your condition.

God grant that we will learn to comprehend what the Word of God says about our need, rather than trying to make the Word accommodate our limited understanding.

Prayer Thought: Your Word, Lord Jesus, has created new life and joy within me. Praise the Lord!

SUGGESTED READING: LUKE 24:24–35

Thy word is a lamp unto my feet, and a light unto my path.

—Psalm 119:105

GOD'S PEOPLE GET OFF ON unreasonable lines when they begin to live by their own instincts, impressions, and vague ideas. That is when they will suffer from the "creepers."

Do you know who the "creepers" are? People of reprobate minds who creep into the congregation of the saints to lead them astray (2 Timothy 3:1–7). There are a number of religious creepers nowadays. They will steal into your soul, just where you are wandering from the Word of God.

Has something been said to you recently from the Word of God that has awakened you with a startling sensation, and yet you have not obeyed God on that point? Then may God bring you face to face with a faithful Christian who will say the same thing to you until you get the victory. Otherwise a "creeper" may lead you further away from the truth.

When the Word of God has pierced your mind, your heart, and your spirit, it will begin its wonder-working way. It will heal and recreate you, and dissipate your stupidity.

Prayer Thought: Protect me, O God, from those who seek to "creep in" and lead my soul astray from You.

SUGGESTED READING: PSALM 119:105–112

And they were astonished at his doctrine: for he taught them as one that had authority, and not as the scribes.

—Mark 1:22

THE RELATIONSHIP OF THE TWELVE disciples to Jesus Christ was unique; we cannot repeat anything like it in our generation. Yet, aspects of their discipleship throw a wonderful light on the subject of our own discipleship today.

For the first three years, the disciples of our Lord were attracted to Him by natural affinity. Thousands of people today are similarly attracted by the Lord Jesus Christ; but they will find a marvelous contrast to the unsatisfactory state of their unspiritual lives if they will study carefully the disciples of Jesus.

Jesus' disciples were not perfect, but they had certain characteristics that are worthy of our study. We shall consider their discipleship over the next several days.

Prayer Thought: Lord Jesus, Your disciples followed You sacrificially. It is my desire to be like them.

SUGGESTED READING: MARK 1:16–22

And the two disciples heard him speak, and they followed Jesus.

—John 1:37

Jesus called His disciples to follow Him, and they did so. Was there any sacrifice in this? Not a bit. It would have been harder to stay where they were. The fascination of our Lord Jesus Christ was on these men, and their natural temperaments fitted the call. So when Jesus said, "Follow Me," they left all and followed Him.

There are scores of people today with that kind of relationship to Christ. They have a natural yen for the higher life; and when Jesus is presented, they say, "Yes, Lord, we will go wherever you want us to go." A sacrifice? None whatever! A lot of people simply like the thrill of walking with Jesus.

The real test of discipleship is not so much a fast start as a faithful ongoing.

Prayer Thought: Lord, I know that faithfulness is the characteristic of a true disciple. With Your help and by Your grace, I will be faithful to You.

SUGGESTED READING: JOHN 1:35–42

Then said Jesus to them again, Peace be unto you: as my Father hath sent me, even so send I you.

—John 20:21

DURING THREE YEARS OF FOLLOWING Jesus, the disciples more and more misunderstood Jesus. Their discipleship grew more and more strained, until the strain grew so intense that it snapped. They all forsook Him!

What happened during those three years when they traveled with and learned from Him? Jesus Christ revealed Himself to them. He put them through crises to reveal to the disciples themselves who they were. After the Resurrection, the disciples' eyes were opened and they understood Him. Then they understood that God had given them the mighty Holy Spirit. But during the early period of discipleship, they were put through crises that revealed their own weaknesses to themselves.

Prayer Thought: Dear Lord, it is necessary that
I understand myself as You see and know me.
Give me that understanding, I pray.

SUGGESTED READING: JOHN 20:19–23

The young man saith unto him, All these things have I kept from my youth up: what lack I yet?

—Matthew 19:20

To whom did the Lord Jesus say, "Marvel not that I said unto thee, Ye must be born again"? It was not said to a moral blackguard, but to Nicodemus–a religious leader, a spiritually minded man who had sterling characteristics. The message for every naturally religious person is, "Be born from above by the Holy Spirit."

Many have been brought up in religious families. They have had religious tendencies put in them, and the fascination of the Lord is on them. When they hear Jesus Christ's claims, they have a sense of heroic duty like Peter and say, "Yes, we will come." They do not realize that Christ calls them to a completely new way of life. Let me share with you a portion from one of our Scottish ministers:

There are young and sheltered lives which have grown up amid the sanctities and in the obediences of a devout home. A godly lineage, a careful training, and the example of a winsome religious life have wrought out in them a natural piety. They grow unspotted from the world. But as years increase their growth in the grace and knowledge of Christ quickens their spiritual insight and gives them a keener sense of sin. The awful power of the world, the flesh, and the devil dismays them as it dismays no one else. They see men and women whom they love, blinded, seduced, desecrated. They see that the gentle rules that bind their own rebellious thoughts snap like Samson's tender withes before the brute-like passions of others. And as they turn their eyes more and more on Christ they discover how far they themselves are from His holiness, and how near akin to the passion-driven profligate.

Prayer Thought: O God, deliver me from self-righteousness. I need You every moment of each day.

SUGGESTED READING: [16]And, behold, one came and said unto him, Good Master, what good thing shall I do, that I may have eternal life? [17]And he said unto him, Why callest thou me good? there is none good but one, that is, God: but if thou wilt enter into life, keep the commandments. [18]He saith unto him, Which? Jesus said, Thou shalt do no murder, Thou shalt not commit adultery, Thou shalt not steal, Thou shalt not bear false witness, [19]Honour thy father and thy mother: and, Thou shalt love thy neighbour as thyself. [20]The young man saith unto him, All these things have I kept from my youth up: what lack I yet? [21]Jesus said unto him, If thou wilt be perfect, go and sell that thou hast, and give to the poor, and thou shalt have treasure in heaven: and come and follow me. [22]But when the young man heard that saying, he went away sorrowful: for he had great possessions. [23]Then said Jesus unto his disciples, Verily I say unto you, That a rich man shall hardly enter into the kingdom of heaven. [24]And again I say unto you, It is easier for a camel to go through the eye of a needle, than for a rich man to enter into the kingdom of God. [25]When his disciples heard it, they were exceedingly amazed, saying, Who then can be saved? [26]But Jesus beheld them, and said unto them, With men this is impossible; but with God all things are possible.

—MATTHEW 19:16–26

The way of a fool is right in his own eyes: but he that hearkeneth unto counsel is wise.

—Proverbs 12:15

SCORES OF MEN AND WOMEN have a sense of personal holiness and self-righteousness. Their fascination of the Lord Jesus is based on an external performance of religion. They read their Bibles, but have no spiritual reality within. They have no consciousness of backsliding; but, oh, the possibility of failure! The feebleness of their lives!

So many Christians fall away from Christ right at this point. They try their best to do what is right, but realize only failure. They slowly feel that Jesus Christ cannot do what He says He can do in their lives. God can show people in that condition who and what they are. He can confront them with the fact that they need to be born from above, of the Spirit.

Consider the cases of Peter. This man was perfectly honest, perfectly earnest, but perfectly shallow in his spiritual experience. Peter had a flash for one second about who Jesus was; but he forgot it immediately. When Jesus talked about the cross, did Peter understand Him? Not a bit. He meant everything he said, but he was simply staggered at Jesus' prediction that he would betray Him. And Jesus was correct. He always is.

Prayer Thought: By myself, I am too weak to wrestle with Satan. But with Christ I can overcome and be victorious!

SUGGESTED READING: PROVERBS 12:1–15

But he turned, and rebuked them, and said, Ye know not what manner of spirit ye are of.

—Luke 9:55

Y OU PROBABLY THINK YOU ARE open-hearted and honest. But if you read about John and Thomas, you will find that sincere disciples may be rebuked.

Jesus Christ was preaching through the villages of Samaria and certain villagers would not tolerate Him. What did John say? "Let us call fire down from heaven and consume them." But Jesus rebuked him and said, "You do not know what spirit you are of." Thomas got his rebuke after the Resurrection, when Jesus told him, "Be not faithless, but believing."

If you have had your natural fascination for Jesus broken, thank God. If you have tried your loyal best to follow Him—if you have worshiped Him, given all you know how to Him, and yet it is failure and defeat and disappointment—you are just in the place to receive the Holy Spirit and be born again from above.

Whenever people who are doing a sincere work for Jesus talk about their sense of failure as "carrying their cross," they simply do not understand. Only the Holy Spirit can expound these things to them.

Prayer Thought: Lord, help me to learn when I receive some rebuke from You.

SUGGESTED READING: LUKE 9:51–56

Then said Jesus unto his disciples, If any man will come after me, let him deny himself, and take up his cross, and follow me.

—Matthew 16:24

JESUS CHRIST, WHILE ON THIS earth, taught all He had to teach. Let me say this very clearly: Pentecost added nothing to the doctrine taught by Jesus Christ or believed by the disciples.

What did Pentecost do? Pentecost made the disciples what they preached. They had heard all of Jesus Christ's doctrines preached in the day of His flesh and had not understood a word He said. Theirs was a life of sentiment. But Pentecost made them living examples of the gospel.

In the dark church she knelt alone,
Her tears were falling fast,
"Help, Lord," she cried, "the shades of death
Upon my soul are cast!
Have I not shunned the path of sin,
And chosen the better part?"
What voice came through the sacred air?
"My child, give me thy heart."

"Have I not worn my strength away,
With fast and penance sore?
Have I not watched and wept," she cried;
"Did thy dear saints do more?
Have I not gained thy grace, O Lord,
And won in heaven my part?"
It echoed louder in her soul—
"My child, give me thy heart."

Prayer Thought: O Lord, I yield my life to the transforming power of Your Spirit.

SUGGESTED READING: MATTHEW 16:21–28

Not every one that saith unto me, Lord, Lord, shall enter into the kingdom of heaven; but he that doeth the will of my Father which is in heaven.

—Matthew 7:21

As Jesus Christ talked to His disciples, they grew more and more mystified. For example, take the question of being a "servant of God." They did not understand what Jesus meant by that, any more than we will until we have received the Holy Spirit.

The difference between a servant of God and an instrument of God is brought out in Matthew 7:21–23. An instrument is a person whom God uses, whether that person is right or not. God will bless His Word, whether a saint or a sinner preaches it. But the servant of God lives in the fullness of His Spirit, evidencing the life of obedience.

Our Lord says in effect, "When you judge the work someone is doing, don't judge by the fact that you see Me at work. Judge him by his fruit." What is that? The fruit of the indwelling Holy Spirit—i.e., character. Many can do the work of God, but no one can imitate the fruit of the Holy Spirit.

Prayer Thought: Lord, I am your servant. Use me as You desire.

SUGGESTED READING: MATTHEW 7:21–23

NOVEMBER

Notwithstanding in this rejoice not, that the spirits are subject unto you; but rather rejoice, because your names are written in heaven.

—Luke 10:20

Jesus Christ emphatically said you must not rejoice in successful service: "In this rejoice not, that the spirits are subject unto you." Only the preacher who lives contrary to true spirituality rejoices in the souls that are saved, the demons cast out, the cases healed.

Jesus says, "Don't do it." Don't rejoice in successful service, but rejoice in your relationship to Him, "That your name is written in the Lamb's book of life." The disciples never understood Matthew 7 or Luke 10 until after the Resurrection; and neither will you and I, unless we receive the Holy Spirit.

Have you never seen an evangelist or preacher, used mightily of God in the salvation of souls, fall into the state of a castaway? This is how he fell—not in deliberate sin, but by deliberately and emphatically rejoicing in his successful service. This surely throws light on the essence of Satanic pride.

Prayer Thought: O God, I recognize the danger of self-importance. Help me to rejoice in You.

SUGGESTED READING: LUKE 10:17–22

In that hour Jesus rejoiced in spirit, and said, I thank thee, O Father, Lord of heaven and earth, that thou hast hid these things from the wise and prudent, and hast revealed them unto babes: even so, Father; for so it seemed good in thy sight.

—Luke 10:21

THE DISCIPLES DISCUSSED AMONG THEMSELVES who would be first when Jesus formed His kingdom. When Jesus asked them what they questioned, they did not answer Him. Why? They felt they missed the mark and did not know how. Then Jesus took a little child and said, "Whosoever shall not receive the kingdom of God as a little child shall in no wise enter therein."

God teaches no other kind of person, but the childlike in spirit.

Prayer Thought: O God, grant that we will understand Your teachings with the humility and simplicity of a child.

SUGGESTED READING: LUKE 10:21–24

And they were offended in him. But Jesus said unto them, A prophet is not without honour, save in his own country, and in his own house.

—Matthew 13:57

THE DISCIPLES BECAME MORE AND more confused by Christ's teachings. They were perplexed. The strain of service grew so intense that, in the last year of Jesus' life, it was too much for them. He predicted, "You shall all be offended in Me, and you will leave Me alone."

Can you blame them? I cannot. It is natural to be perplexed until we receive the Holy Spirit, who alone can expound all God's truth.

Prayer Thought: Lord, enlighten my understanding so that I may fully comprehend Your teachings.

SUGGESTED READING: MATTHEW 13:53–58

And the Lord said, Simon, Simon, behold, Satan hath desired to have you, that he may sift you as wheat: but I have prayed for thee, that thy faith fail not: and when thou art converted, strengthen thy brethren.

—Luke 22:31–32

CHRIST PERMITTED HIS DISCIPLES TO be sifted, for He emphatically stated, "Satan hath desired to have you, that he may sift you. . . . But I have prayed for thee, that thy faith fail not." Not "that you do not fall into sin" but "that your faith fail not."

As a result of that sifting, every one of the disciples suffered from a broken heart. Did you ever notice what John Bunyan in *Pilgrim's Progress* calls the "excellency of a broken heart"? The sacrifice which God requires is not "obedience in sacrifice," but a broken heart. "A broken and a contrite spirit, O God, thou wilt not despise" (Psalm 51:17).

Peter denied with oaths and curses that he ever knew Jesus. That was the supreme point of self-revelation. The other disciples also fell away; and I am sure that when they realized their weakness, they too were broken-hearted.

Prayer Thought: Self-revelation is at times painful, but always helpful. Heavenly Father, I desire to know who I am, for the eternal well-being of my soul.

SUGGESTED READING: LUKE 22:31–38

And he cometh, and findeth them sleeping, and saith unto Peter, Simon, sleepest thou? couldest not thou watch one hour?

—Mark 14:37

JESUS WAS TORN WITH AN agony that these poor, broken-hearted disciples could not understand. They looked up at Him with an answer unspoken, "Lord, how could we watch with you? Our hearts have been broken. We thought you were going to restore the kingdom to Israel." They were sleeping for sorrow.

Peter said he would go with Jesus even to death. But did he ever think for one moment that Jesus would give himself over meekly to the world? When he did, Peter's heart broke.

When a man is brokenhearted and despairing, he becomes weary and sleepy. He fails to be vigilant against the enemies.

Prayer Thought: Lord Jesus, lift me up when I grow weary.

SUGGESTED READING: MARK 14:26–41

And this is the confidence that we have in him, that, if we ask any thing according to his will, he heareth us: and if we know that he hear us, whatsoever we ask, we know that we have the petitions that we desired of him.

—1 John 5:14–15

THE MAJORITY OF US MAKE the blunder of depending on our own earnestness in prayer, not on God. But, dear friend, we must not have such confidence in ourselves. Our confidence is in God!

All our fuss, all our earnestness, all our so-called gifts of prayer are not the slightest atom of use to Jesus Christ. He pays no attention to these. Our Lord taught His disciples the pattern of prayer (Luke 11) and emphasized in that prayer the importance of faith and trust.

Moreover, the Lord warns us about wrong motives in praying. Surrender to the will of God is primary to genuine praying. Guard against selfish asking and greedy wants as you pray.

Prayer Thought: Teach me to pray, Lord,
as You taught the first disciples.

SUGGESTED READING: 1 JOHN 5:1–15

The LORD is nigh unto them that are of a broken heart; and saveth such as be of a contrite spirit.

—Psalm 34:18

Lord, I HAVE STRIVEN. I have prayed. I have agonized. Lord, I have experienced blessings and benedictions; but the thing has snapped, and I feel I have forsaken and fled from Thee." Blessed be the name of God! If that is your confession, you will have to come into the kingdom by the same road the publican and harlot came.

Too many preachers and teachers are losing sight of the atonement of Jesus Christ. They preach salvation through a natural affinity to Jesus. But God wants people who are broken-hearted, broken-minded, and broken-prided.

> *This cruel self, oh, how it strives,*
> *And works within my breast,*
> *To come between Thee and my soul,*
> *And keep me back from rest.*
> *How many subtle forms it takes,*
> *Of seeming verity,*
> *As if it were not safe to rest,*
> *And venture all on Thee.*
> *In Thy strong hand I lay me down,*
> *So shall the work be done;*
> *For who can work so wondrously,*
> *As the Almighty One?*

Prayer Thought: I praise You, Lord, for my redemption!

SUGGESTED READING: PSALM 34:12–22

Wherefore henceforth know we no man after the flesh: yea, though we have known Christ after the flesh, yet now henceforth know we him no more.

—2 Corinthians 5:16

To apply our terms of salvation to the early disciples seems entirely misleading and unwarranted by Scripture. Yet, the disciples' experience with their Lord throws a luminous interpretation on the spiritual experience of many today.

A problem arises today from the fact that the average evangelist regards conversion and regeneration as the same thing. In numbers of cases, conversion and regeneration actually do happen at the same time. But there are many cases in which conversion is a long process that takes place before the point of regeneration, which is the moment when a sinner's need for Christ is consciously realized or entered into.

The men and the women who are fascinated by the Lord Jesus, and who consecrate their lives to Him, but who know nothing experimentally about being born from above, are converted. But they are not yet regenerated—born again. They yet need a disappointing revelation of themselves, as the disciples received during Jesus' arrest and trial.

Prayer Thought: O Lord, search my heart and reveal where I stand in relation to You.

SUGGESTED READING: 2 CORINTHIANS 5:11–16

Therefore if any man be in Christ, he is a new creature: old things are passed away; behold, all things are become new.

—2 Corinthians 5:17

EVERY PERSON—GOOD, BAD, OR INDIFFERENT—MUST be born from above by the Spirit of God.

At the point of being born again, one who has been a wild and externally wicked sinner will be conscious of God's forgiveness of sins. On the other hand, one who has been naturally good and religious will sense the spiritual poverty of the past. Both will realize their need to be born anew by the sovereign grace of God.

Supernatural signs will accompany those saved by the grace of God. (The opening of this question will produce much confusion; that cannot be helped.) We must proclaim the one thing the New Testament demands, which is right relationship to the Lord Jesus Christ.

Prayer Thought: Oh, the bliss of knowing that all my sins are forgiven! Help me today to tell someone else how to become a new person in Christ.

SUGGESTED READING: 2 CORINTHIANS 5:17–21

And when he had said this, he breathed on them, and saith unto them, Receive ye the Holy Ghost.

—John 20:22

SOME PEOPLE BELIEVE THAT RECEIVING the Holy Spirit and the baptism with the Holy Spirit are one and the same thing, which in Scripture they certainly are not.

The men to whom Jesus said, "Receive ye the Holy Ghost," had been put through crises that had revealed their true nature to themselves. This could have been done only by the quickening of the Holy Spirit, who enabled them to understand Christ's teachings and prepared them to receive Christ in His fullness, as promised by the Father.

Christ did not ask the disciples to believe in some person He called the Holy Spirit; instead, He told them to receive the Holy Spirit. No soul was ever, or will ever be, born into the kingdom of God except by the Holy Spirit.

Prayer Thought: Spirit of God, I need You daily.

SUGGESTED READING: LUKE 24:46–49

Whose soever sins ye remit, they are remitted unto them; and whose soever sins ye retain, they are retained.

—John 20:23

WHEN THE DISCIPLES WERE QUICKENED by the Holy Spirit, "the Scriptures were opened to them." We read in John 20:9 that their condition before this time was that they "knew not the scripture." This is the first striking experience of every soul born from above, by the Spirit of God: The Bible becomes a new book.

Yet the quickening of the Spirit is not enough for Christian service. When Jesus ascended back to His Father, He would not allow His disciples to work for Him, in spite of the fact that they were Spirit-quickened. They were to do only two things: first, witness to the fact that He was risen from the dead; and second, tarry until they received the mighty baptism with the Holy Spirit.

Have you tried to rush into Christian service, not having received the promise of the Father?

Prayer Thought: I remember my sinful days of spiritual darkness. But I thank You, God, that the blessed Holy Spirit has brought new life and fresh light.

SUGGESTED READING: JOHN 20:19–23

And Elisha prayed, and said, LORD, I pray thee, open his eyes, that he may see. And the LORD opened the eyes of the young man; and he saw: and, behold, the mountain was full of horses and chariots of fire round about Elisha.

—2 Kings 6:17

O PENED SIGHT" IS A PROMINENT result of spiritual regeneration. When the disciples were born again, they got their eyes opened to who they were, not only who the Lord was.

The Holy Spirit can anoint our spiritual eyes with salve. By His quickening, He performs a kind of surgical operation, which is necessary before we can see in any light other than that of our prejudices.

This is not the sanctified life we are talking about; this is the spiritually regenerated life. Examine yourself to see whether you have ever received this quickening of the Holy Spirit of God.

Prayer Thought: Open the blinded eyes of the human spirit, O Lord, so that we can see You in all Your beauty.

SUGGESTED READING: 2 KINGS 6:8–18

And when he had said this, he breathed on them, and saith unto them, Receive ye the Holy Ghost.

—John 20:23

OUR LORD SAID IN MATTHEW 16:19, "And I will give unto thee the keys of the kingdom of heaven: and whatsoever thou shalt bind on earth shall be bound in heaven: and whatsoever thou shalt loose on earth shall be loosed in heaven." This is a section of Scripture that scares Protestants, simply because a misuse has been made of it by the Roman Catholic Church. But we are not called upon to safeguard truth; we are called to let truth safeguard us.

The characteristic, then, of discipleship is spiritual life, which is as solid and as real as natural life. The view that looks on spiritual life as an acquirement of the intellect, and an accomplishment that is gained from prayer and consecration, is altogether foreign to the New Testament. Spiritual life is life proceeding from the Holy Spirit, whom we received when we were born again from above.

Prayer Thought: Life eternal is my hope! Oh, what anticipation and expectation!

SUGGESTED READING: MATTHEW 16:13–20

Jesus saith unto them, Come and dine. And none of the disciples durst ask him, Who art thou? knowing that it was the Lord.

—John 21:12

THE DISCIPLES QUESTIONED JESUS ABOUT many things. His answers surprised and confused them. The Spirit of God alone understands the things of God, and so they did not understand Him until they had received the Spirit of God, "that no flesh should glory in his presence."

But now, after His resurrection, our Lord began questioning the disciples. He questioned them in such a way it would have been impossible for them to have answered Him unless they had received the Holy Spirit. The first question was about love. John 21 records the famous incident of the seashore breakfast. For us, the point of interest of this incident is our Lord's questioning of Peter; but through Peter He questioned all the rest of them about love.

Love is not an emotional ecstasy. Love is the sovereign preference of the whole being for another. In asking "Lovest thou Me?" our Lord meant no empty sentiment; He meant a love full of such an extraordinary passion that all the relationships and loves of earth are hatred in comparison to it. If Peter and the other disciples had not received the Holy Spirit, they could never have answered Him, because the Holy Spirit alone loves our Lord Jesus Christ that way.

Prayer Thought: Yes, Lord, I love you with all my heart, soul, mind, and strength.

SUGGESTED READING: JOHN 21:1–17

And Zacchaeus stood, and said unto the Lord: Behold, Lord, the half of my goods I give to the poor; and if I have taken any thing from any man by false accusation, I restore him fourfold.

—Luke 19:8

ONE MUST BE VERY CAREFUL to place spiritual things in their right sequence and relationship. It is perilously easy, for instance, to suppose that restitution is a necessary work before salvation; but that is thoroughly unscriptural. Spiritual regeneration leads one to restitution.

It is possible to preach mistakenly a baptism of power and of the Holy Spirit which totally ignores Romans 12:1—namely, the presentation of the body to God. A person can obey such a statement only if he has first of all received the Holy Spirit and been born from above.

Restitution and cross-bearing for the Lord are possible only after the glorious transformation of spiritual quickening.

Prayer Thought: With Paul I rejoice that "I have been crucified with Christ," and in Him I now live by faith.

SUGGESTED READING: EXODUS 22:1–6

Feed the flock of God which is among you, taking the oversight thereof, not by constraint, but willingly; not for filthy lucre, but of a ready mind.

—1 Peter 5:2

OUR LORD'S QUESTIONING OF PETER about love (John 21) is intensely involved with the question of feeding His sheep. The characteristic of one who has the love of the Holy Spirit is intense activity in doing God's will, not in working for God. Love and service are made one in an abstraction of delight, in which the individual is completely transfigured and the self totally effaced.

It is very helpful for modern Christians to remember that we are to feed Christ's lambs and carry Christ's sheep. We are not sent into the world to make our converts, or to run our movements, or to conserve our beliefs. May the Lord's penetrating question paralyze every answer, save the answer of the Holy Spirit in His way, "Lord, Thou knowest all things; Thou knowest that I love Thee."

Prayer Thought: Lord Jesus, I love You. I am seeking new ways to express it. Help me to live my love in service to others.

SUGGESTED READING: 1 PETER 5:1–4

And, behold, I send the promise of my Father upon you: but tarry ye in the city of Jerusalem, until ye be endued with power from on high.

—Luke 24:49

EVERY SPIRITUALLY MINDED PERSON OUGHT to study the difference between testifying and preaching. It is the duty of every born-again person to testify to what the Lord has done; but it requires a new discipline and the mighty baptism of the Holy Spirit before one is sent out to preach.

Our Lord distinctly told His spiritually quickened disciples that He would send the authoritative "promise of the Father" upon them (Acts 1:4) to prepare them for the work of preaching. However, in subsequent generations, there has not been sufficient distinction made between receiving the Spirit for spiritual quickening, and the baptism with the Holy Spirit for service.

The following notation from one of the most profound European scholars on this very matter ought to carry considerable weight. I refer to Bishop Westcott, in his commentary *The Gospel According to St. John*. The bishop says:

The presence of this new life of humility in the disciples, communicated to them by Christ, was the necessary condition for the descent of the Holy Spirit on the day of Pentecost. The spirit which the Lord imparted to them was His Spirit, or, as it may be expressed, the Holy Spirit as dwelling in Him. By this He first quickened them and then sent them, according to His promise, the Paraclete, to be with them and to supply all power for the exercise of their different functions. The relation of the Paraclete to the Pentecostal gift is therefore the relation of quickening to the endowment; the one answers to the power of the resurrection; the other to the power of the ascension. The one to victory; the other to sovereignty.

Prayer Thought: Spirit of the Living God, fall fresh on me!

SUGGESTED READING: [1]The former treatise have I made, O Theophilus, of all that Jesus began both to do and teach, [2]Until the day in which he was taken up, after that he through the Holy Ghost had given commandments unto the apostles whom he had chosen: [3]To whom also he shewed himself alive after his passion by many infallible proofs, being seen of them forty days, and speaking of the things pertaining to the kingdom of God: [4]And, being assembled together with them, commanded them that they should not depart from Jerusalem, but wait for the promise of the Father, which, saith he, ye have heard of me. [5]For John truly baptized with water; but ye shall be baptized with the Holy Ghost not many days hence. [6]When they therefore were come together, they asked of him, saying, Lord, wilt thou at this time restore again the kingdom to Israel? [7]And he said unto them, It is not for you to know the times or the seasons, which the Father hath put in his own power. [8]But ye shall receive power, after that the Holy Ghost is come upon you: and ye shall be witnesses unto me both in Jerusalem, and in all Judaea, and in Samaria, and unto the uttermost part of the earth. [9]And when he had spoken these things, while they beheld, he was taken up; and a cloud received him out of their sight. [10]And while they looked stedfastly toward heaven as he went up, behold, two men stood by them in white apparel; [11]Which also said, Ye men of Galilee, why stand ye gazing up into heaven? this same Jesus, which is taken up from you into heaven, shall so come in like manner as ye have seen him go into heaven. [12]Then returned they unto Jerusalem from the mount called Olivet, which is from Jerusalem a sabbath day's journey. [13]And when they were come in, they went up into an upper room, where abode both Peter, and James, and John, and Andrew, Philip, and Thomas, Bartholomew, and Matthew, James the son of Alphaeus, and Simon Zelotes, and Judas the brother of James. [14]These all continued with one accord in prayer and supplication, with the women, and Mary the mother of Jesus, and with his brethren.

—ACTS 1:1–14

But ye shall receive power, after that the Holy Ghost is come upon you: and ye shall be witnesses unto me both in Jerusalem, and in all Judaea, and in Samaria, and unto the uttermost part of the earth.

—Acts 1:8

LUKE 24:50–53 RELATES A POWERFUL revelation to the disciples as they saw the ascending Christ disappear. In Acts 1:11, the angelic proclamation says that this same Jesus will come back again. Many a commentator has spiritualized these passages to say that the promise was fulfilled at Pentecost. But the Holy Spirit has no wounds in His hands; the Holy Spirit has no atonement. Therefore, Pentecost cannot be the fulfillment of the angelic proclamation.

Pentecost is the fulfilling of the promise of the Lord, not the manifestation of a new Lord. We are to receive the Holy Spirit for quickening; and this quickening is preparation for a sacramental life of service. Our submissive waiting until the mighty fusing of the baptism with the Holy Spirit will allow us to be carried into the mystic body of Christ, for the mighty purposes of omnipotent God.

Prayer Thought: Thank You, Lord, for the promise of Your return. Let me live and serve in the fullness of Your Spirit until that great day.

SUGGESTED READING: LUKE 24:50–53

But unto every one of us is given grace according to the measure of the gift of Christ.

—Ephesians 4:7

JUST AS THERE IS ONLY one kind of human nature, there is only one kind of divine nature. And the holiness which the Bible teaches is the positive characteristic of the Christian is the kind Jesus had. God made His disciples one in holiness with Him.

They were not only made one in holiness, but one in love. Every Bible student must realize that there is an important kind of love taught in the Bible, and that is the love of God. The baptism with the Holy Spirit does not "patch up" natural human love to reach the standard of divine love, but makes the disciple one in love with his Lord.

The characteristic of Spirit-baptized ones is that they show the same unmerited mercy, the same unmerited love to others that Jesus showed to them.

Prayer Thought: I will earnestly seek to love my fellow man as I have been loved by Christ—with all my heart.

SUGGESTED READING: EPHESIANS 4:1–10

And the glory which thou gavest me I have given them; that they may be one, even as we are one.

—John 17:22

Not only are Spirit-baptized Christians made one in holiness and one in love, but they are to be made one in glory. Glory might be described as the place where Christ is enthroned in the fullness of consummating power and has all things subdued to Himself. There the Spirit-baptized are to be one with Him.

And as we are always with Christ, He is always with us. He, by virtue of His ascension, has become omnipresent. "Lo, I am with you always, even unto the end of the world" (Matthew 28:20) is an incomprehensible statement to human intelligence, but a blessed certainty to the Spirit of God and to the Spirit-baptized saint.

Prayer Thought: Lord, I appreciate the assurance of Your presence.

SUGGESTED READING: JOHN 17:17–26

Fear not, little flock; for it is your Father's good pleasure to give you the kingdom.

—Luke 12:32

THERE IS A SUPREMACY IN the persons that are Spirit-baptized—not a supremacy of power attached to the person, but a supremacy of the personality itself. We read in Acts 4:13: "Now when they saw the boldness of Peter and John, and perceived that they were unlearned and ignorant men, they marvelled; and they took knowledge of them, that they had been with Jesus." This aura of the Lord's presence surrounds the personality of everyone who is baptized with the Spirit of Christ.

Remember that Jesus said the Holy Spirit would glorify Him. Consequently, when Spirit-baptized people do good works, they will glorify the Lord who is in heaven. There is no distinction between service, sanctification, and supremacy; all three are fused into one transfiguring devotion to the Lord Jesus Christ. Spiritual supremacy is vested only in consecrated persons.

Further, this supremacy is void of self-interest. Read carefully Luke 24:47 and Acts 1:8. These passages clearly indicate that the baptism with the Holy Spirit removes all parochial notions, gives the disciple a worldwide view of God Himself, and endues him with love for the entire world.

Prayer Thought: O God, I revel in the opportunity to serve in Your kingdom.

SUGGESTED READING: LUKE 12:31–40

And I will pray the Father, and he shall give you another Comforter, that he may abide with you for ever.

—John 14:16

INDIVIDUALS WHO ARE SPIRIT-BAPTIZED RECOGNIZE that they are not their own. Their prayerful attitude is, "Lord, direct me by Thy Holy Spirit to choose what Thou hast ordained for me!"

Consequently, God is always uprooting the saints and scattering them far and wide. He does this to remind them, first, that this age is not their age; and, second, that there is a better time coming. And in that age, the spiritual supremacy of the saints will mean the supremacy of position.

In Luke 22:28–30, our Lord distinctly said that the position of His kingdom will ultimately be over everything. He said, " I appoint unto you a kingdom, as my Father hath appointed unto me, that ye may eat and drink at my table in my kingdom, and sit on thrones judging the twelve tribes of Israel."

Be patient with the Lord when He directs you into unaccustomed paths. He has a greater plan for you than the human mind can fathom.

Prayer Thought: Lord, remind me that this world is not my home; so I must seek Your will, rather than my own comfort or security.

SUGGESTED READING: JOHN 14:15–21

And hath raised us up together, and made us sit together in heavenly places in Christ Jesus.

—Ephesians 2:6

ONE OF THE MOST WONDERFUL things in our spiritual experience is the way God alters and develops our sensitivity to other people. There was a time when our feelings were amazingly sensitive to what certain other people thought of us. Now God has made us absolutely indifferent to what they (the world) think of us (Christians). We are now sensitive to what another Person thinks. Ultimately, we are sensitive only to what God thinks of us.

Is this the way you view your situation? If you do, you will obtain victory.

Prayer Thought: O God, You are the only One I desire to please. Forgive me if I succumb to the judgment of others.

SUGGESTED READING: PSALM 35:1–10

Because thou hast kept the word of my patience, I also will keep thee from the hour of temptation, which shall come upon all the world, to try them that dwell upon the earth.

—Revelation 3:10

God would have His children remember that this is not His or their day. It is man's day; and we must abide in prayerfully centered patience until He sees fit to put an end to man's day. The patience of the saints is not the patience of exhaustion, nor the patience of pessimism, but the patience of sovereign confidence in almighty God.

I believe the reason that most Christian people will not accept the counsel of patience is that the majority take their notions from preachers and books, instead of from the Bible itself.

The perils that we well might shun,
We saunter forth to meet;
The path into the road of sin,
We tread with careless feet.
The air that comes instinct with death—
We bid it round us flow;
And when our hands should bar the gate,
We parley with the foe.
The ill we deem we ne'er could do,
In thought we dramatize;
What we should loathe we learn to scan
With speculative eyes.
. . . .
Alas! for ignorance profound
Of our poor nature's bent
The wakened sympathy with wrong
Becomes the will's consent.

Prayer Thought: Lord Jesus, I know that patience is a virtue. I need more.

SUGGESTED READING: [1]And unto the angel of the church in Sardis write; These things saith he that hath the seven Spirits of God, and the seven stars; I know thy works, that thou hast a name that thou livest, and art dead. [2]Be watchful, and strengthen the things which remain, that are ready to die: for I have not found thy works perfect before God. [3]Remember therefore how thou hast received and heard, and hold fast, and repent. If therefore thou shalt not watch, I will come on thee as a thief, and thou shalt not know what hour I will come upon thee. [4]Thou hast a few names even in Sardis which have not defiled their garments; and they shall walk with me in white: for they are worthy. [5]He that overcometh, the same shall be clothed in white raiment; and I will not blot out his name out of the book of life, but I will confess his name before my Father, and before his angels. [6]He that hath an ear, let him hear what the Spirit saith unto the churches. [7]And to the angel of the church in Philadelphia write; These things saith he that is holy, he that is true, he that hath the key of David, he that openeth, and no man shutteth; and shutteth, and no man openeth; [8]I know thy works: behold, I have set before thee an open door, and no man can shut it: for thou hast a little strength, and hast kept my word, and hast not denied my name. ⁹Behold, I will make them of the synagogue of Satan, which say they are Jews, and are not, but do lie; behold, I will make them to come and worship before thy feet, and to know that I have loved thee. ¹⁰Because thou hast kept the word of my patience, I also will keep thee from the hour of temptation, which shall come upon all the world, to try them that dwell upon the earth.

—REVELATION 3:1–10

For I know that my redeemer liveth, and that he shall stand at the latter day upon the earth.

—Job 19:25

PREACHING IN ST. PAUL'S CHURCH IN London, Father Frere is reported to have said the following on "The Fourfold Attitude Towards Suffering":

Have you ever, I wonder, had to do something to a pet dog, which hurt very much, so as to get it well—to pull a thorn out of the foot, or wash out a wound, or something of that sort? You may remember the sort of dumb eloquence there was in the eye of the dog as he looked at you. It hurt tremendously, and yet there seemed to speak from his eyes trust of you. It looked as if he meant to say, "I do not in the least understand what you are doing, but go on." And that is the picture of trust. It is a very necessary stage into which we have to be brought in our experience of suffering. Perhaps when we most acutely turn to it in the case of those whom we love, we have to look mutely up to God, and say to Him, "I do not understand it at all, but go on." It is a real state of trust in God, and a step towards something further. Spiritual experience has begun, suffering has already deepened the soul.

We must learn to trust the Lord as we suffer. Christ is our example. Follow Him! Trust Him!

Prayer Thought: Lord, help me to trust and follow You today.

SUGGESTED READING: JOB 19

Who also hath made us able ministers of the new testament; not of the letter, but of the spirit: for the letter killeth, but the spirit giveth life.

—2 Corinthians 3:6

BEWARE OF PAYING TOO MUCH attention to the talk of the soul that is in trouble. Keep your heart and mind alert to what God is saying to you; and if you do not hear God, then get to the place where you can. Get to the place where you will know when God brings His Word to your remembrance.

There is a wrong use of God's Word and a right one, in counseling the troubled soul. The wrong one is this sort of thing: I cast about in my mind what sort of man you are, and then I hurl a text like a projectile at you. The Spirit of God is not in that. That use of the Word of God kills your own soul and the souls of the people you deal with. Jesus Christ said, "The words I speak unto you, they are spirit, and they are life" (John 6:63).

Keep your soul in touch with the directions of the Spirit, for your own sake and the sake of those with whom you talk.

Prayer Thought: O Holy Spirit, help my conversations with others to give life, not wounds.

SUGGESTED READING: 2 CORINTHIANS 3:1–6

For to this end also did I write, that I might know the proof of you, whether ye be obedient in all things.

—2 Corinthians 2:9

LET ME SHARE A VERY puzzling situation. You have all had experiences, I'm sure, in which people listened to clear Bible teaching, but failed to enter the kingdom of God. Yet, before that same congregation, a speaker gets up and shares a rambling testimony and—to your astonishment—people are born again.

I have attended the City Mission in New York City several times, for example, and I have never once heard correct biblical teaching there. But recently, I heard a man who had been wonderfully saved get up and tell what he was and what he had been. Then four or five others did this too. The Spirit of God got hold of the people in the congregation. Before I knew it, people went to the altar. These rough men knelt down and prayed with them, and the seekers "struck something," as they say there. Something struck them!

God works in mysterious ways. Correct biblical teaching is a must. But so is obedience from the heart. This is true, no matter how strange or odd the circumstances happen to be.

Prayer Thought: Lord Jesus, I long to be obedient in every detail of Your will for my life—even if others do not understand.

SUGGESTED READING: 2 CORINTHIANS 2

But refuse profane and old wives' fables, and exercise thyself rather unto godliness.

—1 Timothy 4:7

YOU CANNOT PREDICT HOW GOD may operate. Many dear souls are living specimens of what God has done and how the Spirit of God has worked, even though you may not fully understand them nor their methods. Many times some poor, ignorant servant, who seems to scarcely know how to put anything together, is mightily used of God in the salvation of souls—while others, who have a clear understanding of the gospel, explain the way of salvation ever so clearly, yet nothing happens.

This illustrates once again that a right relationship with God is more important than right teaching about God.

Ask yourself, Do I experimentally know what full salvation is? Do I know what entire sanctification means, in my own experience? The worker for God must be in a healthy, vigorous spiritual condition himself. Are you?

Prayer Thought: O God, work out Your will in my life as You desire. Your ways are above my ways.

SUGGESTED READING: 1 TIMOTHY 4:1–9

We are bound to thank God always for you, brethren, as it is meet, because that your faith groweth exceedingly, and the charity of every one of you all toward each other aboundeth.

—2 Thessalonians 1:3

I WANT TO OFFER A WORD of criticism about the choosing of Sunday school teachers. The way we are apt to choose Sunday school teachers is this: A person gets introduced into the kingdom of God and immediately we put that one into a Sunday school class to teach.

When a soul enters into the kingdom of God, that person must grow in obedience until he is consolidated in the ways of God. Why is this necessary? Because dealing with souls is tenfold more dangerous than dealing with bodies. Unless you are in a healthy, vigorous condition with God, you will catch the disease of the soul you are dealing with, instead of helping to cure it. Unless you know how to walk through that Bible, inhale the air of God's truth, and get thoroughly robust, you are sure to catch the disease of the souls with whom you are dealing.

New Christians need time to grow before they are placed in positions of leadership.

Prayer Thought: Lord, as I deal with sinsick souls, insulate me from their disease. Enable me to be spiritually healthy so that I can help them find the Great Physician.

SUGGESTED READING: 1 THESSALONIANS 1

The trees of the Lord are full of sap; the cedars of Lebanon, which he hath planted.

—Psalm 104:16

THE CEDARS OF LEBANON HAVE a most extraordinary power. Instead of nourishing parasites, they kill them. The life within each tree is so strong and so robust that, instead of feeding the parasites, it chokes them off.

God grant that we may get so filled with His life, and be so spiritually flourishing, that He can trust us to work among the souls of our fellow men—so that He may be able to pour His tremendous health and power through us!

Beware of working for God when you have very little Christianity yourself. And you cannot develop your own Christian life unless it exists. The advice that is too often given to Christian workers is, "If you work for God, you can develop your own Christian life." You must learn to live with God first.

Prayer Thought: Help me to flourish like a cedar of Lebanon, so that I can be more effectively used by You.

SUGGESTED READING: PSALM 104

DECEMBER

For I say unto you, That except your righteousness shall exceed the righteousness of the scribes and Pharisees, ye shall in no case enter into the kingdom of heaven.

—Matthew 5:20

OUR STANDARD OF MORAL CONDUCT must exceed that of the morally upright man or woman who lives apart from the grace of God. Our Lord does not lower the standard of moral conduct for His people; instead, He pushes it higher. We not only have to do right, but our motives must be right. The springs of our thinking must be right.

That is the standard of moral conduct we shall be able to meet if we are born again of the Spirit of God and if we obey the Spirit.

Prayer Thought: Help me, Lord, to surrender myself fully to You so that I may be all that You expect me to be.

SUGGESTED READING: PSALM 26

No man can serve two masters: for either he will hate the one, and love the other; or else he will hold to the one, and despise the other. Ye cannot serve God and mammon.

—Matthew 6:24

CHRIST'S TRUE VICTORIES ARE NOT made in moments of revival, but when my will is in the ascendancy.

It is an easy business to make decisions for Christ in a camp meeting.

Everything is in my favor. The revival tide is high; it is easy to float over on the Lord's side. But His mighty, tremendous triumphs are made after the revival—when I am in the ascendancy, when Christ stands on one side of an issue and my will on the other. Then I have to choose whom I have to serve. Then is the time when true decision is made.

During a revival, the Holy Spirit can sway the whole church with His presence. The atmosphere is marvelous. People are rejoicing. But only one tenth of them ever victoriously serve Christ.

Prayer Thought: I resolve to follow Christ, regardless of the price or sacrifice.

SUGGESTED READING: MATTHEW 6:24–34

And unto this people thou shalt say, Thus saith the LORD; Behold, I set before you the way of life, and the way of death.

—Jeremiah 21:8

DURING THE REVIVAL IN SOUTH Wales, God swayed and wooed the people, trying to convince them to make a decision for Him. But as long as they were blessed, they would not decide. When God withdrew the revival, down they went, spiritually—further than before He came in revival. Only those who transacted serious decisions with God came through the aftermath and stood true.

Have you been going to an altar of decision over and over again? Have you been praying, fuming, perspiring, and struggling? You must decide once and for all whether you will serve the Lord.

People will spend nights in prayer rather than resolve to obey God. They will do anything rather than decide. They will ask God to bring fire from heaven or show them other miraculous signs . . . anything to get them out of this horrible position of decision! Oh, God grant that we may get to the point of decision!

Prayer Thought: O God, deliver me from just riding the tide of religious enthusiasm.

SUGGESTED READING: JEREMIAH 21

And Elijah came unto all the people, and said, How long halt ye be-tween two opinions? if the LORD be God, follow him: but if Baal, then follow him. And the people answered him not a word.

—1 Kings 18:21

MANY TIMES, GOD LEADS US along with no clear point of surrender; and then suddenly, like a flash, He draws the line straight. He strikes straight through the joints and marrow with His words. He forces us to decide.

When Jesus Christ comes on the scene, the truth of God stands out clear. All the praying and all the struggling are to no avail. You must act. You must surrender. God cannot help you do it; human friends cannot help you do it. You must decide of your own volition whether you will surrender to Jesus Christ.

As soon as you surrender, He saves. As soon as you present your body as a living sacrifice, He entirely sanctifies.

Oh, may God stop our asking Him to save us! Christ has already died to save us. Oh, may God stop our pleading with Him to sanctify us! He already sent Jesus Christ to sanctify us. We must decide whether we will let Him do His work.

Prayer Thought: Praise the Lord! Victory is mine. I claim it.

SUGGESTED READING: 1 KINGS 18:1–21

And they were astonished at his doctrine: for his word was with power.

—Luke 4:32

As Christians, we must testify of the grace of God to our family and friends. Jesus preached His first sermon in His hometown, Nazareth. He told His disciples that they were to begin their ministry at Jerusalem, their capital. What was the reason? Did Jesus expect great success in Nazareth and Jerusalem? He had exactly the opposite expectation. But He insisted that His disciples begin their ministry where they were.

Our Nazareth or Jerusalem is unquestionably among our own relations. It is easier to testify to strangers than to our own flesh and blood. But we cannot wait for others to bring our relatives to salvation. They are our personal responsibility.

Prayer Thought: Enable me, heavenly Father, to share the good news of Christ at home first.

SUGGESTED READING: MATTHEW 13:53–58

And if it seem evil unto you to serve the LORD, choose you this day whom ye will serve; whether the gods which your fathers served that were on the other side of the flood, or the gods of the Amorites, in whose land ye dwell: but as for me and my house, we will serve the LORD.

—Joshua 24:15

CHRIST IS PARALYZED WHEN YOU will not surrender to Him. He prayed for you. He died for you. He sent the Holy Spirit to woo you. When are you going to let Him have His way?

Never mistake blessings for His mighty regenerating work. Never mistake the external blessings of God for entire sanctification. If you want to be saved, you must repent of your sins and ask for God's forgiveness. If you want to be entirely sanctified, you must bind the "sacrifice with cords" to the altar.

When God gives you such a clear choice, why not decide now?

Prayer Thought: Forgive me, Lord, when I hesitate in obeying You.

SUGGESTED READING: JOSHUA 24:1–16

And the LORD said, My spirit shall not always strive with man.

—Genesis 6:3

Y OU MAY TALK ABOUT YOUR Christian experience all you like; but unless you have been invaded by the Holy Spirit, and every determination of your nature has been fixed on the Lord, your experience amounts to nothing. Consecration is not enough. Obedience is not enough. Only your decision to let the Lord have His way can give you the victory.

You may have spiritual ecstasies. You may see angels. You may spend nights in prayer. But the thing that really counts is not what you experience, but what you allow God to do for you.

Prayer Thought: Thank You, Lord, for spiritual experiences. But I bless Your holy name for flooding my soul with Your Spirit.

SUGGESTED READING: JOSHUA 24:17–31

Lead me in thy truth, and teach me: for thou art the God of my salvation; on thee do I wait all the day.

—Psalm 25:5

GOD CANNOT MAKE US COMMIT ourselves to Him. We must do that. So many of us will do anything under heaven before we truly surrender. We pray and cry, but cannot let go of ourselves. Pride is the reason.

We must stop our reminiscences about the joys and blessings we have had; all the blessings God brings to our lives will never take the place of our surrender to Christ. We must let Him have His own way. God may bless us beyond all measure, but that is not a sign we are sanctified. He longs to give us more.

When Jesus was on this earth, He cried, "I am come that they might have life" (John 10:10).

Prayer Thought: Lead me, O Lord, and
teach me the way of holiness.

SUGGESTED READING: PSALM 25

The Lord is my rock, and my fortress, and my deliverer; my God, my strength, in whom I will trust; my buckler, and the horn of my salvation, and my high tower.

—Psalm 18:2

Do not insult Him by asking Him for the witness of the baptism of the Holy Spirit. Decide; that is the thing for you to do.

When you come to the altar, the Holy Spirit will tell you why you cannot let go. And if you are willing to be sanctified, you will decide without a moment's delay. God grant that if you are in the valley of decision, you may decide quickly.

God gives us unsearchable riches in Jesus Christ. All things are ours because we are Christ's, and Christ is God's. We have a spirit of heaven to go to heaven in. Christ offers us a superabundant life here and now—for body, soul, and spirit—to the end that Jesus Christ Himself may be glorified. Yet we cannot begin to live it unless we decide to let Him have His way.

Would to God that everyone would draw Him to the heart, to have the joys of His fullness!

Prayer Thought: O God, I present my whole being to You as a living sacrifice. Consume me with Your Holy Spirit.

SUGGESTED READING: PSALM 18:1–6

Judge not, that ye be not judged.

—Matthew 7:1

OUR LORD SAYS TO ABSTAIN from critical judgment of others. This sounds very strange, because one characteristic of the Holy Spirit in a believer is His way of revealing things that are wrong and sinful. But the discerning power of the Holy Spirit is not for purposes of criticism; it is for the purpose of conversion.

Criticism is not a healthy habit for a wholesome spiritual life. When criticism becomes a habit, it destroys moral energy, kills faith, and paralyzes spiritual force. Criticism becomes deadly as it decomposes. If you are criticized much, it has the effect of decomposing you. That is never the work of the Holy Spirit, nor the work of a saint; it is the work of the Devil.

Abstain from criticizing others. Beware of any attitude that puts you in the place of superiority.

Prayer Thought: We human beings are given to being judgmental. Forgive us, Lord. You are the only true Judge.

SUGGESTED READING: LUKE 6:37–45

Blessed are ye, when men shall revile you, and persecute you, and shall say all manner of evil against you falsely, for my sake. Rejoice, and be exceeding glad: for great is your reward in heaven: for so persecuted they the prophets which were before you.

—Matthew 5:11–12

Our Lord says that His disciples are to rejoice when they are reviled, persecuted, or slandered for His sake. So many times we are told that if we suffer for "conviction's sake" or "conscience's sake," we have suffered painfully. Not so. We are supposed to suffer for Jesus' sake. Our whole motive in suffering is to be well-pleasing to God.

The true blessedness of the saint rests in determining to make and keep God first. The disadvantage of a saint in our present world is that he must make confession of Jesus, not in secret, but glaringly in public. The tendency to be holy and say nothing about it is right from every standpoint but God's.

Do not hesitate to speak out for God and His Word. It is the greatest need of this world. Be faithful to share the good news of Christ, even if sharing it brings ridicule.

Prayer Thought: Give me grace to rejoice when people persecute me for Your sake, O Lord.

SUGGESTED READING: PSALM 30

For thou art my hope, O Lord God: thou art my trust from my youth.

—Psalm 71:5

How long have you been crying for help, and your god hasn't answered? Step over your god of earnestness. Throw away your god of obedience. Turn to the Lord Jesus Christ. He says, "Come unto me, all ye that labour and are heavy laden, and I will give you rest" (Matthew 11:28).

Nothing will avail but your decision to let the Lord have His way. You may say you have done this and that; but have you done the thing He has told you to do? Let go and let Him change your life.

I do not care how earnest you have been, how great your restitution has been, or how many "tracks" you have cleaned up. Until you decide to cast it all on Christ, there is no hope.

Prayer Thought: I know that Christ is the answer to all my seeking. In Him I place my hope, trust, and faith.

SUGGESTED READING: PSALM 71

As the hart panteth after the water brooks, so panteth my soul after thee, O God.

—Psalm 42:1

Now we come to the great and grand idea of the universal and spiritual aspect of the work of a Christian. There is no respect of persons with God. There is no respect of nations with God. Anywhere and everywhere—here, there, and wherever—God likes to fling us out to disciple all nations. The entire world belongs to Him.

Behind every face besotted with sin is the face of the Lord Jesus Christ. Behind every downtrodden mass of human corruption is Calvary. Deep within each person is the potential for a life incandescent with God's Holy Spirit.

Prayer Thought: I am truly thankful for the blessings You have given me, Lord. Help me introduce others to these blessings.

SUGGESTED READING: PSALM 42

And hath raised us up together, and made us sit together in heavenly places in Christ Jesus.

—Ephesians 2:6

THE GOSPEL OF JESUS CHRIST has the "any man" aspect; "whosoever will" may come to Him and find salvation. So many times we hear people say, "Those experiences are not for me. My past life has been so mean, so sordid, that surely God doesn't mean me." But God does mean you; He means by His marvelous grace and power to create Jesus Christ in you.

God makes no distinction between Jew or Gentile. Anyone may, at the Cross of Jesus, find forgiveness of sins and entire sanctification. God stoops to the very lowest, the very weakest—yes, to the "sons of disobedience"—and raises them up, if they will let Him.

Prayer Thought: O God, I know that Your marvelous grace is the secret to spiritual victory. Hallelujah!

SUGGESTED READING: EPHESIANS 2:1–7

For by grace are ye saved through faith; and that not of yourselves: it is the gift of God.

—Ephesians 2:8

GOD LIFTED ME OUT OF sin, infidelity, inability, weakness, disobedience, and wrath, to the heavenly places where Christ lives in the fullness of His power. Oh, the wonder of being lifted into that inviolable place! God raises me up to that place even now.

"[Sitting] together in heavenly places in Christ Jesus" is manifested in our lives as we look to the Creator and see in that marvelous Being our divine Head. Thank God, when He raises us up, He manifests in us the very mind that was in Christ Jesus—unhurried, calm, steady, and strong.

Prayer Thought: The peace of Christ strengthens, empowers, and gives assurance to me.

SUGGESTED READING: EPHESIANS 2:8–13

He that dwelleth in the secret place of the most High shall abide under the shadow of the Almighty.

—Psalm 91:1

STUDY THE LIFE OF JESUS Christ. Read the story over again. Study the thirty years of quiet subjection at Nazareth. Stand amazed before the three years of service. Think of the slander, the spitting, the backbiting, the hate—think of everything that Jesus endured that was unfathomably worse than you will go through. Yet His peace was undisturbed. It could not be violated. It is that peace that God exhibits in us when we sit in "heavenly places"—not a peace like it, but that very peace.

The circumstances of our lives will not hinder our peace. The rush and turmoil of the world will pass us by practically unnoticed. Why? Because we are sitting in "heavenly places" in Christ Jesus. Oh, "He that dwelleth in the secret place of the most High shall abide under the shadow of the Almighty," where he is secure and safe.

Prayer Thought: Jesus is all the world to me. The security of His love and peace is sufficient.

SUGGESTED READING: EPHESIANS 2:14–22

The LORD will give strength unto his people; the LORD will bless his people with peace.

—Psalm 29:11

WATCH THE SAINT. IN TUMULTS oft, tribulation, turmoil, trouble, affliction—but the peace of Christ will manifest itself in the saint's life. The peace of Christ will hold that person's soul in a poise above outward circumstances and battlings. The old way of looking at things, the old way of doing things, the old fuss and fume are all gone. The saint has become a new creation, and that creation has the very nature that was manifested in Christ.

When you have His nature, then you will have His peace. The sovereign, overflowing power of God—as it was exhibited in and through our Lord Jesus Christ—is exhibited in and through us when He has raised us up from sin to sit in the heavenly places.

How blind we get sometimes! There is a danger, even to those who are the children of God, of getting too familiar with sublime things. We talk about the wonderful realities of God, and yet seem to forget that they are to be exhibited through our lives. Have you asked God to help you realize His peace? Have you allowed God to exhibit His peace through you?

Prayer Thought: O God, may Your peace be seen in me.

SUGGESTED READING: JOHN 14:22–31

Blessed are the pure in heart: for they shall see God.

—Matthew 5:8

W HAT DOES "PURE IN HEART" mean? Nothing less than what the Son of God is. God imparts to us the identical purity that characterized Jesus Christ. The sanctified life is the undisturbed range of His peace, the unshakable power of His strength, and the unfathomable depth of His purity.

Jesus never had secular moods. The heart of the Lord Jesus Christ wanted God's glory most. Entire sanctification means the impartation of this to you and me.

The wonder of a pure heart is this: Its motives are as pure as Jesus Christ's. Our Lord had a wonderful sensitiveness to the things of God.

Prayer Thought: Purity of heart and life is my need. Cleanse me, O God, and make me pure in Your sight.

SUGGESTED READING: JOHN 15:14–27

Yea, in the way of thy judgments, O LORD, have we waited for thee; the desire of our soul is to thy name, and to the remembrance of thee.

—Isaiah 26:8

GOD SOFTLY BREATHES STERN MESSAGES to His children. And what is the result? Are His children stricken with fear? Never.

You will find, as you walk with your mind stayed on God, that nothing will take you by surprise. You will not be panic stricken. God will not permit it; He will keep you in perfect peace. But there is a condition: If you keep your mind stayed on Him.

Why are so many of us panic stricken when some trouble or trial suddenly faces us? Because we get our eyes off of Him. Keep your eyes on Jesus and you will be kept steadfast and immovable.

Our joy is unspeakable and full of glory. Let the Lord sanctify you wholly. Then you will know the "peace of God, which passeth all understanding."

Prayer Thought: This world is full of problems and perplexity, Lord. But You are my peace!

SUGGESTED READING: ISAIAH 26:5–11

And he trembling and astonished said, Lord, what wilt thou have me to do? And the Lord said unto him, Arise, and go into the city, and it shall be told thee what thou must do.

—Acts 9:6

AN EMINENT MINISTER OF THE gospel once wrote, "Sanctification is a supreme desire not to want to have your own way." This quote is rather quaintly expressed but gloriously true, and has about it the fragrance of Gethsemane. It carries one back to the time when the Man of Sorrows went "a stone's cast" further into the garden and cried, "Not as I will, but as thou wilt."

Some have written about the "tragedy of Calvary," but I am inclined to believe it was one of the great triumphs in God's plan. When Saul of Tarsus met Jesus on the way to Damascus, he cried, "What wilt thou have me to do?" In that surrender of all, Saul's own plans came into such obedience to the divine will that God, in the darkness of three days, revealed to him his work. It was a prelude to the days in which Saul would see what he must suffer for Jesus' sake.

When one gets a vision of God, the supreme desire of the soul is "Thy will, not mine."

Prayer Thought: Your will, not mine, be done, O Lord.

SUGGESTED READING: ACTS 9:1–9

And saying, If thou be the king of the Jews, save thyself.

—Luke 23:37

THE SHAME OF THE GOSPEL is its unwillingness to answer its critics. The Christian is at loss to think that, when Jesus hung upon the cross, men said, "He saved others, Himself He cannot save." But Jesus had no answer. Jesus was concerned, not about what mankind thought of Him, but to do what God had sent Him to do.

The shame of the gospel is increasing in this church age. The church becomes discouraged when it stands up for Jesus, and finds Jesus turning to heal the breach it made with the world. Yet Jesus is more concerned with redeeming the world than with preserving a good reputation. That draws criticism, yet Christ remains silent in the face of His critics.

Prayer Thought: Impressing others is not my goal, Lord. I am willing to pay the price of shame in order to serve You.

SUGGESTED READING: LUKE 23:34–45

But he that received seed into the good ground is he that heareth the word, and understandeth it; which also beareth fruit, and bringeth forth, some an hundredfold, some sixty, some thirty.

—Matthew 13:23

WE MUST ALWAYS REMEMBER THAT God is our Father. He loves us. We can never think of any need that He will forget.

Thus, we must not worry. It is not only wrong to worry, it is real infidelity to God; because worry means that we are saying, "God cannot look after my practical details."

Did you ever notice what Jesus said would choke out the spiritual life He puts in us? Was it the Devil? No—the cares of this world (Matthew 13:22). The little worries of life hinder us. A businessman who is filled with the Spirit of God can do his work ten-thousandfold better than a man without the Spirit, because the responsibilities of his daily affairs are off his shoulders and on God's.

The secret of Christian health and prosperity is concentration on the compassionate care of God.

Prayer Thought: Heavenly Father, You know that I worry sometimes. Increase my faith in You. Strengthen my trust in You. Forgive me when I do worry.

SUGGESTED READING: MATTHEW 13:18–23

And every one that hath forsaken houses, or brethren, or sisters, or father, or mother, or wife, or children, or lands, for my name's sake, shall receive an hundredfold, and shall inherit everlasting life.

—Matthew 19:29

JESUS MUST BE ABSOLUTELY FIRST in our love. He will curse anything we love most—that is the burden of today's Scripture text.

If I love this present age more than Him, the Lord will rebuke me. If I love myself more, the Lord will convict me. But if I love Him most, He will not be offended by me, nor I by Him. "And blessed is he, whosoever shall not be offended in me."

Prayer Thought: Dear Lord, I love You—above and beyond all others and everything else!

SUGGESTED READING: MATTHEW 19:23–30

And I will sanctify my great name, which was profaned among the heathen, which ye have profaned in the midst of them; and the heathen shall know that I am the Lord, saith the Lord God, when I shall be sanctified in you before their eyes.

—Ezekiel 36:23

THERE IS AN ATTITUDE TODAY that I call "Pharisaic holiness." People with this attitude have forgotten the horrible pit and miry clay from whence they have been dug out by the mighty atonement of Jesus Christ. These people thank God, with an arrogant offensiveness, that they are not as "other men are."

The Holy Spirit continually takes back the saint of God, in memory, to what he once was. For as God told the children of Israel in Ezekiel, He sanctified them "not for their sakes but for His own."

We need to remember that
Every virtue we possess
And every victory won,
And every thought of holiness
Are His alone.

Prayer Thought: To God be all glory and honor for the victory I have in Jesus as my Lord and Savior.

SUGGESTED READING: EZEKIEL 36:21–38

But made himself of no reputation, and took upon him the form of a servant, and was made in the likeness of men.

—Philippians 2:7

WE ARE NOT TO STAND up for our own honor, only for the honor of others. Jesus' critics called Him a glutton, a winebibber, demon-possessed, and a madman. Yet He never opened His mouth against their criticism. But when His accusers said a word against His heavenly Father, He not only opened His mouth; He said some very stern things.

Jesus made Himself of no reputation, and we are to follow His example. When people slander us, we should not worry about it. But when they dishonor our Lord, we must be disturbed.

The best illustration of what I am trying to explain to you is that of mud on your clothes. If you touch it while wet, you will rub it into the texture of the fabric. But if you leave the mud till it is dry, you can flick it off, and it is gone without a trace. Leave criticism alone; do not touch it.

Prayer Thought: Give me the discipline of refusing to answer my accusers, Lord. You are my example in this.

SUGGESTED READING: PHILIPPIANS 2:1–8

Wherefore he is able also to save them to the uttermost that come unto God by him, seeing he ever liveth to make intercession for them.

—Hebrews 7:25

GOD WANTS PRAYING PEOPLE WHO will vicariously take on the difficulties of the various churches and denominations and communities in which they live. He wants us to present these difficulties before God, being identified with them.

The New Testament teaches that we are raised up "together" to sit "in heavenly places in Christ Jesus"—not raised in isolation, but together. God grant that we may learn the tremendous meaning of intercessory prayer!

Intercession includes vicarious repentance—feeling all the distress and all the pain of the sins of the people to whom we belong, as if they were really our own. Are you willing to make this your ministry?

Prayer Thought: Like You, Lord, I want to be an intercessor for others. I will pray for the needs of my friends, relatives, and fellow Christians.

SUGGESTED READING: HEBREWS 7:14–28

Brethren, I count not myself to have apprehended: but this one thing I do, forgetting those things which are behind, and reaching forth unto those things which are before.

—Philippians 3:13

PAUL SOUNDS A NOTE OF challenge in Philippians 3:13–14: "Brethren, I count not myself to have apprehended: but this one thing I do, forgetting those things which are behind, and reaching forth unto those things which are before, I press toward the mark for the prize of the high calling of God in Christ Jesus."

This seals forever the most subtle of all heresies, the idea of stagnation in our spiritual life. It cannot be too often repeated that we can do absolutely nothing for our soul's salvation or entire sanctification; these are the gifts of God through the atonement. But we must do everything afterwards with sublime courage. We have to remember Whose we are and Whom we serve.

Christ calls us to carry the sublime dignity of the children of God in the midst of a crooked and perverse world. To that end, we may always strive for greater maturity and godliness.

Prayer Thought: Growth in grace is my aim and aspiration. By Your grace, Lord Jesus, help me to mature.

SUGGESTED READING: PHILIPPIANS 3:7–21

Then saith Jesus unto him, Get thee hence, Satan: for it is written,
Thou shalt worship the Lord thy God, and him only shalt thou serve.

—Matthew 4:10

THE CENTRAL CITADEL FOR THE Devil's attack on Jesus was the same as for his attack upon us—"my right to myself." He tempted Jesus to do God's work in His own way.

Likewise, even when a soul is sanctified, the Devil attempts to get the saint to do God's work in his own selfish way. He will do anything to dethrone the Lord as Lord!

The keynote of Jesus' reply, throughout the temptation, was His steady insistence that " For I came down from heaven, not to do mine own will, but the will of him that sent me." Is this your testimony, too?

Prayer Thought: Forgive me, O Lord, when I insist on my own way. Help me to realize that Satan works through selfishness on my part.

SUGGESTED READING: MATTHEW 4:1–11

And ye shall hear of wars and rumours of wars: see that ye be not troubled: for all these things must come to pass, but the end is not yet.

—Matthew 24:6

S AINTS ARE AS THE PROPHETS of God: They portray in their individual lives what God's purpose is for their community. The events of our day point toward an unparalleled catastrophe which marks the sudden coming of the Lord and the birth of a new epoch, known as the kingdom of God, visibly established on earth. God's people are to be harbingers of that new age.

By contrast, the sin of this age has peculiar and definite characteristics. It is true that we still have the sins of all the other ages. But the dominant characteristic of the sin of our age is imitating the Holy Spirit; first, by attempting to impose an organized interpretation upon the gospel; second, by insisting that each individual's responsibility is based upon that inter-pretation; and third, by boasting about the infallible certainty of having the mind of God.

Prayer Thought: Deliver me, Lord, from ever attempting to usurp the ministry of Your Holy Spirit!

SUGGESTED READING: MATTHEW 24:1–31

Heaven and earth shall pass away, but my words shall not pass away.

—Matthew 24:35

THE FIRST FEW CENTURIES OF the church were among the greatest, the purest, and the most blessed that the world has ever seen. Those early Christians had an unquestioning love for God. All of the subsequent reformations and revivals have been spurts of spiritual energy to get back to those primitive Christian days.

Yet the present church age continues to manifest three prime characteristics of the apostolic church. The main features of this church age are: (1) individual responsibility for letting God cleanse the heart from sin, readjust our nature, and infill it with His divinity, on the sole ground of the substitution of Jesus Christ for the sin of the world; (2) personal realization of a personal God, by making the response of perfect love and devotion; and (3) consciousness of each individual's accountability to God alone.

These fundamentals are what Satan is trying to undermine. Yet all of our work as Christians must spring from these elements. The worldly never fight God, but religious people do so by letting Satan work through them.

Prayer Thought: O God, let me realize when I am playing into the hands of Satan as he attempts to undermine Your work.

SUGGESTED READING: MATTHEW 24:32–44

Having a form of godliness, but denying the power thereof: from such turn away.

—2 Timothy 3:5

MATERIALISM WILL CEASE TO BE a power in our world. Spiritualism will be the characteristic force at the end of this age. All of mankind's endeavors will revolve around the "unseen." The dominant feature of this movement will be a certain form of godliness, which will bear many beneficial works.

In fact, so much so will this be the case that even the very elect may be deceived.

As the end of the age approaches, we shall see a higher type of morality than there has ever been. Better forms of government, higher forces of civilization, greater intellectual understanding, better physical development will be seen at the end of this age.

Suddenly, though, everything will be shattered to pieces by the second coming of Jesus!

Prayer Thought: Lord, help me not to be deceived by the spirit of our age. I want to be ready for Your return to this earth.

SUGGESTED READING: 2 TIMOTHY 3:1–15

SCRIPTURE INDEX

Acts